東京

ロバート スティ

七十一年 二月 五日

ORIGINALLY PUBLISHED BY STANFORD UNIVERSITY PRESS

THE AGRARIAN ORIGINS
OF MODERN JAPAN

Thomas C. Smith

ATHENEUM, NEW YORK
1966

To LMS

THOMAS C. SMITH, Professor of History at Stanford University, is the author of *Political Change and Industrial Development in Japan, 1868-1880*. He has taught at Stanford since 1948 and traveled extensively in Japan since 1945. A Japanese translation of *The Agrarian Origins of Modern Japan* will be published in 1966.

Published by Atheneum
Reprinted by arrangement with Stanford University Press
Copyright © 1959 by the Board of Trustees of
The Leland Stanford Junior University
All rights reserved
Printed in the United States of America by
The Murray Printing Company, Forge Village, Massachusetts
Bound by The Colonial Press, Inc., Clinton, Massachusetts
Published in Canada by McClelland & Stewart Ltd.
First Atheneum Edition

CONTENTS

INTRODUCTION

INTRODUCTION

In the course of its long history, Japanese agriculture has in some respects changed remarkably little. Farming is scarcely less a family enterprise now than it was a thousand years ago; holdings are still tiny and fragmented, tools simple, and rice the main crop. Although a Heian peasant would no doubt be perplexed by many things about contemporary farming—above all about its human relations—the main operations of planting, tilling, and harvesting he would understand. This is an impressive fact which has given rise to imposing theories of Japanese society and history.

But the resistance of Japanese agriculture to change, though notable, is sometimes exaggerated. The impression is even given that nothing essential about it has changed. Although this view cannot be supported, it has many adherents and quietly presides over much earnest discussion of cultural issues seemingly remote from it. One reason for its currency is that in some countries of the West there have been dramatic changes in particular aspects of farming that in Japan have changed scarcely at all, so that it is tempting to dismiss as unimportant such changes as in fact have taken place.

These changes, however, were of great importance for Japanese history, perhaps justifying comparison with the agricultural revolution in Europe. As one might expect, they occurred at widely different times in different regions and were far too complex to capture in a word or phrase; but taking the country as a whole they fell mainly in the Tokugawa period, and their central feature was a shift from cooperative to individual farming. At the beginning of the period, farming was generally carried on through the cooperation of families organized into actual or putative kinship groups, who to some extent shared land, labor, animals, tools, and even food and housing. By the end of the period, however, such cooperation had largely disappeared. Although it lingered on for a generation or more in isolated places, in the end the individual family nearly everywhere clearly emerged as the center of production organization and economic interest.

This mighty change is easier to describe than explain, but if one of its causes may be singled out as especially important, it must be the growth of the market, with all that implies about changes in men's ways and ideas. More than any other influence the market lifted economic life in the village out of the context of traditional social groupings. Economic exchange, which had been merely an aspect of social relations, a necessary concomitant of kinship, became increasingly independent of social organization and created values of its own. Thereafter what goods and services men gave and received, on what occasions and in what amounts, was less a matter of obligation than whether the price was right.

This was a disruptive tendency in a society based even among the peasants on a hierarchy of birth. Economic life in the village had been organized around lineages, which provided a distributive as well as a productive system; now it ignored or worked against them. As family gain became the chief end of economic activity, new productive energies were released and income was more and more distributed without regard to status. Old wealthy families laden with prestige came on hard times; new cadet lines added field to field, moving into the landlord class. Thus the power of status, traditionally defined, was greatly reduced, and new routes were opened to social position and political power. The results were far-reaching. Peasant society took on an unprecedented mobility of which the effects were felt far beyond the boundaries of the peasant class; agriculture became competitive, productivity increased, commercial and industrial activity in the countryside flourished; there were even profound shifts of political power in many villages.

This book attempts to sketch these changes in bare outline and to suggest their significance for modern Japan. But first I wish to make a disclaimer lest readers without a knowledge of Japanese be left with the false impression that this book is based mainly on original materials. Parts of it are (especially Chapter 12) and I have tried to check sources everywhere, but I have been unable to do this consistently since many of the most important materials are still unpublished. As a result, I have had to depend heavily on the researches of Japanese scholars, who since the war have devoted themselves with awesome energy to collecting and studying the Tokugawa manuscript materials that are scattered in profusion about the countryside. I hope my notes provide an adequate acknowledgment of indebtedness, but I wish to mention especially the work of Professors Ariga Kizaemon, Furushima

Toshio, Miyagawa Mitsuru, and the late Toya Toshiyuki; I can hardly express the debt I owe to the researches of these four men.

I also wish to thank Professor Andō Seiichi and Mr. Kanai Madoka, both of whom helped me in more ways than I can enumerate here; Mrs. Elizabeth Spurr for editing the manuscript; Professor Mary C. Wright, Professor Bruce F. Johnston, and Mrs. Jeanne M. Smith for reading parts or all of the manuscript and making helpful criticisms. Finally, I wish to express my gratitude to the Social Science Research Council and to the Ford Foundation for financial aid, to Mr. John Rich of the National Broadcasting Company for sharing his house with me at a difficult time in Japan, and to the Stanford University Press for uncommon liberality and efficiency in the making of this book.

Part I

THE TRADITIONAL VILLAGE

PROVINCES OF JAPAN IN 1868

Aki 48
Awa 42
Awa (Bōshū) 13
Awaji 41
Bingo 50
Bitchū 49
Bizen 51
Bungo 63
Buzen 62
Chikugo 64
Chikuzen 61
Echigo 16
Echizen 20
Etchū 18
Harima 52
Hida 24
Higo 66
Hitachi 8
Hizen 65
Hōki 58
Hyūga 67
Iga 32
Inaba 56
Ise 33
Iwaki 6
Iwami 60
Iwashiro 7

Iyo 44
Izu 28
Izumi 37
Izumo 59
Kaga 19
Kai 26
Kawachi 38
Kazusa 12
Kii (Kishū) 35
Kōzuke 10
Mikawa 30
Mimasaka 57
Mino 23
Musashi 15
Mutsu 1
Nagato 47
Noto 17
Ōmi 22
Ōsumi 69
Owari 31
Rikuchū 2
Rikuzen 4
Sagami 14
Sanuki 45
Satsuma 68
Settsu (Sesshū) 40
Shima 34

Shimōsa 11
Shimotsuke 9
Shinano (Shinshū) 25
Suruga 27
Suō 46
Tajima 55
Tamba 53
Tango 54
Tosa 43
Tōtōmi 29
Ugo 3
Uzen 5
Wakasa 21
Yamashiro 39
Yamato 36

REGIONS

Hokuriku 16–21
Kantō 8–15
Kinai 36–40
Kyūshū 61–69
Sanyō 46–52
Shikoku 42–45
Tōhoku 1–7
Tōsan 22–26

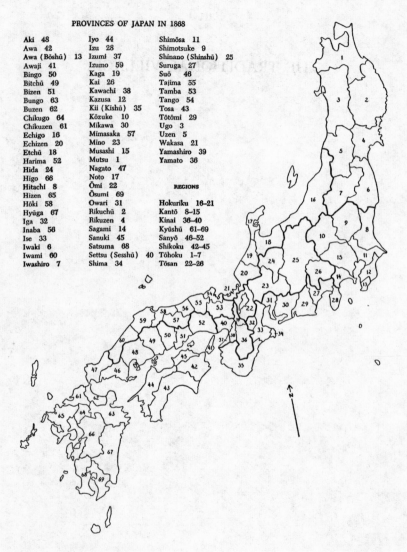

1

THE LAND SYSTEM

No one of its aspects alone provides a satisfactory understanding of agrarian society as a whole, but none perhaps reveals the broad contours so clearly as the system of landholding. We get our first glimpse of the Tokugawa land system toward the end of the sixteenth century when Nobunaga's brilliant successors, Hideyoshi and Ieyasu, were completing their work of conquest and beginning the task of building a stable political order. [Agrarian policy inevitably claimed their early attention: land and peasants were the ultimate bases of military power, and government could ill afford laxness in either controlling or exploiting them.] To avoid any such failure, the conquerors made cadastral surveys of their own territories and of new ones as these were brought under control. The surveys served to tie the peasant population to the land, to tighten the collection of the land tax, and to permit the assignment of fiefs with secure knowledge of their value. But the surveys did even more: they allowed overlords (*ryōshu*) to collect taxes directly from the peasants and so to remove armed retainers from the land to castle towns. By thus cutting off the lower-ranking warriors from the bases of independent power and making them mere stipendiaries, the overlords eliminated at a stroke one of the chief sources of political instability in the previous era.

The work of surveying went slowly; it could proceed no faster than the pacification of the country, and until 1600 fighting was a continuous distraction. But by the end of the first decade of the seventeenth century surveys had been completed nearly everywhere,[1] and they continued to be made periodically thereafter to take account of changes in the extent of arable and the size and productivity of fields.[a]

[1] Numbers refer to Notes (pp. 215–27), primarily citations of sources and relevant collateral material. Footnotes are designated by letters.

[a] Ideally, surveys should not have been more widely spaced than about ten years, but in fact they were commonly less frequent, probably owing to the enormous administrative effort required to survey and classify and register the thousands upon thousands of fields in the domain of even one of the smaller *daimyō*; the result was

lord's register

None of Nobunaga's surveys has survived; the earliest extant survey dates from 1583 in Hideyoshi's time,[2] but after that <u>land registers</u> or *kenchichō*, as the recording documents were called, survive in ever-increasing number. The earliest registers differ in detail from the later, which permitted less land to escape registration and were far more rigorous in classifying and surveying fields. But they all had the same objective: to register within a small and more or less carefully defined area—usually a village[b]—each taxable field; to record the name of its holder, its extent, the quality of its soil, and its estimated yield. The last datum, called *kokudaka*, was a figure arrived at by test-harvesting (*tsubo-kari*) scattered squares in the field, taking into account whether the current yields were good or bad and production costs in the particular village high or low. Factors that officials were often enjoined to take into consideration in setting *kokudaka* were how far tax grain had to be transported, the number of animals and the extent of common land in the village, the expense and difficulty of maintaining irrigation works, whether the village had sources of income other than agriculture, and whether it was rich or poor. The *kokudaka* therefore was an estimate of normal yield with adjustments for factors affecting taxable capacity.[a] The *kokudaka* of each holding and of the village as a whole could be derived from the *kokudaka* of individual fields.

The data contained in the *kenchichō* permit us to go far beyond the general statements of literary sources in understanding the land system and its place in rural life. They nevertheless do not give us as full a picture as we could wish since they registered land from but one of two relevant points of view—the lord's, which did not always coincide with that of the village. The disparities in the registration of land that sometimes resulted from the divergence of these viewpoints are very revealing, but they are not important at the moment. It will suffice for the present to see landholding as the lord did, through the *kenchichō* only, noting however that land was *more equitably* distributed in these registers than in those compiled from the viewpoint of the village. (See Chapter 4.)

---

that *kokudaka* did not always fully reflect taxable capacity, to the great advantage of the peasant.

[b] In the late sixteenth and early seventeenth centuries, *kenchichō* often corresponded to the boundaries of *shō* or *gō*, older units of local administration which frequently contained more than one village. But *kenchichō* compiled after about 1615–24, with few exceptions, were confined to individual villages, whose exact boundaries they were often instrumental in defining—a function called *mura-kiri*. (Endō Shinnosuke, "Kinsei shoki kenchi ni okeru 'mura' no seiritsu," *SKSG*, XX, 2 (1954), 46–49.)

The *kenchichō* reveal a remarkably uniform pattern of landholding in all parts of the country. Typically they show in each village a few large holdings, somewhat more middling holdings, and a great many more small holdings, with some large holdings bulking many times the size of some small—ten or twenty times was very common and even a hundred or more not unknown. But within this pattern, which is illustrated in Table I, there was considerable difference be-

TABLE I

LANDHOLDING IN SELECTED VILLAGES*

(Figures show yield or *kokudaka* of individual holdings:
1 *koku* = 4.96 bushels of rice or rice equivalents)

Village	Province	Date	Number of Holdings						
			0–5 Koku	5–10 Koku	10–20 Koku	20–30 Koku	30–40 Koku	Over 40 Koku	Total
Shimo	Echigo	1587	13	4		1			18
Kibuchi	Shinano	1666	1		5	10	5	2	23
Tsukiyama	Yamashiro	1694	8	2	2	1			13
Makuuchi	Iwashiro	1691	5	8	14	2	1		30

* Kitajima Masamoto, "Echigo sankan chitai no okeru junsui hōkensei no kōzō," *SGZS*, LIX, 6 (1950), 9; Suzuki Hisashi, "Kinsei nōson no ichi keitai," *RGKK*, 149 (1951), 37; Fujita Gorō, *Kinsei ni okeru nōminsō no kaikyū bunka*, Tokyo, 1949, pp. 190–91; Furushima Toshio, "Edo jidai ni okeru Kinai nōgyō to kisei jinushi," *RGKK*, 144 (1950), 8–9; and Furushima Toshio, *Kinsei Nihon nōgyō no kōzō* (Tokyo, 1948), p. 593.

tween the Kinai region and the rest of the country. As Professor Miyagawa has shown by study of land registers from the late sixteenth and early seventeenth centuries, holdings in the Kinai tended to be substantially smaller than elsewhere, partly because the largest holdings were less large, but mainly because the proportion of very small marginal holdings was extremely high.[c] It is to be understood, of

[c] According to Professor Miyagawa's data, the proportion of holdings of three *tan* or less was over 70 percent in most Kinai villages and over 80 in some, although outside the Kinai such small holdings rarely accounted for more than 50 percent of all holdings and in some places for as few as 20. (Miyagawa Mitsuru, "Gōson seido to kenchi," *NSKK*, 19 (1953), 15–16.) It has been suggested that Professor Miyagawa's figures are skewed by the fact that some holdings were scattered through more than one village. This would make most villages appear to have more small holdings than they actually did. But there is no reason to believe that this tendency would have been especially strong in the Kinai; besides, when it is possible to identify and eliminate holdings not lying entirely in one village, the land registers show much the same pattern of landholding as before. For examples see Akiyama Hideo, "Kinsei shotō ni okeru Kinai sonraku no kenchi ni tsuite," *Hisutoria*, 5 (1952), 46.

course, that these regional patterns represented statistical tendencies only and that many villages in both regions conformed more closely to the other regional type than their own.

[The two patterns of landholding, as we shall see, reflected different stages of economic development, not immutable regional types imposed by terrain and climate. The pattern outside the Kinai had prevailed earlier in the Kinai, while the present pattern there was destined to become increasingly common in other areas as time passed. As to why the Kinai should have been economically in advance of other parts of the country in 1600, one need but recall that it was uniquely urban[d] owing to a constellation of favoring factors, among them a relatively benign climate that permitted double cropping, a central geographical location, easy communications with other regions, and the location in the area since very early times of the Imperial Court and its fisc. Urban life and commerce had developed first in the Kinai and centered there ever since; in Kyoto, Fushimi, Osaka, and Sakai the Kinai still boasted the country's only real cities as late as 1590— and these four cities totaled approximately 400,000 population, all comfortably within a circle with a diameter of perhaps forty miles.[e] By comparison the rest of the country was a rural fastness broken, when at all, merely by small local markets and widely scattered port and castle towns that rarely counted 5,000 inhabitants each.[e] [The villages adjoining these towns were probably very similar to Kinai villages where commercial agriculture flourished; holdings were small and intensively worked, and farming was combined with other occupations.] But beyond them lay a limitless hinterland of villages where subsistence farming still held sway and men had yet to feel the first sharp tremors of change emanating from the towns.

Thus, variously shaped by different rates of economic develop-

---

[d] Urban influences seem universally a dissolvent of older agrarian forms. Speaking of one phase of the agricultural revolution in Europe, Marc Bloch notes: "Les pays de peuplement intense et plus particulièrement de fort développement urbain furent partout les premiers à abolir la jachère: telles les banlieues de quelques villes allemandes, quelques campagnes de Normandie ou de Provence,—mais surtout les deux grandes contrées de civilisation urbaine qu'ait connues l'Europe, dès le moyenâge: Italie du Nord et Flandre." (*Les caractères originaux de l'histoire rurale française*, Paris, 1952, p. 220.)

[e] The only notable exception may have been Kamakura, in which twenty thousand people are said to have perished in the great famine of the thirteenth century, but it is uncertain what the population was in 1590. Edo at that date had just come into the hands of Ieyasu and was not yet a significant population center. ("Kamakura," *Sekai rekishi jiten*, IV, 193 ff.)

ment, regional patterns of landowning pointed to different modes of farming. How different these modes were, with what consequences, might easily be overlooked since differences were obscured by a general similarity of landscape and technology. Differences were to be seen mainly in the organization of labor on the larger holdings. Unlike small holdings, which in both regions were worked by family labor, these large ones required more labor than the ordinary family could supply. In the Kinai and other economically advanced areas, this problem was solved by surrendering the management and cultivation of the excess land to tenants, and this practice was carried so far on some holdings as almost to reduce them to mere legal entities. Over the rest of the country, though an inconveniently located plot here and there might be given over to tenant cultivation, large holdings were worked as farming units by the holder and his various dependents. The latter mode of farming was called *tezukuri* to distinguish it from the former, called *kosaku*.

That tenancy had little importance outside the Kinai until the eighteenth century is attested by the fact that not until then did administrative handbooks give it more than passing attention, although from that time on they began to regard it as the crux of the agrarian problem.[5] This conclusion from literary testimony is supported by the history of individual holdings outside the Kinai. Rarely was the shift to tenant cultivation noticeable before 1700 and in many instances it did not begin until considerably later; in any case it started only under the stimulus of commercial farming, which cannot be dated as a powerful movement in most parts of the country until well into the eighteenth century.

The social relations characteristic of the two modes of farming were of course very different, though historically closely related. Specifically, landlord-tenant relations had evolved from the social relations of *tezukuri*, and much of the history of agrarian institutions is implicit in that subtle but radical transition. Since a major part of this book is devoted to tracing the intricate course and consequences of this change, it is essential to understand the web of social relations characteristic of *tezukuri*, the prior of the two modes.

At the center of the web was the immediate family of the holder, a nuclear family consisting of a married couple and their unmarried children. This group usually did not constitute the whole population of the holding, but it was always distinct within the larger group, its rights in the land infinitely stronger, its ceremonial position superior. The nuclear group was generally small, rarely numbering more than four or five persons, not all of whom could be regularly employed in farming, some being engaged in household occupations and others too young or too old to work. With the occasional help of neighbors such groups were able to work the average holding, and the majority of families were consequently of this type. But it is evident that on large holdings these groups were by no means autonomous agricultural units. A seventeenth-century treatise on farming, the anonymous *Hōnen zeisho*, states that the full-time labor of about four or five able-bodied adults was required to work one *chō* of arable, eight or nine to work two, and about 12 to work three—the holding in each case being part paddy and part unirrigated land.[6] From the land registers it is known that at this time holdings ranging between one and a half and five *chō*—requiring seven to twenty full-time workers—were not uncommon, especially outside the region of tenant cultivation.[7]

Most of the supplementary labor needed for holdings of this size, as the village population registers reveal, came from members of the extended family. Perhaps the most convenient way to visualize this larger group is to think of it as composed of three concentric circles. The first or smallest circle consisted of the nuclear family of the holder; the next larger consisted of affinal and cognate relatives none of whom were in direct line of descent; and the third or largest consisted of persons related to the holder by neither blood nor marriage but who were nevertheless registered as part of his family and incorporated in it ceremonially. The number of persons in each circle varied considerably from one family to another, and a family might have either one of the outer circles without the other. There were likely to be marriage groups in either of the outer circles.

The population registers, in which the population of the village was periodically recorded, indicate that there was a generous sprinkling of these large extended families almost everywhere outside the Kinai—one, two, or three to a village.[f] The practice of tenant cultivation made this type of family organization less useful in the Kinai, but even there

---

[f] Professor Furushima's data on three Shinshū villages in the latter half of the seventeenth century are perhaps typical. Counting affines and cognates only, there were in the three villages a total of 65 families with between one and five members, 35 with between six and ten, five with between ten and fifteen, and one with twenty. Fifty-four of the families had one married couple, 31 had two, seven had three, three had four, and one had six. (Furushima Toshio, *Kinsei Nihon nōgyō no kōzō*, pp. 104–5.)

instances of it were to be found.[8] Counting the first two circles only, the extended family usually consisted of two or more marriage groups and eight to twelve members, but occasionally even this restricted group would run to twenty or more persons. A peasant family in Shinano Province in 1661, for example, was composed as follows (ages in parentheses) :[9]

```
            family head (41)
              wife (39)
                son (22)
                son (17)
              mother (82)
              cousin, son of paternal uncle (67)
                wife
              cousin, son of paternal uncle (61)
                wife
                  son (24)
                  son (33)
                  son (35)
                    wife
                  son (38)
                    wife (34)
                      son (1)
                      daughter (12)
                      daughter (10)
                      daughter (8)
            wife of deceased cousin, son of paternal uncle (51)
              daughter (21)
              daughter (9)
              daughter (7)
```

The identification of this type of family with the large holding is brought out clearly by the land and population registers for 1645 of a village in central Honshū.[g] Families in this village with holdings of less than 20-*koku* yield were significantly smaller and more often nuclear families than those with larger holdings. They averaged exactly four members per family; very few had any members in the second circle and none had members in the third. Families on larger holdings,

---

[g] The tendency of family size and organization to follow labor requirements is still noticeable, especially in Tōhoku, where it is reduced to an aphorism used as advice to the man short of labor—namely, *"Uma ka yome ka,"* which means get either a horse or a bride. The tendency is clear in the 1938 agricultural census, which showed that the average family size increased according to the amount of arable land held, as follows (family size in parentheses): 10.2 *tan* (5.50 members), 12.1 (7.67), 12.3 (7.75), 20.2 (7.78), 20.6 (8.36), 21.5 (8.00). Ōuchi Tsutomu, *Nōka keizai*, Tokyo, 1957, p. 115.)

however, averaged 5.5 members in the nuclear family, 7.7 in the first two circles, and 22.5 in all three!

The proximate reason for the differences in respect to the first two circles is evident from a more detailed breakdown: the larger families held members in the group, especially married children and brothers of the family head, whom the smaller family regularly eliminated.[a] This was no doubt because the larger family needed the labor of the additional members or at least could support them, while the smaller family did not. Thus the peasant family could evidently expand and contract its boundaries, alter its size and organization within the first two circles, as the economics of the holding might require. But its adaptability went even further: it could also, when necessary, adjust its organization and bring within its boundaries persons from the outside without benefit of blood or marriage relationships; that is, add a third circle. We must now briefly consider who occupied this third circle.

Persons in the third circle consisted of members of one or both of two broad status groups—servants and persons called *nago*. Servants were at different places and times held under widely different conditions, but in the early seventeenth century most of this class were either hereditary servants called *fudai*, who together with their children passed down in a family from generation to generation, or indentured servants bound for exceedingly long terms ranging from ten years or so to life. Both types of servants lived with the master, who by custom was deemed responsible not only for their food and clothing but also for their upbringing, their conduct in the village, and their

[a] This is clear from the following breakdown (figures in each group based on 100 for family head) (Furushima, *Kinsei Nihon nōgyō no kōzō*, p. 106):

	Families with More Than 20 *koku*	Families with Fewer Than 20 *koku*
Family head	100	100
Father	0	5
Mother	0	4
Wife	100	86
Children	283	159
Daughters-in-law	50	9
Grandchildren	25	0
Uncles	0	0
Brothers	50	27
Sisters-in-law	42	5
Nephews and nieces	63	0
Wives of nephews	8	0

general welfare. Consequently, the assimilation of servants to family members in the population registers, though accompanied by a notation to the effect that they were servants and not kin, was no conceit of administrative officials but a sound and even necessary administrative practice.

We shall call such servants generically *"genin,"* to distinguish them from servants of shorter term who normally were not listed with the family and were not common until a later time. (See Chapter 8.) *Genin* were to be found in considerable number in every part of the country, no less in the Kinai than elsewhere. One must be cautious about making broad statistical estimates, but scattered population registers suggest that *genin* accounted for about 10 percent of the total peasant population in the seventeenth century.[10] They were of course not spread uniformly through the farms of any locality, being confined mainly to large holdings, though some were scattered about on middling and even small holdings where for unusual reasons labor was short. On some large holdings they were present in startling numbers; families who maintained between five and ten *genin* were not uncommon and one occasionally finds a family with 20 or more.[11] But, on the other hand, some large holders used no servant labor at all; one supposes because other types of labor were ample in these cases.[i]

The second group of people, whom we have called *"nago,"* went by a variety of local names—*nago, hikan, sakugo, kado, kamado, shita-byakushō, tsukuri-byakushō, fudai, takashita, uchi no mono.* There were innumerable variations of status within this group, but its members almost universally held small plots of land and separate dwellings from holders to whom they owed labor services in return, and this is perhaps the single most reliable way of identifying them.

Nago were sometimes unmarried, but more often they were husbands and fathers whose offspring would either inherit their status or become *genin.* Although the land worked by a *nago* was registered in the holder's name, the *nago's* name was sometimes entered after the holder's to indicate that he was the cultivator. This subordinate form of registration presumably confirmed his limited rights in the land, but it did not make him the holder recognized by the lord and legally

---

[i] Hikozaemon, who lived with a family of 18 in a certain village, for example, had no servants; but in the same village Hirosaemon with a family of three and a holding about the same size as Hikozaemon's employed two servants, and Kiyosuke with a family of 20 but an extremely large holding of 54 *tan* employed six servants. (Miyagawa Mitsuru, "Taikō kenchi to kazoku kōsei" (4), *Hisutoria*, 11 (1955), 39–40.)

responsible for taxes. [Since, therefore, *nago* nominally bore no share of the tax burden laid on the village, even though they might actually pay taxes in the holder's name, they were not considered members of the village in several important respects.] They had no share in village common land and water rights; they could not hold village office or take part in the selection of village officials or even join the village assembly in discussing the formal business of the community; they were normally not even members of the five-family groups into which the village was divided for administrative purposes. Insofar as they took part in the public life of the village, they did so through the holder to whom they were subordinate.[12]

Nago constituted a much larger proportion of the population in some parts of the country than in others, and they were almost wholly absent from some. Of the four major regions of the country whose seventeenth-century land and population registers have been intensively studied, Kyūshū, Tōhoku, and Tōsan had large *nago* populations which survived, much reduced, into the twentieth century; this is perhaps the main reason the social and economic history of these areas has been so intensively studied. The Kinai region, whose economy was far more advanced than that of any other, stands at the other extreme. *Nago* either did not exist there in significant numbers or did not exist in the form familiar to us elsewhere. But, since *nago* tended to disappear from other regions as the market developed, it is probable that they were once common in the Kinai also but had largely disappeared before the earliest modern land and population registers. In this connection it is suggestive that parts of the country not much studied until now, and which fall economically between the Kinai and backward areas such as Tōhoku and Kyūshū, are yielding increasing evidence of a widespread and surprisingly heavy *nago* population.[13]

Nago in the seventeenth century were unevenly distributed in the various localities as well as over the country as a whole. A census of five counties of Buzen Province in northern Kyūshū made between 1681 and 1684 shows a *nago* population comprising just over half of all households, but from one county to another the proportion varied from as low as 36 to as high as 60 percent.[14] There were sometimes even greater differences between villages in the same area.ʲ One hesitates to assign reasons for these sharp local variations. Judging from

ʲ In a cluster of 14 villages in Echigo, for example, *nago* accounted for 40 percent of all households, but the figure in particular villages was as low as 4 percent and as high as 70.

the rather clear tendency for *nago* populations to be heavier in mountainous areas than in broad open valleys, one is inclined to think that degree of accessibility to market influences may have been the decisive factor; but it must be admitted at once that the relative thinness of the *nago* population in lowland plains and valleys would equally support the conjecture that *nago* were less efficient than other kinds of labor in rice culture.

To summarize: the land registers of the seventeenth century reveal the existence in most-villages of one or two holdings very much larger than the average. Although in the Kinai and a few other places these holdings were given over mainly to tenant cultivation, in the more backward regions typical of the time they were worked mainly by the holders. From population registers it is clear that part of the needed labor was supplied by expanding the family of kin beyond the limits usual on small holdings. This was accomplished by holding in the family the younger generations after marriage and retaining members of collateral lines of descent.

But frequently even this type of expansion failed to provide enough labor, and then additional labor was recruited in one or both of two forms. One was *nago* who were settled on the land and given dwellings in return for their labor; the other was hereditary or other servants held for very long terms. The two had this in common: both were usually in some degree incorporated in the holder's family since the family was the unique means of organizing labor for farming. There was a natural tendency to consider as part of the family anyone brought more or less permanently into its farming organization—a fact accurately reflected by the land registers.

We may go a step further. The reader may have noticed that the farming organization on large holdings in backward areas linked, through the extended family, the two main classes of Tokugawa peasant society—those who held land and those who did not. These classes corresponded respectively to the inner and outer circles of our imaginary diagram. But to understand their relations as parts of a functioning system it is necessary to see how and why those without land were brought within the system. It will be convenient for this purpose to speak first of *genin*, or servants, and then of *nago*.

2

AGRICULTURAL SERVANTS

In the seventeenth century family and farming were indivisible. Successful farming could be sustained only insofar as the family provided a legacy of land and capital and a disciplined labor force in which youth with its energy and age with its authority were mingled. Since life in the village, for all but a few, was impossible without farming, those whose families could not use their labor and so provide for them took refuge in other families. Such people might occasionally escape to the city or into another occupation, but until the market greatly widened such opportunities, most took the only course open and became *genin*. In fact, the father or elder brother or uncle, or whoever was the family head, usually made that decision for the unwanted member and put him out to work, taking whatever compensation his person or labor would bring.

Genin typically came from families whose size had outrun the resources of their small holdings. The anonymous author of the *Hōnen zeisho*, writing in the latter half of the seventeenth century, remarked: "Everywhere fields are divided and redivided, until finally holdings of seven, five, and even one *tan* or less appear. The holders of such small farms put their children out in the service of others."[1] His statement is confirmed by the population registers, which sometimes listed, along with current residents of the village, persons who were presently serving elsewhere as *genin*.[a] It was this, rather than partitioning or a lower birth rate, that kept the family on small holdings small *and* nuclear.

Faced with the necessity of eliminating someone if the group was to survive, the family naturally unburdened itself of least valuable

---

[a] Of 69 persons serving as servants outside a village in Ōmi Province in 1678, all but one came from families with fewer than five *koku* of arable and 41 came from families with fewer than three *koku*. (Imai Michiko, "Kinsei Ōmi no nōmin keizai," *NSKK*, 26 (1955), 45.) Sixty-nine servants from a single village and all but one from the same class: no wonder family size and composition varied notably with class.

members first. Other things being equal, these were persons presently or potentially members of collateral lines—daughters, younger sons, brothers of the family head. Even the poor peasant family, which had few means of creating social distance among members, made a distinction between main and collateral lines. As a Tokugawa writer put it, poor families sent out as *genin* "children from the second son down."[b] We need not take the statement to mean literally that younger sons only were put out, but simply that who went was generally determined by genealogy.[2]

We have already seen that the person sent out as a *genin* typically joined a family larger than his own, and in doing so not only made his own smaller and simpler but made the other larger and more complex. This is not to say that he became immediately and in all respects a member of the new family, but in time he did so to some degree—especially if he were a *fudai*, or hereditary servant.

Fudai were acquired for the most part in two ways: either they were born of *fudai* who were already held, or they were acquired by purchase or gift from poor families with a surfeit of members. A famous traveler in the eighteenth century tells us that wealthy peasants in Kyūshū usually owned *fudai* whose children, suggestively called *"niwa no ko"* (children of the garden), belonged to the master. He could sell or otherwise dispose of them as he wished, and it was usual for him to give one or two as servants to each daughter upon marriage.[3] *Fudai* were acquired by birth in other areas also, but it is possible that the powers of the master were especially strong in Kyūshū.

Occasionally population registers from the same village at different dates permit us to follow a *fudai* line through more than one generation in a family. In the excerpts below from population registers of 1689, 1721, and 1744 for a village in Shinshū, we see a certain Hachi- suke—"*genin*"—marrying, growing old, and having his children take his place in the largest holding family in the village. We do not know when and how Hachisuke came to this family, but he belonged to it as a *genin* in 1689, at the age of 18. When we hear of him next in 1721 (1722?), he was 51 and married to a woman who was 43; he and his

---

[b] Kodama Kōta, "Edo jidai nōson ni okeru kazoku seiin no mondai," *Rekishi chiri*, LXV, 4 (1935), 52. There is much testimony to this effect; for instance, Suyama Don'o (1657–1732), writing on Sado Island at the end of the seventeenth and in the early eighteenth centuries, tells us: "Second and third sons who have ability become the adopted sons of peasants without heirs, or they become *nago*, or, again, they are hired for public tasks in the village. . . ." ("Dokokudan," *NKSS*, IV, 147.)

wife had a son whom the scribe neglected to register, but of whom we
learn later. By this time Jin'emon, who was the master and family
head in 1689, had been succeeded by his son Sakunai. In the last of
the three registers, Hachisuke had reached the venerable age of 74
(73?), his wife was 69 (66?), and his son, Kiyokichi, was 33 and married. Once again the headship of the master's family had changed,
Sakunai having been replaced by his youngest son, filially named
Jin'emon after his grandfather.⁴ Such careers must have been very
common, for seventeenth-century population registers show not only
a high proportion of young children among *genin* but also a nice balancing of the sexes among the adult *genin*.ᶜ

CAREER OF HACHISUKE, "GENIN," 1689–1744, IN IMAI FAMILY,
IMAI VILLAGE, SHINSHŪ⁵
(Ages in parentheses)

Date	Family Head	*Genin*
1689	Jin'emon (73)	Hachisuke (18)
1721	Sakunai	Hachisuke (51)
		Wife (43)
1744	Jin'emon	Hachisuke (74)
		Wife (69)
		Kiyokichi, son (33)
		Wife (28)

Not all *fudai*, of course, were born servants. Many were the sons
or daughters of impoverished holders who had given them away or,
more likely, sold them, usually as children when they were most bur-
densome and could make no resistance. All parental rights were surrendered along with the child in such cases; at least our Kyūshū
traveler stated that the parents could make no complaint even if the
buyer subsequently mistreated or sold the child.⁶ But since the parents
were usually frightfully poor, they could scarcely have ventured a
complaint against a well-to-do and influential family anyway. Although
no doubt marked by pathos and bitterness, the sale of children was not
without its happy side; for it often gave the child opportunities which,

ᶜ Of 59 *genin* serving in a village in 1652–54, five were between one and five
years old, four were between six and ten, and four were between eleven and fifteen.
Indicative of the balancing of sexes, suggesting family groupings, is the composition
of the *genin* population on individual holdings, as on this one: adult males: aged 32,
31, and 28; adult females: aged 28 and 25; children: aged 9, 5, 4, and 1. (Takeuchi Harutoshi, "Higashi Shinshū chihō ni okeru kinsei sonraku no seiritsu to
hatten," *Nihon rekishi*, 77 (1954), 19–20.)

however limited, were beyond the means of the parents to offer, and
not infrequently it was even the only alternative to infanticide—not of
the child in question, perhaps, but of an infant sibling.[d] Moreover, if
genin were subject to especially harsh treatment, we do not hear of it.
Possibly we would not anyway.

In any case sales were very common, as is attested by contemporary
witnesses and extant "bills of sale." A journal kept during the eighteenth century by a peasant family in present-day Iwate Prefecture repeatedly mentions crop failures and in the same breath states that local
families were selling members as *fudai* in Sendai;[e] we learn elsewhere
that about six thousand persons were sold as *fudai* between 1622 and
1629 in a single county in northern Honshū.[7] There is much testimony
of this kind; but even without it we should guess that such sales were
commonplace and even socially sanctioned, since the Bakufu was forced
repeatedly to prohibit the practice after first outlawing it in 1619.[8]
Even the Bakufu seemed at times to admit that the practice might be
socially useful, as in 1675, when it issued a directive to officials stating:
"Because of the flood that affected several provinces last year, the
people are in terrible distress. This year, therefore, even if people are
taken as servants for *long terms or made fudai,* no objection shall be
made. . . ."[9]

Let us follow in imagination the career of the typical new *fudai.*
Having been separated from his parents, the young boy (or girl) was
brought up by the master along with his own children; he lived with
them under the same roof, ate from the same board, played the same
games. Though in some respects treated differently from the master's
children (who were by no means all treated alike),[f] he was taught the

[d] It is well known of course that infanticide was prevalent in the Tokugawa
period among the rural poor. It was possibly because they had been saved from
this fate that many *fudai* were named by their masters "Kaisuke" (Bought-and-
Saved).

[e] The journal runs from 1689 to 1824; one hand-written copy is in the
author's possession and another is in the *Shiryō hensanjo* at Tokyo University.

[f] It should be noted that sons were not treated identically. This is nicely illustrated by the following quotation from the house laws of 1798 of a wealthy
Echigo family:

"Item: Until the main heir (*sōryō*) is ten he may wear silk, but after that he
should dress the same as the master of the family. It is especially important for him
to pay the closest attention to farming and to the traditional business of the family.
Of course he must learn the way of cultivating and of governing the family. He
shall follow the way of his ancestors always, neither changing the family business nor

same elementary social lessons: respect for elders, seating arrangements
at meals, the proper forms of address for the various family members—
above all, concern for the traditions and good name of the family.
A written code of conduct accepted by the inhabitants of one village
says: "Man's character is originally neither good nor bad. If a person
becomes accustomed to good he will be good, but if he becomes accustomed to bad he will be bad. Every man must therefore instruct
his children and *genin* in proper conduct."[10] It behooved the young
genin to take the lessons taught him to heart, for his present treatment,
acceptance by the village, and future prospects depended on winning
a recognized place in the family in which his life now centered. As he
learned its lore, worked and celebrated and mourned with it, and as the
memory of his own parents grew dim,[g] he came eventually to feel that
he belonged where he was, to accept the family as his own.

By imperceptible degrees the family also accepted him.[h] Not only
would the *fudai*, upon reaching a suitable age, be permitted to take a
wife and bring her into the group, but the master, taking the role of
parent, might arrange the match. The young man would now move

---

undertaking new things. If he violates the teaching of his parents and is thus unfilial he shall be disinherited.

"Item: The second, third, and other sons may wear silk to the age of seven,
but thereafter they shall wear nothing but cotton right down to their undergarments.
Until seventeen they shall study letters and arithmetic, but thereafter they shall devote themselves to work in the fields. It is strictly prohibited that they indulge in
fashionable and frivolous pastimes. Each son who founds a branch family shall inherit one-fifteenth of the family land. . . . But no more than twenty *ryō* may
be given to a son who is adopted into another family." (Kitajima Masamoto,
"Watanabeke no jinushiteki seikaku ni tsuite," *Essa kenkyū*, 2 (1952), 56.)

[g] *Genin*—particularly *fudai* or servants with very long terms of service—more
often than not served *outside* the village of their birth. Mr. Ichikawa estimates
that, in the late seventeenth century in northeastern Shinano, only 20 percent of
all *genin* were serving in their native villages. (Ichikawa Yūichirō, *Saku-chihō Edo
jidai no nōson seikatsu*, Nozawa, 1955, p. 84.)

[h] The practice of taking persons of low status associated with a family into it
as members was by no means confined to Japanese peasant society. Many other
examples might be given, but it will suffice perhaps to cite one notable case. Mr.
Evans-Pritchard tells us that the Nuer of the Sudan incorporated Dinka captives
into the family. "Captured Dinka boys," he writes, "are almost invariably incorporated into the lineage of their Nuer captors by rite of adoption, and they then rank
as sons in lineage structure as well as in family relations, and when the daughters
of that lineage are married they receive bride-cattle. A Dinka boy is brought up
as a child of his captor's household. He is already incorporated into the family and
joint family by his acceptance as a member of these groups by their other members
and by outsiders. People say . . . 'he has become a member of the community,'
and they say of the man who captured him that 'he has become his father,' and of
his sons that they have become his brothers." (E.E. Evans-Pritchard, *The Nuer*,
Oxford, 1940, pp. 221–22.)

from the main house where he had been living into one of the surrounding outbuildings, just as a son did upon marriage. Though the new dwelling was small and rough, probably a one-room hut with earthen floor, it was his to use and make home.

Despite the move he was still carried in the village population register as part of the family. Now, however, he would usually be listed as the head of a distinct conjugal group within it; that is, the names of his wife and eventual children were grouped after his, perhaps with notations showing the individual relationships to him. In addition, the conjugal group might be so registered as to show that it also formed a separate residential unit.[4]

The change did not, however, make the *genin* significantly less dependent on the family head, who must still provide him with clothing, bedding, cooking implements, and—if he were to have any—pocket money to spend on festival days or at the nearest market. Nonetheless the change in living arrangements was significant. The *genin* was no longer constantly under the master's scrutiny, ever at his beck and call, for now he cooked, ate, and slept separately. This meant not only greater freedom for the *genin*, but the necessity for the family head of taking into account the times when the *genin* would be absent, perhaps even of keeping account of the *genin's* food and other expenses separately from those of the rest of the family. Thus a new organizational unit, a new focal point of economic interest and a new nucleus of social life, emerged within the extended family.

In this respect the new *genin* household was no different from one formed by kin. Such households appeared within the family whenever sons and brothers of the family head married, for peasant houses were rarely larger than 40 by 20 feet[11] and would usually accommodate no more than seven or eight persons comfortably. Thus families on large holdings, by keeping younger generations in the group, tended to increase but in so doing to spill over by conjugal groups from the main dwelling into subsidiary buildings.[5] The residential pattern of the extended family coincided in considerable measure with the three concentric circles of its kinship structure. The nuclear family of the holder,

---

[4] In Awa Province, for example, separate households called "*koya*," or "small family," were listed within the extended family in the population registers. The Kyūshū registers of 1633 first recorded population by holding families and then again, in a separate section, by households.

[5] For example, a village just north of the Yoshino River in Shikoku consisted of 23 families with a total of 58 households in 1672; three of the families had between five and seven households each. (Ōtsuki Hiroshi, "Awahan ni okeru kinsei sonraku no keisei katei," *Keizai ronsō*, LXXIV, 2 (1954), 13.)

perhaps with the addition of a few unmarried members from the outer
circles, lived in the main dwelling (*honya*), and the members of the
two outer circles occupied small attached dwellings (*soeya*) disposed
around it. Testifying to this arrangement, the attached dwellings were
sometimes known after their respective occupants, as "parents' hut,"
"younger brother's hut," "*nago's* hut." Persons who occupied subsidiary dwellings were often called *kadoya* (gate-house), *yashiki no
mono* (persons of the *yashiki*), or other names indicating that they
resided on someone else's homestead.[12]

It would not do to give the impression that *genin* were treated
exactly like kin. But there were sharp distinctions among kin themselves; for the extended family, to a much greater degree than the
small nuclear one, was severely hierarchical. But in at least one very
important respect *fudai* were treated like kin; that is, the family took
responsibility for them through the entire life cycle, including marriage, children, sickness, old age, and death. One sees, if sketchily,
something of this life cycle in the following group of *genin* listed as
part of a peasant family in Echigo in 1679:[13]

> Jiyuemon (66)
> Wife (61)
> Children (and grandchildren?)
>   Kahei (26)
>   Ken (18)
>   Katsu (14)
>   Hachi (10)
>   Hana (3)

We have said that *genin* and kin were held in the family on large
holdings, rather than eliminated in the various ways practiced by
families on small holdings, because their labor was needed. But this
is not quite accurate: it states the relationship between family organization and farming one-sidedly, as though the former were passively
determined by the latter. Actually the family had a built-in dynamic
of its own—natural increase—which acted powerfully on the organization of farming. Steadily increasing numbers might be accommodated
on the holding for a while, but inevitably there came a time when numbers pressed dangerously on resources. Even before that the labor

---

[k] Family size was sometimes remarkable when *genin* were counted: in a cluster
of Shinshū villages in the late seventeenth century, there were a total of eight families which by this count had 36 or more members; the largest had 46. (Ichikawa,
Saku-chihō, p. 94.)

force might become ineffectually large,[1] or vitiating tensions might arise between various groups within the family, as members in the second circle became more numerous and more distantly related to the center. When any of these events occurred, the family had to be reorganized, and that required reorganization of the holding also.

Custom, pride, and public opinion would not permit the large family with ample resources to solve these problems as poor families did: by merely eliminating surplus members, cutting them off summarily from the resources and protection of the group. This interdiction, moreover, applied to the treatment of *fudai* as well as kin. There was, however, one sanctioned recourse open to families with large holdings and it had been practiced since the beginnings of agriculture. That was to divide the holding, or, more accurately, to *give* a small piece of land to a conjugal group from one of the outer circles.

This "division" of the holding was typically very unequal: the main line took much the greater share of the property—in fact, all but barely enough to support the collateral line. The result was to reduce the size and responsibilities of the family far more than its resources; and this was not the only important advantage of partitioning, for by reducing an unwieldy labor force to manageable size, productivity might at the same time be increased.[m]

The losses to be set against these certain or possible gains were remarkably slight. There was, to be sure, the loss of income from a small piece of land, but the land in question was often of such poor quality or so awkwardly located that it scarcely paid the family to work it.[n] For the recipient family, however, it was the main source of income, and it would therefore be worked more intensively than before. In some cases actual title to the land was not surrendered but cultivation rights only;[o] this was invariably the practice when the recipient family

[1] Intensive farming and particularly rice culture (as practiced in Japan) requires an immense amount of hand labor. One result is that the labor force quickly loses efficiency as it is expanded owing to the difficulty of supervising cultivation and the fact that incentives are weakened as numbers increase.

[m] The partitioning of holdings is discussed in considerably more detail in Chapter 4.

[n] Holdings were characteristically highly fragmented, the larger ones frequently being composed of upward of 50 fields. Fields moreover were widely dispersed. Even in 1922, when much recent consolidation had taken place on government initiative, it was found that in Kanagawa Prefecture fields ten minutes from home were considered close, and 30 minutes average. (Ono Takeo, *Nihon sonrakushi gaisetsu*, Tokyo, 1948, p. 114.)

[o] In which case the head of the new branch family might be registered—as in

were *genin* rather than kin. Nor was the labor of the new family necessarily lost since labor services were often made a condition of the grant
of land, and nearly always were in the case of *genin*.

Land by itself, of course, was not enough to give a family even the
poorest living: animals, tools, and housing were necessary as well.
But these needs could be met without diminishing in any way the older
family's capital. The new branch family was given the use of animals
and tools when they were needed until it acquired its own, and it
continued to occupy the same dwelling as before. It might be given the
dwelling outright, but that was uncommon except when the dwelling
in question stood apart from the family homestead, which would otherwise have to be divided.ᵖ It will be evident that in most cases the branch
family—even if kin—was certain to be dependent on the main family
for a considerable time. The dependence, which required frequent help
of various kinds, was sometimes recognized in the village by failure to
register the new family separately, at least until it had achieved a
measure of economic independence. This is a practice to which we shall
return, and merely note now in passing.

To the reorganization of the extended family just described, *fudai*
contributed as well as kin, for they also married and procreated in the
family and could not, any more than kin, be summarily ejected as
though merely employed. And, at the moment of family reorganization, they were treated like kin in that they might be given cultivation
rights to a piece of land and so established in some degree as autonomous. Even if kin were frequently given actual title as well, it also
happened that they were sometimes merely given cultivation rights.

---

the case of *nago*—alongside the holder in the land register; this practice was
sometimes also followed in the case of *fudai*. A passage in the *Jikata hanreiroku*
(pp. 439–40) states: "If fields be inherited by a second or third son or a grandson in addition to the main heir (*sōryō*), the field in question may be registered in
the latter's name with merely a notation of the former's name. This is called subordinate registration (*buntsuke*). . . . Fields given to a *genin* are also registered
in this way (*buntsuke*). . . . In both cases all dues on the land are paid to the main
heir (*sōryō*), who then pays the officials in his capacity as *honke* (main family)."

ᵖ Sometimes homesteads *were* divided. This is clearly what happened in a
village in Tamba Province where the number of homesteads increased from 35 to
48 between 1678 and 1820, whereas the aggregate acreage of homesteads remained
unchanged. This suggests incidentally how difficult it was, after a certain density
of settlement had been reached, to appropriate new land for homesteads. (Miyagawa Hidekazu, "Nayosechō kisai ni kansuru nisan no mondaiten ni tsuite," *NHRS*,
90 (1955), 21–22.)

Nor did the similarity of treatment end with the grant of land. With that event the kinsman became the founder of a branch family which traced its descent, through him, from the ancestors of the main family. The basis for continuing to acknowledge this relationship to the main family, which was one of severe subordination and often persisted through many generations, was economic dependence. Dependence was most marked when the branch family borrowed farm implements and animals from the main family, and in such cases it commonly performed labor services in return.[q] Formal acknowledgment of the main-branch relationship was given annually by the head of the branch family joining in the ancestral rites of the main family, thus affirming descent from common ancestors by a collateral and inferior line.

A very similar relationship ensued when the new family were *genin*. Economic dependence was then even more marked, and the obligations it gave rise to were rationalized as flowing from main-branch relations.[r] Whether this was always the case seems doubtful, but it is certain that it commonly was, since there are recorded instances of the practice in widely scattered places where hereditary servants survived until recently.

In Nagano Prefecture, for example, until the latter part of the nineteenth century it was customary for well-to-do peasant families to keep servants. Many of these servants were literally adopted, from impoverished parents, usually at the age of about ten. Since adoption entailed heavy responsibilities on the one side and risks on the other, adoption agreements were usually confined to families between whom close social relations already existed. The adopted child was taken into the home, raised, and made to work there like one of the family. At a

---

[q] This dependency had its counterpart among the town merchants. A compilation on customary law made early in the Meiji period records: "In towns a merchant often portions off a faithful employee in the manner of a branch family, but the relationship of master and servant is in form preserved." (*Materials for the Study of Private Law in Old Japan*, edited by John H. Wigmore in *Transactions of the Asiatic Society of Japan*, XX, Supplement, Part V, Yokohama, 1892, p. 107.)

[r] The practice of making a branch family of an "employee" with whom the master was related by neither blood nor marriage was not restricted to peasants, but was common among merchants as well. In Aki Province, for instance, we are told: "A merchant sometimes gives a faithful employee the right to use the house-name . . . and a branch house so formed ranks second only to a branch established by a son or brother." Again, in Buzen Province: ". . . a merchant often portions off a faithful employee in the manner of a branch family. . . ." (Wigmore, *Private Law*, pp. 105–7.)

suitable age the adoptive father would arrange his or her marriage, taking the spouse under his protection also; he might in addition give the new couple the use of a house and land and make them a branch family, even bestowing his surname on them.[14]

A document found some years ago among the papers of an exceedingly wealthy landed family in Echigo testifies to this practice in another part of the country and provides circumstantial details. It is dated the fourth moon of 1805 and records how a certain Shōhei became a hereditary servant (*fudai*) of the Watanabe family, with the understanding that he would eventually be given property and made a branch family. The document, which is signed by Shōhei and addressed to "His Honor, Watanabe Sanzaemon," reads in part as follows:[15]

1. My father, Buhei, sent Yozaemon as middleman to discuss my future with Sanzaemon of Tamagawa village. As a result Sanzaemon consented to take me as a *fudai*, and it was decided as follows:

2. Sanzaemon most graciously agreed to take me as his blood brother, for which kindness I am exceedingly grateful. However, my line is to be his "brother" for my generation only, and my sons and grandsons will be his *fudai* as originally. However, if among my line there should appear one of outstanding merit, he may be graciously treated the same as me; but I express no wish about such matters; my children and grandchildren shall be treated as His Honor decides.

3. I shall live with Sanzaemon and serve him until the age of 40, at which time it is agreed that I shall be made a branch family (*bekke*).

4. At that time I shall be given either land worth 200 *ryō*, or 200 *ryō* in cash, whichever Sanzaemon prefers. If it be land, its registration in the record (*nayosechō*) kept by the headman shall not be altered but remain in His Honor's name; but I shall discharge all dues and obligations attached to it just the same.

Not only were *fudai* similar to kin of the master in that they might be given land—or cultivation rights—and made branch families by him; but in acquiring land they also assumed a status in relation to the master very similar to that of *nago*. Consider the similarities: they were listed in the population register subordinately to the holder rather than separately; they held house and land from him; and they gave him labor and other services in return. These underlying similarities are far more impressive than any difference in names.

But even the distinction in names was by no means invariably made. Japanese scholars have found documents from the Tokugawa period in which the same persons are referred to in one place as "*genin*" and another as "*kado*"—one of the many local terms for *nago*.[16] Indeed

"fudai" was itself the equivalent of *"nago"* in some places. This blur-
ring of the distinction between the terms suggests the movement of
people from one status group to the other, without an immediate change
in the status term by which they were known. But more frequently the
distinction between the terms was successfully maintained. Then, apparently, the status term of the individual changed when he passed
from one group to another. Ōishi Kyūkei says that in Kyūshū *fudai*
who were given land were called *"nago,"* adding that they were also
thereupon considered branch families. A government compilation of
the customary law in the early Meiji period makes a similar statement:
"In the countryside servants are sometimes given a share of the holding and made branch families (*bekke*); such branches, *which are called
nago*, do so many days of labor a month in perpetuity for the master's
family."[17]

Before going further it will perhaps be well to review the main
points. We saw that the extended family, which constituted the labor
force on large holdings, consisted of three elements: the nuclear family
in the center, affines and cognates in the next circle, and servants and
nago in the third. Servants were taken into the family as children,
educated in its values, and, later, through the dynamics of natural
growth and differentiation in the family, often established as branch
families. Since upon receiving land *fudai* became indistinguishable from
nago, and in many cases were even designated as *nago*, it is probable
that a large part of the *nago* class sprang from hereditary servants. If
so, *nago* were not an outside element taken into the family to meet a
temporary labor shortage, but one that the family itself produced, and
the relationship between them and the holder must have been similar
to that of branch and main families.

3

LABOR SERVICES

We have seen that *nago* accounted for a large fraction of the peasant population in the seventeenth century, and seem to have been present in some numbers everywhere in the country, except perhaps in a few scattered areas of commercial farming. Cultivating the land in close dependence on certain large holders—whom we shall call "*oyakata*"[a] to distinguish them from ordinary holders without *nago*—*nago* families were not autonomous farming units. They and their *oyakata* were cooperators who together formed an important element of the agrarian system and a pervasive and influential social relationship in the village. Any description of their relationship should begin with an account of its economic basis; since something has already been said on this subject from the *oyakata's* side, we shall look at it now chiefly from the *nago's*.

Nago had access to land only in the form of allotments from the *oyakata*, on whom they were usually also dependent for the necessary means of working land—among others, housing, tools, animals, compost, fuel, fodder, and water. Access to village common land and water was a right associated with the holding of arable, and since *nago* held land only by private arrangement with the *oyakata*, they had access to communal resources in his name only. With the market in a rudimentary state of development, moreover, materials taken from the common were essential to the self-sufficient farm economy. From the common came wood to repair the peasant's house and farm tools, twigs and dead branches to keep his family warm through the winter, grass and leaves for compost. If any one of these was more important to him than the others, it may, surprisingly, have been compost, owing to the intensive character of Japanese farming, which planted fields year after year to the same crop without rest. Water was another critical communal resource to which the *oyakata* gave access; it came through his irrigation rights and often even from his very ditches. In that case

[a] "*Oyakata*"—one who takes the role of parent—was perhaps the commonest term for such holders; the corresponding term for *nago* was "*kokata*," or "*child.*"

the *nago* could not transplant rice seedlings until the *oyakata* had finished his planting and could release water, thus synchronizing the work of the two and encouraging the exchange of labor for tools and animals.

If, from the point of view of the communal rights essential to farming, the *nago* allotment could be worked only as a part of the holding to which it legally belonged, it was no less part of the holding in respect to capital equipment. *Nago* no doubt themselves owned the simplest farm tools; but for tools with expensive iron parts, which could not be made in the village, let alone fashioned at home, they had to rely on the *oyakata*. And the same was true of draft animals; even if the initial cost of a horse or bullock was not prohibitive, the size of allotments made animals an uneconomic investment.[b] Yet for certain farm operations they were indispensable. Crops had to be hauled from fields to an open space in front of the houses for threshing; tax grain had to be transported to official warehouses or collecting points; firewood, building materials, and compost had to be carried from the mountainside and remote meadows and wasteland to homes and fields for use. From time to time animals were necessary to move these heavy and bulky loads the required distances, often over the most difficult terrain. Not only *nago* but small holders generally depended on wealthier neighbors for the loan of animals when needed, a practice still to be found in parts of rural Japan.

But it was not only for access to land and the means of working it that *nago* depended on *oyakata*. Allotments in themselves rarely gave even a meager living; before taxes and production costs were deducted, most allotments yielded less than three or four *koku* annually—and one *koku* would barely feed one adult for a year.[c] Then too, *nago* fields were usually the poorest in the village, vulnerable to flood or drought, the soil thin and rocky and unsuitable for the more desirable but demanding crops. Rice, which was high in nutritive value, and cotton and indigo, which were readily marketable and brought a good price,

[b] Such scattered data as exist on the animal population show that draft animals averaged less than one per family in most villages; their ownership, however, was heavily concentrated in the hands of large holders. For example, in 1679, there were 39 holders and 34 work animals in a village in Shinshū—an average of nearly one per family; but the two largest holders in the village owned four animals each. (Hirasawa Kiyoto, "Kōshinchi ichi jinushi no nōgyō keiei kibo no hensen," *SKSG*, XIII, 1, 97–98.)

[c] Seventy-one *nago* scattered through neighboring villages in Tōhoku in 1852, for instance, held allotments that averaged less than one *koku* yield each! (Mori Kahei, *Nago seido to nōchi kaikaku*, Tokyo, 1951, pp. 18–21).

were crops that could not usually be grown on allotments. The standard crops for *nago* were soy beans, red beans (*azuki*), radishes, buckwheat, and *hie*.

Nago eked out the income from their allotments in a variety of ways, all with *oyakata* help. During the eighteenth century and later, tenant farming was the most important source of supplementary income, even at times surpassing allotments in economic importance; for by that time most *nago*, in addition to their original allotments, held land in tenancy (on which a rent in kind was paid). But, in the seventeenth century, this was no considerable source of earnings outside the Kinai where holder cultivation (*tezukuri*) was still firmly established on large estates.

Nago in these areas managed to survive in large numbers because labor services, which were essential to holder cultivation, were indirectly compensated. Merging with the family labor force on workdays, *nago* received their meals from the *oyakata's* kitchen along with *genin* and others;[d] it might almost be said that on such occasions *nago* temporarily became family members, reverting to *genin* status. The stipulated annual number of workdays for *nago* varied sharply from one place to another, from one or two in some localities to as many as two hundred in others; and in many cases no maximum was fixed at all, the number depending wholly on the *oyakata's* needs. But since, for obvious reasons, the need for labor services was reduced as *nago* were assigned tenant land by the *oyakata*, and since tenancy appeared on a significant scale only with the growth of trade and industry, one may take upward of thirty or forty days as typical of the seventeenth century. Where workdays were considerably fewer, they represented a more advanced phase of economic development. Workdays, then, were a major source of *nago* income in the early Tokugawa period and were probably willingly given for that reason.[e] Thus in the seventeenth century, resources flowed continuously from the *oyakata's* farm to the *nago's* allotment and back again in different form: capital in many shapes going one way, labor the other. This exchange was the visible mark of economic interdependence; but interdependence went even further. Since the

[d] In some cases at least, the adult *nago* were accompanied on workdays by their children, who did not work but nevertheless ate; Professor Ariga reports a case of this kind in which the *oyakata* normally provided four meals on workdays. (Ariga Kizaemon, *Nihon kazoku seido to kosaku seido*, Tokyo, 1943, p. 635.)

[e] In addition to workdays, there were a number of festivals during the year when *nago* were usually given food and drink at the *oyakata's* house; this was also the practice on the occasion of marriages, births, and deaths in the *oyakata* family.

oyakata's animals and implements and the *nago's* labor could be used on but one farm at a time, there was a kind of breathing, organic unity between the two farming units, one resting when the other worked. (For a vivid illustration, see Chapter 4, note *n* on page 47.)

Of still other kinds of help from the *oyakata*, several need be mentioned, because of either symbolic or economic value. The *oyakata* loaned his *nago* suitable clothing for dress occasions, gave them cast-off furniture and cooking utensils, and in modern times paid the doctor when they fell ill, perhaps counting the payment a loan, though at the same time neither expecting nor pressing for repayment.[1] In other words, he treated the *nago* very much as he would a needy kinsman.

More important, however, he helped *nago* survive the ever-recurring crop failures that were the marks of agricultural backwardness, and which hit everyone periodically but hit the weak most often and hardest. Custom and self-interest, both, obliged the *oyakata* to open his storehouse at such times, to provide his *nago* with food and seed until the next harvest lest he be thought pitiless for thus driving them onto the highways in search of sustenance and a more reliable protector. If that happened, it was usually because famine conditions prevailed and the *oyakata* was himself short of food. Except for such times when no one was safe from hunger, *nago* had greater security than many small holders; indeed, small holders frequently gave up their land to an *oyakata* in return for the protection *nago* status afforded.

The continuous exchange between *oyakata* and *nago* of labor, capital, food, and protection for labor was unlike the exchange familiar to modern economies;[2] it was an economic exchange in the guise of a social relationship, not a direct exchange of economic values defined by an impersonal market. For one thing, there were no individual transactions to which prices might apply; there was only a continuous trading of certain resources for others that was felt to be equitable in the long run, though not exactly or in any particular time period. For another, there was no market to price diverse commodities in a common unit, so precise comparisons of value could not be made nor accounts struck, even had this been thought desirable. Something nevertheless kept the exchange tolerably equitable from the point of view of the participants, or it could not have been sustained, as it was, generation after generation. The governing factor was the reciprocal obligations of kinship or kinlike relations, which were not only understood and observed by both parties but insisted upon by community opinion.

Professor Ariga has shown very clearly through a comparative study of *nago* labor services the personal character of the exchange. If the exchange had been an impersonal market transaction, there would have been a determinant relationship between the size (value) of allotments and amount (value) of labor services—but in fact there was none. There were two types of labor services: those fixed at an annual number of workdays and those not so fixed. In the case of those *not* fixed, the *oyakata* used his *nago's* labor without constraint, just as he did the labor of *genin* or of a member of his immediate family; if he nevertheless used part rather than all of it, that was merely because he needed no more.

The other type of labor services seems at first essentially different: the amount of labor, being fixed, appears to be determined by the value of the allotment. But on closer scrutiny this turns out not to be so. Even when held from the same *oyakata*, allotments of identical size often carried the obligation of a different number of workdays, and allotments with the same number of workdays rarely happened also to be the same size.[1] The relationship between workdays and allotment, then, was manifestly adventitious. There were even cases of "fixed" labor services being altered as to amount at the convenience of the *oyakata*. An *oyakata* in northern Japan, for example, between 1872 and 1920 commuted labor services into money payments for about half of his *nago*; the resulting loss of labor, for which he had received monetary compensation, he made good by increasing the labor services of the remaining *nago*![3]

We shall see later how labor service in general became "fixed" at so many workdays. Here it will be enough to say that the evidence is that they became fixed, or rather customary, at a particular level when for years on end the *oyakata* asked for no more. In short, even when there was a customary limit, it was the *okayata's* need that determined the number of workdays,[9] not any limitation on him set

---

[1] Among 72 *nago* of the same *oyakata* in 1852, no two held allotments of precisely the same yield, but many were burdened with the same number of workdays. Nor was there even a *general* correspondence between number of workdays and the yield of allotments; many allotments with relatively high yields bore relatively few workdays and vice versa. (Mori, *Nōchi kaikaku*, pp. 18–20.)

[9] This comes out very clearly in a set of regulations drawn up for his *nago* by an *oyakata* in Kyūshū, in 1721. In it are first listed the number of workdays each *nago* family was obligated for on various occasions during the year; then follows a state-

by the size of the *nago's* allotment. Far from being a means of payment, for land, then, labor services were clearly part of a far-reaching system of personal obligation.

Another circumstance points to the same conclusion. It frequently happened that individual *oyakata* held considerably more *nago* than the cultivation of their respective holdings could conceivably have required. Why? One suspects that in such cases family growth, through the proliferation of *genin*, had conspired to produce more *nago* on some holdings than were needed. But however that may be, it is clear that *nago* were often maintained by virtue of an obligation to keep them rather than for strictly economic reasons.

Nago, generally, perhaps even universally, owed their respective *oyakata* certain services in addition to workdays. Although these services varied endlessly in detail, all had one feature in common: unlike labor services, they had little or no economic value, consisting of ritual acts unmistakably expressing personal subordination. A single illustration should suffice. Among the many services the numerous *nago* of a certain Saitō family in Iwate Prefecture performed for it in 1935 were the following at the New Year:[4]

On the thirtieth of the twelfth month by the old calendar, each *nago* family sent one person to the *oyakata's* to help him make rice cakes. During the two or three days previous to this, the *oyakata* gave each *nago* a salted fish and paper for repairing the panels of sliding doors; he gave those who had done a notable amount of labor services during the year hand towels in addition. *Bekke* [consanguine branches of the Saito family] were each given a large salted fish, but no paper.

On the first day of the New Year, *nago* who had gone the night before to the *oyakata's* to help him went to his house early in the morning; there they were entertained and given rice cakes to take home. At about noon, men from *bekke* families and the other *nago* began arriving to pay their respects and present the *oyakata* with gifts; *bekke* gave from five to ten cents each and *nago* from two to five cents. In making their greeting, *nago* stopped

---

ment to the effect that at the planting *nago* were to do such work as the author directed. The pertinent parts of the document are as follows: "At the time of my ancestor Hachihei, it was decided that *nago* labor services (*yatoi*) were to be as follows: (1) Men and women were to do three workdays each month, but in case of need women might be required to do one more. (2) In addition, the following workdays per family were required: one full day when the seedbeds were prepared for the rice seedlings; one full day when the rice seedlings were taken from the beds; work at the transplanting was to be *as directed*." In short, labor services were fixed at so many workdays—except when the *oyakata* required more. (Miyamoto Mataji, *Nōson kōzō no shiteki bunseki*, Tokyo, 1955, p. 85.)

at the kitchen, but *bekke* crossed the threshold. All were given food and drink, and after talking for a while returned home drunk.

On the following day, the women of *bekke* and *nago* families came to pay their respects, and each brought what present she could—for instance, chestnuts, rice cakes, and fruit; the *oyakata* gave the women hair oil and hand towels in return.

On the fifteenth of the first month, *nago* assembled again at the *oyakata*'s to help him make rice cakes. This time they ate three meals at his house, and each received in addition several rice cakes; these were taken home uneaten. When the rice cakes were finished, the *nago* performed the "Ceremony of the Planting" (*taue gyōji*). The most important part of this ceremony was the election by the *nago* of one of their number as their representative for the year. This ceremony was performed not only by the *nago* of the *oyakata* but by the *nago* of the *bekke* as well. The person so elected was a man of upright moral character, and if nothing untoward happened he was continued in his office year after year. The duties of the office included going periodically to the *oyakata*'s house and offering ceremonial wine at the altar (*kamidana*). He performed this ceremony on behalf of the other *nago* at the New Year, on the eleventh, fifteenth, and nineteenth of the first month, on the first three days and on the fifteenth day of the second month, on the third day of the third month, the fourth day of the fourth month, the fifth day of the fifth month, the fifteenth day of the eighth month, the twenty-ninth of the ninth month, and the twentieth of the tenth month.

Such ritual acts we shall distinguish as "ceremonial services." It is significant, however, that the participants themselves made no consistent distinction between ceremonial and labor services, often calling both by the same name.[h] It would seem—one cannot speak with certainty in such cases—that the two services were thought of as being essentially the same. This is not because people failed to observe that one had economic value and the other not, but because this difference though evident was insignificant in view of the fact that the two had the same social character.

In the annual cycle of ceremonies that described the orbit of family and village life, there were many occasions that called for ceremonial services to the *oyakata*. These occasions differed considerably from one locality to another, as did the form of the ceremonies themselves.

[h] Thus, in the Saitō case, both ceremonial and labor services were called *suke*; this seems to be a typical case, for many other examples of the kind are encountered. It sometimes *appears* that a distinction is made between the two types of services, because in some places a distinction is made between services done indoors and those done outdoors; but this does not consistently distinguish services having economic value from those having none. (Ariga, *Kazoku seido*, pp. 652–55.)

But there were two occasions that seem universally to have called for such services and to have been most elaborately observed: New Year's and All Souls' (*bon*). A common feature of these two occasions, indeed the central element of both, was in the rites performed to ancestors. Not only were *nago* required to be present at these rites in the *oyakata's* home, but they often had an active role in them. We have already seen how New Year's was celebrated in the Saitō family. All Souls' was observed as follows:[5]

The celebration of the festival began on the fourteenth of the seventh month. However, on the thirteenth day preparations were made for the arrival of the souls of the deceased by sweeping ancestral graves, and repairing and sweeping the roads that passed through the village and led to the graves. The graves of the *oyakata's* ancestors were swept by the *bekke* and *nago*. Early on the morning of the fourteenth, the *bekke* and *nago* both went to the *oyakata's* to do *suke* (labor services)—the *nago* cleaning the grounds and the *bekke* decorating the altar. When this work was finished, all went together to the graves, carrying offerings; after Buddhist prayers were said at the graves, the party returned to the *oyakata's* house to partake of rice with red beans. After another meal later in the day, each *bekke* and *nago* returned home to decorate his own altar. Each night during the celebration, a faggot of pine was left burning in front of the gate as a welcome to the returning souls. On the sixteenth the souls were seen off.

Other accounts exist of *nago* participating in the *oyakata's* ancestral rites,[6] but this one is especially suggestive because in it *nago* and *bekke* are shown participating in a similar way. *Bekke* — the consanguine branches of the Saitō house—were required to be present at the main house because in this way they acknowledged the authority and genealogical precedence of the main family. Is it not possible that these ceremonies had a similar meaning in the case of *nago*? Even if they did not symbolize main-branch relations, they certainly bespoke obligations characteristic of such relations.[4]

Nor is this the only evidence on the point. It was customary in

[4] In many cases, of course, main-branch relations between such persons were explicitly affirmed. This is perhaps easier to understand if one thinks of main-branch relations being a genealogical rather than a blood relationship. The former, which could be fabricated, was the important one in defining obligations whereas the latter, which could not be contrived but was biologically given, was not; it merely seemed to be because it so often coincided with the former. We have seen above (p. 21–22) that in some parts of Shinshū, *fudai* were adopted and later given land and made the heads of branch families. Many other instances of main-branch relations without benefit of blood relationship might be cited.

many places for *oyakata,* their consanguine branches, and *nago* to perform group rites to a common protective deity. This deity was known
by a variety of names, but perhaps most widely as *"ujigami."* Though
the identity of the *ujigami* was frequently quite obscure, in some cases
he was explicitly identified with the *oyakata's* ancestors:[j] the annual
festival to him was called "ancestral festival" (*senzo-matsuri*); the
rites on that occasion were performed before the grave of the alleged
original ancestor; the object enshrined was the written genealogy of
the *oyakata.*[j] If in such cases the group was not acknowledging common descent, it was clearly affirming the obligations appropriate to
common descent—solidarity, mutuality, protection, obedience. A village "law" code of 1748 likens an *oyakata* to one's parent or elder
brother, saying: "One must not go against the wishes of one's father,
mother, elder brother, or *oyakata.*"[8] Moreover, *nago* were actually
designated as "branch families" in some documents.[k]

Just as the evolution of *fudai* gave some hint of the origins and
character of the *nago* class, so—if we trace their evolution—*nago* may
lead us to a better understanding of the holder class. *Oyakata-nago*
relations changed very little so long as the village economy remained
largely closed to outside market influences; the same crops were tilled
in the same way, and there was very little change in the stock of possessions of individual families. But conditions became less stable as
trade and industry began to modify the self-sufficient agrarian economy.
This development generally belongs to the late Tokugawa period, but
even in the seventeenth century it was already a powerful force in some
areas, and at least dimly felt in others.

The growth of rural trade and industry brought two significant
though very gradual changes in the economic position of the *nago* class.
Of both, the immediate cause was a steady increase in the price of labor, a phenomenon characteristic of periods of economic growth. One
change was that *oyakata* were obliged to give land in increasing amounts

---

[j] An interesting reconstruction of the process by which certain ancestors were
at first celebrated merely as spirits (*tama*) but later became deities (*kami*) who were
objects of supplication and thanksgiving, is to be found in Wakamori Tarō, *Kokushi
ni okeru kyōdōtai no kenkyū,* Tokyo, 1945, I, 370–83.

[k] An *oyakata* in Sendai in 1872 addressed his *nago* as "branch families" (*bekke*)
and exhorted them to be forever loyal to their duties as such. (Mori, *Nōchi kaikaku,*
p. 67.) According to a government document of early Meiji, *nago* were normally
considered "branch families" in northern Kyūshū. (*Fukuoka-ken nōchi kaikaku
shi,* edited by Fukuoka-ken nōchi kaikaku shi hensan iinkai, Fukuoka, 1950, I, 406.)

to *nago* as tenants, in order to hold them on the land against the pull of rising wages in the town—a practice also encouraged by the fact that, with *genin* becoming more expensive and difficult to find, *oyakata* could work less and less land themselves. The second change was that *nago* families could now increasingly supplement their farming income by working at domestic handicrafts, or other part-time employment. No sudden improvement in the *nago's* position occurred, nor were all *nago* equally affected, but for some there was for the first time hope of achieving a significant measure of economic independence.[1]

With industry and good fortune, *nago* (in some places) might now accumulate farming capital of their own. There are occasional entries of "*nago* horse" and "*nago* bullock" even in the seventeenth century registers;[9] and one may be sure that if some *nago* were buying animals, many more must have been acquiring the far less expensive farm implements. The possession of animals, in particular, suggests that the scale of *nago* cultivation was being greatly expanded, no doubt largely through tenant farming.

Here and there, wherever tenancy was spreading, the vital integration of *nago* and *oyakata* farming was gradually disrupted. One mark of the disruption was the reduction of labor services, to which even the *oyakata* could have no objection, for he had less land to work than before and he must give the *nago* more time to farm as a tenant. The upshot was that the *nago* was increasingly self-employed, and he increasingly sought rewards for his labor on his own land, rather than on the *oyakata's*. Very slowly, out of the matrix of the *oyakata's* holding, the *nago* with his allotment and tenant land was emerging as an autonomous producer.

Growing economic competence eventually brought a change in *nago* legal status. *Nago* were registered neither as holders of land nor as family heads, being subordinate to the *oyakata* in both respects. This system of registration greatly simplified administration; it not only reduced the number of holders and family heads to be dealt with but, by making *oyakata* responsible for their *nago*, avoided dealing with a class of peasants who were so to speak neither socially nor economically competent.

But the conventions of registering land and population were subject to change whenever they became administratively inconvenient.

[1] For fuller discussion of the transformation of *nago* worked by the market, see Chapter 9.

This happened increasingly as *nago* came to manage more and more land: it then became expedient to register *nago* autonomously, in both the land and the population registers. That was very easily accomplished, merely requiring that *nago* be listed now as separate families and as the *holders* of their allotments. These simple changes made *nago* directly accessible to administration and directly taxable as holders. With *nago* accumulating property and winning some degree of social autonomy, this had great juridical and fiscal advantages.

One consequently finds evidence throughout the Tokugawa period of the elevation of *nago* to the status of separate families and independent holders.[m] It is even possible occasionally to follow, from one village register to a subsequent one, the progress of an individual *nago* to holder status.[n] We should not imagine, however, that such advancement occurred on a massive scale—it happened sporadically. Nor should we suppose that it greatly altered the *nago's* relations with his *oyakata*, for such relations were economic and social as well as legal. The achievement of economic and social autonomy was a gradual process which legal autonomy, an either-or matter, cut across midway. On the day after registration as a holder, the former *nago* was as dependent on the *oyakata*—for housing, for land as a tenant, for capital, for everything except his allotment—and as tightly bound to him by obligations recognized by the community as he had been the day before.[o] This is broadly hinted in the fact that he often continued per-

[m] An edict of Hideyoshi, apparently applying only to certain parts of the Kinai, stipulated that persons holding even cultivation rights be registered as holders. This order has been widely interpreted as having transformed *nago* into holders throughout much of the Kinai. Professor Araki offers evidence of a somewhat similar development in the Kantō. (Araki Moriaki, "Taikō kenchi no rekishiteki igi," *RGKK*, 167 (1954), 16.) In still another area, the lord of Sendai in 1717 ordered that *nago* in his domain be given full title to their allotments and thereby made "new holders" (*shimmen hyakushō*). (Mori, *Nōchi kaikaku*, p. 86.)

[n] A population register of 1650 for a village in modern Hyogo Prefecture, for example, lists five persons as "*kerai*"—another of the common local terms for *nago*—who are entered in a land register of 1656 as holders. (Oka Mitsuo, "Kinsei sonraku no tenkai to inasaku kankō," *RGKK*, 193 (1956), 25–26.) For other examples, see Takao Kazuhiko and Wakita Osamu, "Genroku jidai ni okeru Kinai sonraku no hatten," *NSKK*, 20 (1953), 3–4; Takao Kazuhiko, "Edo zenki ni okeru Kinai sonraku no kōsei," *Kenkyū* (Kōbe daigaku bungakkai), 3 (1957), 63–65; and Miyagawa Mitsuru, "Gōson seido to kenchi," *NSKK*, 19 (1953), p. 13.

[o] This is obvious from the size of holdings belonging to former *nago*; for example, five who became holders between 1650 and 1656 in a village in modern Hyogo Prefecture held land yielding 5.8 *koku*, 1.05 *koku*, 0.34 *koku*, 0.09 *koku*, and 0.06 *koku* respectively. (Oka, "Kinsei sonraku," pp. 25–26.)

forming labor services,[10] that the very persons recently named "holder" in one document were sometimes designated in other contemporaneous documents as "*nago*," that persons recently raised from *nago* status were often not granted full political rights in the village.[p]

Not only, then, were *fudai* continuously entering the *nago* class from the bottom; after 1650, *nago* at the top were moving into the holder class. In doing so, they shed *nago* legal status but carried *nago* social and economic relations with them into the holder class. That is, the obligations to an *oyakata* were not peculiar to *nago*: they might be found also among the holder class. This begins to suggest that the familial organization of farming was not confined to large holdings, but extended beyond them, to form a network of relations encompassing the entire range of holdings from large to small.

[p] As in a village in Awa Province: there a land register of 1612 listed four holders whose names, nevertheless, bore this notation: "*Genin*, not qualified to serve as village elder." (Ōtsuki Hiroshi, "Awahan ni okeru kinsei sonraku no keisei katei," *Keizai ronsō*, LXXIV, 2 (1954), 8–9.)

4

SMALL HOLDINGS

Prior to the eighteenth century, when the growth of trade and industry began radically to alter the economic environment, new holdings were created mainly by the division of existing ones among elements of the same family. This is what happened when a hereditary servant was given an allotment and in time came to be registered as its holder. But it happened more commonly when a collateral blood line of the family was given land and simultaneously registered as holder; it is this type of new holding that will mainly concern us here.

True, new arable holdings were sometimes created out of waste and forest land; but this was the rare exception, for such land could ordinarily be brought under cultivation only by an established holder. Families without arable already were unlikely to have the necessary resources for so formidable a task, requiring as it did a stock of tools and sustenance until the new land could be made productive.

Nor, except early in the history of a village, when land was plentiful and the sense of community not yet strong, was an outsider with the necessary resources eligible to claim and open land in the village. Land belonged to the village, which reserved to members the exclusive right of bringing it under the plow.[a] Whether they exercised the right at a given moment or were content with the existing cultivated area depended on a variety of factors: on the quality of the new land, on the cost of bringing it under cultivation, on whether or not population pressed severely on food resources.

Old holdings were most frequently partitioned to create new ones when the cultivated area was being steadily expanded; but, frequent or not, there was always some partitioning and it was the primary factor in the growth of most villages. This is evident from the fact that, except where there has been heavy immigration in recent years owing to

[a] The tendency to restrict immigration, even to the extent of enforcing community endogamy, is characteristic of peasant communities in widely scattered places outside Japan. Eric R. Wolf, "Closed Corporate Communities in Mesoamerica and Central Java," *Southwestern Journal of Anthropology*, XIII, 1 (1957), 1–19.

industrialization or other forces almost wholly absent in the seventeenth century, only a few surnames—often no more than two or three —are to be found in a village; and persons who have come into the village from the outside are often known as *kitarimono* or by some other term that equally marks them as outlanders.[b]

Partitioning also worked powerfully to shape the class structure of the village. How property is divided among heirs is always one of the determinants of class structure, powerful in proportion as other ways to wealth are closed. When completely closed, what a man inherits must fix his class position permanently, and perhaps even that of his descendants through several generations. This situation was approximated in most parts of rural Japan in the seventeenth century.

Peasant inheritance practices, however, are among the least known subjects of Japanese social history, partly as a result of neglect by scholars, partly because relevant historical materials are exceedingly scant.[c] Still, it is possible to make out the broad contours of the inheritance system from scattered materials, and by inferences from both traditional class structure and contemporary practice.

Before describing the system, however, it is essential to understand the distinction between the inheritance of the family headship, on the one hand, and the inheritance of property, on the other. [Property, especially land, might be divided among heirs; the family headship could not.] Along with heirlooms, the main dwelling, ancestral graves, and plaques—indeed everything symbolizing family continuity—headship of the family passed to a single heir. It was this heir who perpetuated the family and through whose issue descent was traced, who performed the ancestral rites that linked the family to the remotest past and projected it indefinitely into the future. A family that partitioned its holding between two sons, let us say, did not divide into two new

---

[b] In most cases we cannot actually trace any considerable part of the growth of a village before the eighteenth century, but it is possible in a few cases where growth during the seventeenth century was exceptionally rapid. For example, between 1667 and 1680, the number of holding families living in a village in Aizu Province increased from 17 to 36; each of the 19 new families was a consanguine branch of one or another of the original 17. (Endō, "Kinsei shoki kenchi," *SKSG*, XX, 2 (1954), 64; also *Sanson no kōzō*, edited by Furushima Toshio, Tokyo, 1949, p. 164.)

[c] Written wills were rare and survive in scant number; more useful potentially are the land registers, but to serve the purpose they must be in long series, from the same place, in close chronological sequence—otherwise it is impossible to follow the vicissitudes of individual holdings. To discover a number of such series is not impossible but would require a long and intensive search.

or equal parts; rather, the existing family passed to the head in a new generation, at the same time establishing a branch representing a new, collateral line of descent. Equality between two such lines—old and new, senior and cadet—was not to be expected. Not only was the branch new and its descent inferior—a matter of extreme importance in a society that valued few things so highly as age and lineage—but the branch was also founded by a grant of land which came to it, not as a matter of right or course, but as a gift from the main family.[1]

No member of a family had birthright to an individual share of the family patrimony, or even to freedom to separate from the group in order to establish a family of his own. As the population registers show, a member could be held indefinitely in the family, as part of its labor force, without individual property, if that were advantageous to the group—even when it meant living under the authority of someone decidedly his junior, such as a nephew. If, on the other hand, a man were given land and freedom to found a family, it was an act of generosity for which eternal gratitude to the family head was the only proper sentiment.

Under these circumstances, holdings were not customarily "divided" equally, or anything like it, for that was not the intention. The absolute amount of land given to a branch family upon founding varied widely, since so many factors were relevant to determining the minimum requirements of the branch, and partition ideally aimed at satisfying no more than these minimum requirements. Two factors were especially important. One was the status within the family of the founder of the branch; generally speaking, the higher he stood in the family hierarchy (that is, the closer he stood to the family head), the larger his portion was likely to be. Thus, he would probably receive somewhat more if he were the eldest son rather than a younger son, more if a brother than an uncle, more if a kin than a servant. The second factor was the stage of economic development in the area—chiefly, the level of income from by-employments. If such income were high, how much or how little land was given to the branch obviously was a less critical question than if land were the sole source of support. Land might then be "divided" either more or less evenly. It was, however, *likely* to be less rather than more equally divided, except where there was considerable commercial or industrial property to divide also. In that case agricultural property might be of so little relative importance that it was simpler to divide it evenly. But such extreme cases were rare and may be ignored in this account.

These two factors—status in the family and the stage of economic development—tended to fix the absolute size of the land grant to the branch family. Its relative size—that is, compared to what the main family retained—depended therefore mainly on the size of the original holding.[d] ⌈Partitioning, it must be remembered, did not have as its major aim establishing a new branch under the most favorable conditions possible, but benefitting the main family—relieving it of the support of one of its elements at as little sacrifice of land as possible.⌋Thus the main family could not only check its growth and enhance its efficiency as a farming unit, but at the same time actually increase its per capita acreage. To come close to achieving this ideal, however, it was necessary to keep the grant of land to the branch family as small as possible. The larger the holding to be partitioned, therefore, the smaller the *relative* share of the branch was likely to be.

Geographically, the most comprehensive data on partitioning come from a government survey of customary law made in the early Meiji period.[2] Although conditions at that time were not dissimilar to those of the late Tokugawa period, they were of course very different from those in the seventeenth century, and one must therefore take care not to read the Meiji data back mindlessly to the earlier period. It is necessary in particular to remember that, at the time of the survey, income from nonagricultural employments was at an unprecedentedly high level, a condition that made for more equal partitioning than was possible two centuries earlier. One other characteristic of the Meiji data must be kept in mind: though they provide a description of inheritance in several provinces of each major region, only the dominant practice in each province is described; thus we get no notion of how often or how widely practice in a given locality varied from the norm. We know only what was the norm in each locality.

Taking the country as a whole, the inheritance system at the end of the Tokugawa period was characterized by four main features.

1. Nowhere, apparently, was there any customary rule obligating a family to partition under certain prescribed circumstances.[3]

2. On the other hand, partitioning was severely discouraged,

---

[d] It bears repeating that the size and productivity of the holding largely determined whether the holding could be partitioned in the first place. There was a minimum size below which partitioning was not practical; it varied from one place and family to another, but every holder knew approximately what it was in his case and that to ignore the minimum was to invite ruin. On the other hand, there was a maximum size beyond which the labor force required to work a holding became unwieldy and was subject to vitiating internal tensions. Families on such holdings had not sanctioned a way of reducing their size *except* by partitioning.

though never absolutely forbidden, by stipulating conditions that had
to be met before a branch family could be founded. For example, the
total number of families in each village was fixed by custom, so that
no new family could be founded until an old one died out or moved
away; or no holding could be partitioned without a will, all those holdings left intestate going automatically to a single heir; or holdings
yielding less than a specified number of *koku* annually could not be
partitioned at all (no doubt to protect the community against the appearance of holdings too small to bear a share of the village tax burden); or, again, prohibitions were placed on the construction of new
dwellings, especially on the use of arable land for building sites.[4]

3. In the event of partitioning, there was no rule requiring the
main family to give a stipulated share of the property to the branch;[e]
on the contrary, in some places there seems to have been community
intervention against undue generosity. In Tōtōmi Province, for example, the usual portion given a branch family was three-tenths of the
property: but "If the amount exceeds this proportion, the relatives . . .
may object." In Ugo Province, the portion assigned a branch family
might not exceed a tenth of the whole;[5] in Bingo Province, the amount
given a branch varied, but in no case could the award be unsatisfactory
to the heir representing the main line.[6]

4. Nowhere was the usual portion more than a third or a fourth
of the estate; indeed, in some areas it was considerably less. In Yamashiro Province, for example, ". . . the part apportioned [to the branch
family] is customarily the property acquired by purchase; that part
inherited from one's ancestors is given only to the one who perpetuates
the main family." In one county in Ugo Province, the usual portion was two-tenths; in another it was not allowed to exceed one-tenth;
in Iki Province, it consisted only ". . . of household utensils and a piece
of residence land, all arable land being reserved for the main line."[7]
These illustrations, of course, represent dominant practices; the portion of the branch family might be considerably smaller in particular instances, especially if the partitioned holding was exceptionally
large. In such cases, the branch's portion was often far less than one-
tenth—one even hears of cases where it was only one-fifteenth.[f]

---

[e] "In Yamashiro *kuni*, Otagi and Kadono *kori*, at the starting of a new family
by a son or younger brother, there is no fixed rule as to the amount to be apportioned." Many examples of this kind might be given. (Wigmore, *Private Law*,
p. 97.)

[f] Thus a set of eighteenth-century household laws belonging to an exceedingly
wealthy Echigo family stipulated that the portion of a branch line should be one-
fifteenth of the holding. (Kitajima, "Watanabeke," p. 56.) For evidence of even

The scattered data available on seventeenth-century partitioning confirm these general principles (for examples, see Table II, page 46). However, at the same time they show one recurring exception: when a father retired as family head in favor of the eldest son and along with his younger sons established a branch family. Then the share of the branch was likely to be unusually large, sometimes close to 50 percent.[9] In some villages, though apparently in no high proportion of them anywhere, this was the customary system of inheritance; elsewhere it was rare or unknown.

Such is the picture of the partitioning of *arable land* between main and branch lines.[8] With a single exception—dwellings (of which we shall presently speak)—neither the Meiji survey nor seventeenth-century materials give any hint as to how other types of property were divided when they were divided at all. The only reliable information on the subject is supplied by a study of 34 postwar partitionings in two villages in Kōchi Prefecture. Admittedly, the sample is small and the partitionings inconveniently recent; on the other hand, they show a division of arable similar to that sanctioned by Tokugawa practice,[9] and it would seem unlikely therefore that they departed drastically from it in respect to other kinds of property.

In the two villages, new branch families were usually given, in addition to land, such tools as hoes, spades, and sickles, but never electric generators, gas engines, or threshers. Large and expensive pieces of equipment were always retained by the main family, although the branch was permitted to use them. The same was true of work animals, though in several cases the partitioning family owned two or more and division of the property was physically possible. Without exception, the branch families were given food to carry them until the next harvest, or a share of the previous harvest corresponding to their portion

---

less equal partitionings, see Fukutake Tadashi, *Nihon nōson no shakaiteki seikaku* (Tokyo, 1949), p. 75.

[9] This might also have been the case when the eldest son was made the branch, at least in some places. The Meiji survey states that in Echizen Province the usual portion of the branch line was one- or two-tenths, but when the eldest son represented the branch line it might be as much as one-half. (Wigmore, *Private Law*, V, 102.)

Of 34 cases of partitioning in Kōchi Prefecture since 1945, the average portion of the arable received by the branch line varied as follows with the relationship of the recipient to the partitioning family head: eldest sons, 28 percent; younger sons, 19 percent; adopted sons, 15 percent; brothers, 16 percent; fathers, 45 percent. (Nakamura Jihei, "Sengo nōson no bunke," *Nōgyō sōgō kenkyū*, VI, 3 (1952), 173.)

of the holding. But never were they given money; which suggests once again that the notion underlying partitioning was not to share the wealth of the family, however unequally, but to give the branch merely the minimum means of support.[10]

In the delicate balance of the economy of individual holdings, meadow, waste, and forestland were scarcely less important than arable; we have seen that they supplied the peasant family with fuel, fodder, compost, and building materials. Nevertheless, such land was either "divided" even less equally than arable,[h] or (in just half the cases studied) held in common by main and branch families after the partitioning of arable. Common ownership, however, did not mean an equal partnership; effective control was vested in the wealthier, influential senior line.[11] Presumably, the practice of partitioning arable land without dividing water rights and rights in common land accounts for the fact that frequently there were fewer holders of such rights than of arable land in villages in the Tokugawa period.

As for dwellings, by no means the least significant class of property, the seventeenth-century land registers provide considerable information. Since these documents registered homesteads (*yashiki*) as well as arable land, it is possible to discover which holders of arable also owned homesteads and which, if any, did not. Approximately one hundred seventeenth-century registers, representing all major regions, have been studied from this viewpoint; astonishingly, they reveal that in most villages between 40 and 80 percent of all arable holders were without homesteads! Even when holders actually resident in other villages can be identified and deducted, the percentage remains astonishingly high—often over 50 percent.[i]

Holders who actually resided in a village without holding homesteads in it must have lived in dwellings belonging to other holders; there is no other possibility. There were several reasons for such a living arrangement, however. Arable holders sometimes lost their homesteads through debt, but continued to occupy them as tenants; *nago* often became holders of their allotments without acquiring title

[h] Data on land other than arable were available in only six cases, and in three of these such land was divided; in those three cases the branch lines received respectively 22 percent, 14 percent, and less than 1 percent of the land available for division. (Nakamura, "Nōson no bunke," p. 173.)

[i] Of 33 holders actually residing in a Bizen village in 1609, only six owned homesteads; in a Kawachi village in 1594, the proportion of resident holders who owned homesteads was 14 out of 36. (Andō Seiichi, "Kinsei shoki nōson kōzō no tenkai," *Rekishi kyōiku*, III, 11 (1955), 59; and Takao, "Edo zenki ni okeru Kinai sonraku no kōsei," p. 59.)

to their dwellings at the same time. But the commonest origin of holders without homesteads was undoubtedly the inheritance system; that
is, by the "division" of arable between heirs without division of the
homestead, in which case, of course, the branch family was left occupy-
ing a dwelling belonging to the main family. And it frequently happened that homesteads were not partitioned along with arable, either
because they were too small to divide, or because the complex of dwellings, outhouses, and work space formed an integral unit, or again because there was reluctance on the part of the main line to relinquish
any of the physical symbols of family continuity. It is true that a new
house was sometimes built for the branch family; but there were often
severe communal restrictions on creating new homesteads (see
pp. 54–58), and such undertakings were expensive in any case.

Owing to the sharply unequal treatment of main and branch lines,
the inheritance system created an economic hierarchy among holders,
shaping the class structure of the village in the image of the hierarchical
family. This was, of course, the stiffly patriarchal extended family on
large holdings, not the more egalitarian nuclear family on small holdings; for, as we have seen, partitioning was confined mainly to the
former. Partitioning tended to divided the village not only into a few
large holders and many small ones, but also into holders with homesteads, capital equipment, and communal rights, and holders who had
none of these. From what has already been said, it is hardly necessary
to add that it was smaller holders who had none, though not all small
holders were without them.[1]

The class structure given the village by the inheritance system was
not, of course, unalterable; even in the seventeenth-century village,
despite the almost complete absence of trade and other volatile elements in the economy, individual families did sometimes move up or

[1] The following situation in respect to homesteads in a village in Higo Province
in 1589 is more or less typical:

Yield of Arable Holding in *koku*	Number of Holders	Number of Holders with Homesteads
Under 1	7	1
1–5	20	3
5–10	8	0
10–20	12	5
20–50	10	8
50–100	2	2
Over 100	1	1
Total	60	20

down in the economic scale. How frequent such movement was is difficult to say, since it is nearly impossible to follow the vicissitudes of all, or even the bulk, of the families in a village over any considerable time period. In the few cases where one can, however, there turns out to have been even less movement than might be expected. Perhaps a single illustration will suffice:[12] one from the Kinai, where the development of commerce and industry favored mobility.

The village in question was located in Kawachi Province, in the center of probably the richest cotton-growing region in the country and very near Osaka. It had a population of 35 holding families in 1657; 17 of this number claimed to be older than the rest, indeed to be the "original" families of the village. They were known as *jūkabu*—a term that might be freely translated as "very important families." Whatever the exact meaning of the term, it was an honorific title by which certain families claiming special antiquity in fact exercised exclusive political and ritual functions in the village. Since these were functions that in other villages as well were associated with family age, it is probable that these 17 were indeed the oldest families in the community, and therefore that the other 18 families had been founded by them as branches. If so, that fact was still evident in the distribution of land in the village in 1657. At that date not all *jūkabu* were large holders, but nearly all large holders were *jūkabu*—in fact, eight out of the ten largest were.[k] In view of the unstable economic environment of the area, this is a very impressive instance of continuity.

[k] Landholding in 1657 was as follows:

Yield of Holding in *koku*	Number of Holders	Number of Holders Who Were *Jūkabu*
Over 100	1	1
50–100	1	0
30–50	1	1
25–30	1	1
20–25	2	2
15–20	4	3
10–25	6	2
5–10	13	5
1–5	5	1
Under 1	1	1
Total	35	17

That not all *jūkabu* were large holders and not all others small proves conclusively that the distinction between *jūkabu* and the other families was *not* purely an economic one. (Furushima Toshio and Nagahara Keiji, *Shōhin seisan to kisei jinushisei*, Tokyo, 1954, p. 49.)

In the more backward areas there were many such cases. Until the land reform, in villages exceptionally isolated from outside influences—in parts of northern Honshu, for instance—the families with the largest holdings in the community were frequently also acknowledged to be the oldest. Before the last century of breathless economic and social change, such villages must have been far more numerous; two centuries before that they were probably the rule.

Two factors seem mainly to account for the stability of family fortunes—that is, for keeping class lines and main-branch relations in close alignment. One is that partitioning was a continuously recurring event; if after several generations there was a tendency for the class lines between main families and their branches to waver, it must be remembered that new lines were continuously being drawn in other cases by partitioning. The other factor was that a branch family was rarely an autonomous economic unit upon being founded; rather, as a farming unit it was an extension of the main family, dependent upon it in a thousand ways.[1] For this reason, though the branch did not necessarily prosper when the main family did, it could hardly prosper if the main family did not. This brings us to a closer consideration of the economic relations between main and branch families—or, to put it another way, between large holdings and small.

The framework of these relations was set by the terms of partitioning. Partitioning, as we have seen, usually took place on large holdings, where the dynamic of population increase was strongest, and it was an event designed by the main line for its own benefit. It was intended to relieve the family of a greater proportion of its members than of its land: to decrease family size drastically but family resources less so.

This objective, moreover, was usually achieved. Four partitionings between 1654 and 1657 in the same Shinshū village may serve as illustrations; they are summarized in Table II. The table shows that the four partitionings were not only absolutely unequal—the main family in all cases receiving the larger share—but also unequal in relation

[1] Another perhaps minor factor that might be mentioned was the at least occasional intervention of the authorities to support the main family's authority in disputes with a branch. The following order from a higher official to a village headman in 1843 is an illustration of the practice: "I have heard that Shigezō is by nature quarrelsome and has fallen out with his [main] family head, Yuemon. It is most important that harmony prevail between main and branch families. Consequently you are instructed to investigate the matter. . . ." (*Kawachi Ishikawamura gakujutsu chōsa hōkoku*, edited by Nomura Yutaka, Osaka, 1952, p. 333.)

to family size. Per capita, the main family in every case received considerably more land than the branch—in one case 13 times more! Other types of property were typically divided less equally than land; indeed, animals and buildings usually went in entirety to the main family, and communal rights less often.

TABLE II*

FOUR PARTITIONINGS IN A SHINSHŪ VILLAGE, 1654–57

	Amount of Arable Received (in *tan*)	Size of Families, Including *Genin*	Arable Per Capital (in *tan*)
Main family	54.244	19	2.854
Branch family	7.816	7	1.116
Main family	10.620	3	3.540
Branch family	7.21	4	1.802
Main family	25.66	9	2.851
Branch family	2.513	5	.502
Main family	29.422	5	5.884
Branch family	.224	5	.044

* Adapted from Miyagawa Mitsuru, "Taikō kenchi to kazoku kōsei," *Hisutoria*, 11 (1955), 39–40.

It is obvious, therefore, that main and branch families tended to be economically complementary. Partitioning divided the resources of a highly integrated farming unit between heirs in such a way that more of some resources (capital and land) went to the main family and more of another (labor) went to the branch. Thus, critical resources that were short in one family were almost necessarily surplus in the other. Since the families were kin living in the closest proximity, sometimes even in the same house, and in an economy with no market to mediate exchange, the inevitable result was continuous cooperative exchange. The branch family gave labor when asked, and received in return housing, tools, animals, water, fertilizer, firewood, and protection. Economic relations, therefore, were similar in kind if not in degree to those between *nago* and *oyakata*: they had a similar origin and were similarly rationalized in terms of the obligations of kinship.

Admittedly, this type of exchange—labor for other resources—is nowadays rare among holders. But *nago* labor services are also rare;

and if they have nearly disappeared, it is hardly surprising that labor services among holders, whose economic and legal position was on the whole somewhat stronger, should have disappeared altogether. There was, of course, nothing in principle against consanguine relatives doing labor services, for such relatives were occasionally even made *nago*.[m] Nor was the holding of land, a legal state, any bar to labor services, which were expressions of an economic and social relationship that had no legal sanction and needed none. [Moreover, cases of holders doing labor services *are* known.] It will suffice to cite one.

A very large holder in Iwate Prefecture in 1912 adopted a young man whom he married to his second daughter. For five years the young couple lived with the parents. Then, in 1917, they were established as a branch family, receiving at the time seven *tan* of arable, a horse, and certain tools; they were obliged to borrow other tools. During the first few years, the branch family performed between 80 and 90 workdays a year for the main family; and according to the records of the main family, it was still doing labor services in 1925. That year it did 22 days' *suke*—significantly, the very word that was applied to *nago* labor services in this area. It is also worth noting that in this same year the main family itself gave the branch seven and a half days' labor, which was also called *suke*.[18] What clearer illustration could there possibly be of the fact that "labor services" were part of a system of reciprocal obligation, not in any way a function of legal status?[n]

[m] Other examples might be cited. It is said that population registers in northern Kyūshū in the late Tokugawa period show many *nago* who were related by blood to *oyakata* and had sprung from his family. (*Fukuoka-ken nōchi*, edited by Fukuoka-ken . . . hensan iinkai, Fukuoka, 1950, I, 405.) The Meiji survey of customary law reported of a county in Hida Province, Gifu Prefecture: "A person who receives less than ten *koku* of land by partitioning . . . is called 'so-and-so' *kadoya* and is a person of more or less inferior rights." (*Meiji bunka zenshū*, VIII, 300.) "*Kadoya*" and "*kado*" are terms commonly used in Gifu, Nagano, and Shimane Prefectures for persons elsewhere called *nago*. (Ariga Kizaemon, *Nihon kazoku seido*, pp. 261–62.)

[n] *Suke* is used for *nago* labor services in the accounts of another family in this very village. (Shimada Takashi, "Bakumatsu, Meiji shoki Kemuyama-mura no rōdō soshiki," *Keizaigaku*, 28 (1953), 78.) It was also the word used for both labor and ceremonial services in the Saitō family mentioned earlier; see Chapter 3, p. 31.

Labor often went both ways in *oyakata-nago* relations. This was particularly notable at the planting, when the *oyakata* mobilized the labor of his *nago* to plant his fields, but also concentrated this large labor force on each *nago's* allotment long enough to plant it. Thus, according to the work records of an *oyakata* family for 1873, each of five *nago* gave between one and three man-days' *suke* each day between the 15th and the 20th of May, and some gave *suke* until the 28th; during

,How common, though, were labor services among holders in the seventeenth century? Judging from the proportion of small holders, especially those without homesteads, they must have been very common indeed. Only by virtue of continuous cooperative support from larger holdings could many of these holdings—mere slips of land incapable of supporting a family or even the necessary capital for farming—have survived. That they were in fact supported by the continuous exchange of labor for other resources is evident from village land registers. These registers, made out from the viewpoint of the village, listed but a fraction of the small holders (especially those without homesteads) who were listed in the lord's register.[o] One suspects that the holdings of those not registered were listed in the names of their respective main families. This is strongly suggested by the fact that holders whose land was listed in the village register in someone else's name were, with few exceptions, small holders without homesteads— that is, branch families living with their respective main families.[p]

---

this time each received the help of from three to ten workers for at least half a day from the *oyakata*. This labor was also called *suke*, and in the case of one *nago* family it actually exceeded in amount the labor it gave that year! (*Ibid.*, pp. 77–78.)

[o] This register was usually called "*nayosechō*" as opposed to the lord's register, which was usually called "*kenchichō*." It was the former that the village used in collecting taxes, as is shown by the fact that it registered land, field by field, according to holders, so that all land belonging to the same holder was listed together; whereas the *kenchichō* listed fields in the order they lay in the village, regardless of ownership; hence it could not have been used to collect taxes. The holders listed in the *nayosechō*, then, were those the village considered responsible for the payment of taxes; and persons listed in the *kenchichō* only, though holders from the viewpoint of the lord, paid their taxes through the *nayosechō* holder of their land.

The *nayosechō* consistently listed fewer holders than the *kenchichō*; but, almost without exception, all holders with homesteads were listed in both documents. In other words, holders listed in the *kenchichō* only were likely to be holders without homesteads. This may be illustrated by the following comparison of the two types of registers for an Ōmi village in the year 1598 (Miyagawa, "Gōson seido to kenchi," p. 24):

	Total Arable Registered	Total Yield Registered	Number of Holders Registered	Number of Holders with Homesteads
Kenchichō (lord's reg.)	26.7129 *chō*	213.963 *koku*	79	36
Nayosechō (village reg.)	26.8914 *chō*	213.896 *koku*	40	37

[p] Sometimes a new branch line, though receiving land in use, was not listed as the holder of it even in the lord's register. In a treatise on administration, a Tokugawa official made the following remarks on this subject: "Although land be inherited by a second or third son or grandson in addition to the main heir, the land of the former may be registered in the lord's register (*kenchichō*) *in the latter's name.* . . ." (My italics.) ("Jikata hanreiroku," p. 439.)

From the viewpoint of the village, such holders were perhaps considered similar to *nago* in that they were not regarded as holding the land themselves. Sometimes holdings were partitioned without the fact being recorded in either the village or the lord's land register; in that case, of course, the land continued to be listed in the main family's name in both registers.[14]

It therefore seems clearly a mistake to regard *nago* as a class sharply differentiated from holders. They were different from the legal viewpoint only, and even then the distinction was not invariably maintained; for some holders were "holders" in one document and "*nago*" in another one. Such validity as the distinction has is merely legal. From other viewpoints it had none: all the multitude of economic and social ties between the *nago* and his allotment on the one hand and the *oyakata* and his holding on the other were characteristic also of relations between small and large holdings. If one were to forget the legal distinction, thinking of allotments and holdings as homogeneous units, one might visualize the agricultural system as consisting of a large number of clusters of such units—sometimes one or two to a village, sometimes more. Each cluster consisted of ten or 20 units (including *nago* allotments) of variable size, with an exceptionally large unit as the nucleus and with lines of obligation running between it and each of the others.

Each of these units was dependent on the large one in the center, but in various degrees. Some were linked to it so tightly that, both socially and economically, they could hardly be distinguished, whereas others were farther removed, located near the edge of the group and nearly independent of the center. The most consistent distinction between those units close to the center and those on the periphery was not the legal one between allotments and holdings, but that between units that had broken off as fragments from the center unit recently and those that had broken off more remotely. Those near the center included both holdings and allotments.

We carry this figure one step further: the central unit was (or had been) an extended family, and the whole group had formed by the pulling away of elements belonging to that family: pulling away very gradually, first becoming branch families and then slowly winning an increasing measure of social and economic autonomy. The structure of the cluster at any given time was therefore a cross section of this process, catching every family at a different stage.

5

THE ORGANIZATION OF POLITICAL POWER

It is evident that we must think of the seventeenth-century village as consisting, [not of a number of autonomous farming units, but of clusters of mutually dependent ones.\ Outside the areas of commercial farming, all these groupings were very similarly organized, each consisting of a large holding and a number of smaller dependent ones (including *nago* allotments, which may be considered holdings from the economic point of view). The size of individual groups varied considerably, ranging from as few as three or four families to as many as 15 or 20; but whatever the number, the group duplicated in miniature the hierarchical economic and social structure of the village.

As cooperative economic units, the groups performed a number of indispensable functions for their members. They mobilized labor for tasks that recurred more or less regularly which no family could cope with individually; when a house was to be built, or a thatch roof was to be replaced, or fields were damaged by flood and needed repair, each family in the group provided labor regardless of who happened to benefit at the moment. The group also provided the framework for day-to-day cooperation in farming, especially between the largest and the smallest holdings. For the large holding provided a pool of capital, of tools, animals, seed, food, fertilizer, storage space, and so on, which the small holding drew on from time to time; the small in turn furnished the large holding with labor when needed. Thus, although in a sense the small holding was worked as an adjunct to the large holding it also gave it crucial support. Through cooperation the group as a whole attained a degree of self-sufficiency that was impossible for any of its members alone—a self-sufficiency imposed by physical isolation and the rudimentary state of the market.

[One function of the group that deserves special notice was to provide a single, large labor force for the spring planting.\ Even in the Tokugawa period, rice was not sown directly in the fields but was started in special beds from which the seedlings were later transplanted.

A group of women planting rice seedlings that are being carried from the beds by the man on the left, who tosses them behind the women in bunches. Other men (not shown) are busy plowing composting, and flooding other fields preparatory to planting. The women shown here are a rather small group; 20 or 30 women in a group was common, the younger women being scattered along the row and covering a greater span than the older women. (*Yamato no kuni hyaku onna.*)

This hard, slow work had to be performed within the exceedingly short period when the seedlings could be transplanted without dangerously interrupting their growth. Since enormous quantities of water were required to work the soil to the consistency of a thick paste preparatory to receiving the young plants, and since few fields could be given the necessary amount of water simultaneously, it was necessary to flood and plant fields one after another in rotation. This reduced the period allowed for planting any one field to a matter of a few hours. To accomplish the planting in the allotted time required a labor force far larger than the individual family could muster. And the various lineages in the village—main family, branches, and pseudo-branches—provided stable groupings for performing this critical work. Mobilizing all its adult members for the planting, the group moved with the water from field to field, without regard for individual ownership; not only did this permit fields to be planted in the extremely short time water was available to each, but it added to the sociability of this exhausting and otherwise wholly disagreeable task. Needless to say, the power to refuse a family this help and sign of solidarity gave the group enormous power over its members.[1]

As the group evolved, its economic functions developed naturally. Each group developed mainly as a result of an extended family expanding and sending out branches through many generations; though there were sometimes families in the group with different origins, they were incorporated as if their history were the same. Since the division of property between main and branch lines created grossly unequal but complementary holdings, as the group grew there was provided not only the necessary social nexus but the economic necessity for cooperation. Even the techniques of cooperation came naturally, for they were merely family practice prolonged and transformed as individual members slowly pulled away from the family core. Thus the group created was, in a sense, an enlarged version of the extended family that stood at its center and from which it had sprung, making it easy to understand the continuous, easy movement of resources from one holding to another within the group.

Fortunately such groups survived in some form in many parts of rural Japan until recently and have been extensively reported;[2] otherwise one would be less confident of their presence in the seventeenth century. They were known by many local names,[3] but despite such diversity, these near contemporary groups had two features in common that identify them all as essentially the same institution and link them to a remote past: (1) they were lineage groups whose members traced their descent through the male line from a common ancestor, and (2) each had a protective deity to whom rites were performed from time to time during the year.

The economic functions of these groups differed widely; but the differences appear to reflect stages of economic development, rather than more radical diversities. Thus in economically advanced areas where the economic functions of the group had been surrendered to the market, little remained to mark the boundaries between groups but organization on ceremonial and social occasions. In areas where economic life had been little affected by outside influences, however, lineage groups functioned very much as they must have nearly everywhere several centuries ago—mobilizing labor for house raising, reroofing, road building, planting and harvesting, and providing a mechanism for day-to-day cooperation. Judging from the reports available, groups in such areas typically formed a hierarchy of holdings of the kind revealed in the seventeenth-century land registers; but, on the other hand, in the more advanced areas the market and other volatile influences had often upset this traditional pattern, and branch families might outstrip their main families economically.[a]

Survival of the lineage group adds details to our knowledge of its social functions. Where its economic functions were still strong, the group had a highly developed social side. Members celebrated or mourned together at births, weddings, funerals, and numerous annual festivals, and although persons outside the group might also participate in the activities on such occasions, the primary roles were reserved for members of the lineage. These recurring events underline the solidarity of the group. Indeed, at times when only members of the lineage were present, one might almost say the assembled group momentarily formed a single extended family. Within this family circle which formed and dispersed from time to time but was always present in the minds of its members, distinctions of seating, address, and costume were strictly observed, and just as in the actual family they distinguished most sharply between the head and the other members. The head of the main family was seated in the position of honor where he presided over the whole assemblage as patriarch. He was addressed by an honorific title and was shown extreme deference in other ways; when visiting a branch family, for instance, he was given the seat at the hearth reserved at all other times for the family head; and he often acted as parent in place of the natural parent at weddings or name-givings in branch families.[b]

Nothing reveals so clearly as ritual that stratification and oneness, hierarchy and solidarity, were simultaneously traits of the group. An-

---

[a] When in such cases the economic functions of the group had not been decisively weakened, the economic, ceremonial, and genealogical role of the main family might be assumed by the now dominant branch family, the former main family sinking to the status of a branch. For a case in point, see Ariga, *Kazoku seido*, pp. 45–50. The assumption by a branch of the main family's genealogical position is difficult to understand unless one comprehends that genealogy and kinship were not biologically given but were ways of defining status and role. This accounts in part at least for the frequency of the adoption of an heir, the assimilation of hereditary servants to family members, and the taking of the surname of a lineage by a family incorporated into it from the outside for economic reasons. (Kitano Seiichi, "Dōzoku soshiki to oyakata kokata kankō shiryō," *Minzokugaku nempō*, III (1940–41), 181–89.)

[b] Cases similar to main-branch family relations have been reported in which the natural parents actually absented themselves from the wedding ceremony to dramatize the relationship of the acting parents to the new couple. (Kawashima Takeyoshi and Ushiomi Toshitaka, "Kaneoya ni tsuite," *Minzokugaku kenkyū*, XII, 1 (1947), 33–38.)

cestral rites—those directed to the common ancestors of the group—
were held in the home of the main family under the direction of its
head (those directed to the ancestors of individual families were held
in their several homes), and the group thus acknowledged common descent by different and unequal lines. These same elements of strict
ordering within a solidary whole were also seen in the annual rites to
the protective deity. In these rites the corporate unity of the group was
obviously asserted since the deity protected members of the group
only; but at the same time the position of the main family was affirmed
by its leading role in the rites. It is true that other arrangements were
possible where the hierarchy of the group had been disrupted by economic change; then, several of the leading families might take turns
presiding over the rites, or, if the disruption were more far-reaching,
this office might rotate among all families without distinction. But
these exceptions merely underline the point that ritual organization
reflected the structure of the group.

The head of a lineage enjoyed a politically powerful position in
the village for obvious reasons. Lineage groups were units of social
and economic life, clusters of interdependent interests that clung together with great force and were broken up only when the competitive
inducements of trade began, much later, to dissolve the internal ties.
These wholes were the integers of village organization of all kinds, and
the families who spoke for them were exceedingly powerful. When,
as sometimes happened, there was but one lineage in a village, the main
family's authority in lineage and village were exactly the same; more
commonly, however, there were several lineages, and then the influence of each head was modified by that of the others. This would
suggest that the political power of a family depended solely on the
size and discipline of its lineage in relation to others; but this is not
quite correct—other, related points of support must be mentioned.
[The most important of these was the restriction of village office to
certain prominent families who perforce included the heads of lineages
and in some cases no one else.] Just how such restrictions on office arose
is difficult to say; but they were evidently closely associated in origin
with the general tendency for formally defined classes to develop in
the village. To cite but a few examples: a certain Kinai village was
divided into classes of families known respectively as *honyaku, han-
yaku, inkyo, karazaike,* and *genin*; a village in Echigo was divided into
shōya, yakunin, inkyo, and *nago*;[4] a village in Tōtōmi was divided into

honke and *karazai*.[5] Documents of the Tokugawa period, whether
originating in the village or outside it, rarely referred to peasants as
a homogeneous class, but listed various classes of peasants, or else referred to the whole by some such locution as "from *hombyakushō* down
to *genin*"—as though the generic term "*hyakushō*" became inappli-
cable as soon as one considered the village at all closely. These classes
cut laterally across lineage groups, and they included fewer and fewer
members as one ascended the social scale. Nor were they ill-defined
shifting groups, such as our modern terms "upper," "middle," and
"lower" class. Rather, they were categories actually used in registering population: they represented differential political rights in the
villlage and their membership was precisely and exhaustively known
at all times.

The names and number of these classes differed from village to
village. But the most pervasive and radical distinction among them,
which often overlapped with others (revealing the character of all?),
was that between "old" and "new" families. Nearly every village had
its *kyūka*, or "old families," and its "new families" who were variously
called *shin'ya, shintaku, shimban, kitarimono*.[c] These were not merely
descriptive terms but designations of differential status and rights that
applied more or less permanently.[6]

It is not difficult to see that these distinctions were merely general-
ized public versions of similar distinctions within lineages between main
and branch families. Not only were main families always older than
their branches, but branches were frequently put by community rules
under certain disabilities as a public mark of inferiority. Thus, in
Kyūshū, new branch families were often not allowed for five generations after their founding to enshrine a household god (*yashikigami*);
during this time they were obliged to worship the household deity of
the main family.[7] Or the distinction between main and branch might
be publicly asserted in other ways; for example, in some Shinshū villages consisting of a single lineage, the location of the houses of branch
families was designated as "upper," "lower," "west," "east," "before,"

---

[c] The Meiji compilation on customary law affords many examples of discrimination against newly established families. For instance: "In Awa . . . the farmers dislike to own descent from a new family, and so . . . younger sons do not
start new families but take the succession of a family about to become extinct." Or:
"The new householder [in Noto Province] pays from 3 to 5 yen to the village
as 'face money.' . . ." Or again: "The house of the new family [in Tamba Prov-
ince] may be covered with straw-thatch only, not with reed-thatch or with tiles."
(Wigmore, *Private Law*, V, 99, 103–4.)

or "behind," depending on the geographical relation to the residence of the main family.

In a society with a strong sense of the past and local reminders of it on every hand, distinctions such as these easily became political, especially if the main families of a village acted in concert to that end. And they did. A village headman, writing on the conduct of his office in the early nineteenth century, emphasized the political significance of family age, stating that "old families should be selected [by a headman as subordinates] . . . for, however prosperous a family may be, if degree is overlooked, things will not go well."[9] This view was widely held and commonly enforced as part of the village constitution. But although most villages restricted political rights to "old families" in some degree, how narrowly they defined that class of families differed greatly; thus we find villages with no more than half a dozen "old families" but others with a great many more.[d] But if the line between "old" and "new" was drawn differently from one place to another, all villages appear to have drawn it under force of the same compelling circumstance.

That circumstance was having reached limits placed on the growth of the village by the amount of available resources, especially in the form of common land and water sources. Until these limits were reached, new families might be created with the same rights in the community as existing families; but once these resources were fully employed, or nearing that stage, no new share could be created without diminishing the actual or future value of existing shares.[e] Rather than suffer this loss existing families restricted or prohibited altogether the creation of new families who could claim shares. The Meiji compilation on customary law contains much evidence of such restrictions. We are told that in Tōtōmi Province ". . . one cannot start a new family at pleasure, and usually one must wait until a piece of residence land

---

[d] Those with the most restrictive constitution, that is, with a single family that monopolized political rights, paradoxically may not have divided families formally into classes, since such distinctions were not needed to bolster power so firmly and exclusively held.

[e] The author of the "Minkan shōyō" tells us how villages tended to expand until they pressed severely against their resources: "As to the origin of villages, one or two families usually settle where the land is good, and fields are brought under the plow surrounding the dwellings of the settlers. Gradually a village forms; new houses are built among the existing ones, new fields are opened up, and land previously neglected, such as valley bottoms and marsh, is filled in, ditches and ponds are built and new fields are developed until not an inch of land is left. . . ." "Minkan shōyō," *NKSS*, I, 381.

is vacated. . . ." In Sado Province ". . . a law prohibits any change in
the number of houses, so that the creation of branch families is not allowable, and it is customary for a younger son to wait for the removal
of some family and take its place. . . . [In Tango Province] in some
villages an increase of the number of houses is not considered desirable,
so even though a branch family be established, the name is recorded
with that of the main family [in the population register], until an opportunity arises to succeed to the name and remaining property of
some extinct family."[10]

[Despite restrictive covenants, however, new families were established—but without equal rights with the old. Nor was the inequality
confined to access to common land and water resources, for these rights
were merely aspects of rights in the community generally, including
political rights.] As illustration: a village in Tōtōmi Province in 1772
was divided into two groups of families, those with and those without
the right to hold village office;[f] each group had a distinct status-name,
was registered in a separate population register, and belonged to a
different temple of the same Buddhist sect. The basis for these distinctions was establishment as families before or after 1741: families established before that date belonged to one group and enjoyed political
rights, those established afterward belonged to the other and were
devoid of such rights. This particular date is significant since no new
land was brought under cultivation after that. This year the absolute
limit on the expansion of arable was apparently reached. Families
founded afterward, therefore, had access to land only as tenants, and
they were probably placed under political disabilities to discourage any
further increase in their number.[11]

Many similar examples, some of surprisingly recent date,[g] might

[f] A village in Shinshū affords a similar case. This village dates from the construction of irrigation facilities in the area in 1630, growing rapidly thereafter.
Families founded before about 1670 became "*hombyakushō*" and had full rights
in the village; the number of such families remained unchanged until the end of
the Tokugawa period at 45. Branch families founded by them were known as
kakae and were without political rights in the village; such families numbered 144
by 1866. (Ōishi Shinzaburō, "Kinseiteki sonraku kyōdōtai to ie," *Tōyō bunka*,
18/19 (1955), p. 20.)

[g] A village in Yamanashi Prefecture illustrates both the tenacity of the system
of differential rights and the tendency of the system nevertheless gradually to
change under the stress of modern conditions. In 1948 there were four distinct
groups in this village of 304 families: 57 *kyūka* or "old families"; 268 *shimban* or
"new families," who were branches of the last few generations of the "old families";
a few *fudai*, that is nonconsanguine branches of *kyūka*, probably formerly hereditary

be cited to show the restriction of political rights to the older families of the village. The practice was seemingly general, with only details differing from place to place. This is evident from the way in which the office of headman was filled and from the character of a village institution called *miyaza*.

There were three usual methods of filling the office of headman: election, rotation, and inheritance, in order of increasing exclusiveness. The least common of the three was election, which seems to have been confined to villages where traditional status patterns had broken down under the impact of commercial farming—a modern feature of agrarian life. In most traditional villages the role of headman either was hereditary within a single family and the office was handed down from father to son with the family headship, or it rotated at regular intervals among a few qualified families only.

Where the headship was hereditary, it is usually clear from oral tradition and other evidence (such as the household deity of the headman being also the protective deity of the village) that a single family had founded the village and that its branches accounted for most of the village's subsequent growth. It is equally clear that, where the role of headman rotated among a number of qualified families, such families represented a number of different lineages each of which had contributed substantially to the establishment and growth of the village.[h]

The other institution illustrating the restriction of political rights to certain old families is the *miyaza*. (See Chapter 12 for fuller dis-

---

servants of those families; and a number of *kitarimono*, or "newcomers," consisting mostly of immigrant doctors, teachers, and other specialists. The first three groups all bore one of four surnames and were divided among as many lineages; on the other hand, the *kitarimono* bore different surnames and stood outside the lineage organization of the village.

Until 1887 the headship of the village had been restricted to 12 especially eminent "old families" who were known as *nanushi-kabu*. Since that date, however, every family in the village has been legally eligible for that office. Nevertheless, of 13 incumbents between 1890 and 1948, 12 were from "old families" and only one was from a "new family." No *kitarimono* or *fudai* had ever held that office as late as 1948. The "old families" dominated other village offices—such as chief of the village Youth Group (*wakashū-gashira*), head of the "children" of the protective deity, and chief of the group of worshippers at the Buddhist temple in the village. (*Sanson no kōzō*, edited by Furushima, pp. 160–200.)

[h] I am told by Professor Ariga that occasionally a fusion of the two systems occurs when one of several lineages in a village is much stronger than the rest; then the role of headman may come to rotate in some such sequence as 1, 2, 1, 3, 1, 4, and so on, rather than in simple 1, 2, 3, 4 order.

cussion.) Especially prevalent in the Kinai, in Shikoku and Kyūshū, though found in nearly every region in some villages, the *miyaza* consisted of a group of families who held the exclusive privilege of ministering to the village deity. The most important aspect of this position was the monopoly of the several offices concerned with the maintenance of the shrine and the organization of the annual rites to the deity. In villages where the *miyaza* has been closely studied, these ritual privileges have been revealed as expressions in one area of village life of a generally privileged position in the community, including the exclusive right to hold village office; and we may assume that this was true of the *miyaza* in other villages as well. As to the origin of these political and ritual privileges there can be little doubt, for everywhere the holders of them claimed to be the oldest families in the village.

It was of considerable importance to the authority of privileged families, of course, that the lord did his utmost to support and exalt the position of village officials. He could not do otherwise; the collection of taxes, the maintenance of peace, the security of administrative centers—all depended ultimately upon the self-discipline of thousands of autonomous villages, in which the most effective advocates of obedience were the local headmen. In all parts of the country, therefore, the lord sought to lift the headman above the ordinary peasants, with the intent of assuring his loyalty and at the same time impressing the rest of the village with the dignity and authority of his office. Thus, for example, the headman and his family were permitted to wear silk and certain articles of dress considered especially elegant, to live in large and elaborately decorated houses, and sometimes even to wear swords and take surnames—all of which were forbidden the peasants generally.[12]

The lord also constantly exhorted the peasants to look upon the headman as a parent, to give him love and respect—but above all obedience. He himself stood ready to give the headman every help including the support of troops if necessary. But it was a clumsy headman who let affairs in his village reach such a pass, for though military intervention might temporarily strengthen his authority, it could serve only to weaken it in the long run. To appeal for such intervention was a confession of inability to get along otherwise—a confession that reduced the headman's value by exposing him to the ruling class as ineffectual and to the villagers as the lord's agent. Rather than thus isolate himself from the approval of village opinion, many a headman in a crisis sided with the village against his lord though the decision to do so often meant almost certain death. Throughout the Tokugawa period, but especially in the first half when the solidarity of the village had not yet been widely disturbed by the influence of competitive farming, many peasant uprisings were led, not by outcasts and ne'er-do-wells, but by headmen.[13]   see Craig - 280 →   (chōshū ↑ .....)

This brings us to another point of support for the power of the leading families of the village: the solidarity of the community itself. For it was essential to their power that they be able to speak with the voice of the village—on behalf of the sanctity of tradition, communal interests, and other similarly approved public goals. If politics is the art of transforming private interests into the public good, rarely have the conditions for its successful practice been so favorable as in the Japanese village before the advent of trade. This is best seen perhaps in the headman's discharge of his office.

Like most group characteristics, the demand for unanimity in the Japanese village is difficult fully to account for, though one may mention numerous relevant environmental and historical influences. Geographically isolated from all but a few neighbors, farming communities since prehistoric times have been compact settlements whose families, linked to one another by innumerable ties of kinship, and trusting for protection in the same local gods, were huddled together physically. This afforded mutual comfort in the face of a menacing natural environment, and enabled them to help one another in their work and in conditions of famine, sickness, and death. But all such factors somehow still do not adequately explain the most important social characteristic of the Japanese village, its fierce and pervasive sense of solidarity.

The urgent sense that the village was a group that could tolerate no genuine internal differences, even in intimate matters of family concern, was evinced in more ways than can be discussed here. It was manifest in the legal personality that history had given the village: its competence to make contracts, borrow money, sue and be sued, and its collective responsibility in matters of taxation and criminal law. The solidarity was acted out annually in collective rites to the community deity who protected his "children," not as individuals, but as members of the community, whose priestly officials were automatically also the village's secular leaders. It was evident in community exclusiveness: in rules against the sale of land to outsiders;[14] against the settlement of outsiders without consent within the village precincts;[15] in the endless disputes and law suits between villages over water rights and wasteland; in the village rule of endogamy except for high-placed families who had to go outside the village to find marriage partners of comparable family rank.[16]

The striving for solidarity was not least evident in the way personal affairs were often given a public character lest they otherwise lead to deviant opinion or behavior.[i] Because anything secret and private was suspicious, a man who had private business with someone from another village might be obliged to conduct it through his headman; thus a face-to-face relationship became one of group to group.[j] Or when a man named a child, he might be required to contribute a certain amount of rice or wine to the village deity who, apparently, permitted the child to be given his social identity and brought into the community.[17] If a villager quarreled with a neighbor or neglected the proprieties of the season, he was likely to be fined:[18] for how could the harmony of the group be maintained if forms of politeness and consideration were slighted? And how much more serious was a crime! Not only did it offend against the village, but brought shame upon it as well. It is no accident that the expulsion of a wrongdoer from the community, a punishment known in all villages, was often known as *mura-harai,* or "cleansing the village"—a term that passes over the punishment inflicted and fastens on the group expiation accomplished by punishment.

With this background of group sentiment, the village was armed with very powerful weapons to bring about conformity. Gossip, by which the humiliation of deviant behavior or opinion was made generally known, usually sufficed to secure conformity; but if not some mild form of public censure normally would. The villagers had in-

---

[i] The following quotation in part of an agreement signed by all the holders of a village in 1831 is an example: "Poor harvests have continued for several years now and the harvest this year was especially bad. The villagers have therefore talked together and agreed as follows:

"1. At the wheat planting and when planting vegetables, *sake* will not be brought out to the fields to give those working there a noontime sip as in the past. . . .

"2. When weeding or otherwise tilling rice, even when help is being received with such work, no one may take any refreshment but tobacco or tea; it is strictly forbidden to bring rice or *sake* to the fields. . . ." (*Kawachi Ishikawa-mura,* edited by Nomura, pp. 90–91.)

[j] We find this explicitly stated in a village code of 1788 (*Nihon kinsei sompō no kenkyū,* edited by Maeda Masaharu, Tokyo, 1950, p. 60.) It is undoubtedly significant in this connection that headmen appear in private written agreements of all kinds as witnesses or surety persons (*ukenin*).

numerable ways of expressing disapproval—placing a mark on a man's door, for instance, or assembling at his gate and beating on pots and pans in unison. But occasionally when harrying did no good sterner measures were taken, leading by degrees to ostracism and expulsion from the village—the severest punishments that could be inflicted.[19]

So severe were these punishments that the mere threat of them could scarcely fail to have effect. Banishment drove a man onto the highway without property or credentials, so that he must soon starve or run afoul of the law. Significantly, banishment was not confined to serious offenses, but might be invoked for any wrong-doing persisted in—the purposeful flouting of opinion apparently being as serious as any crime.[k] Ostracism was scarcely less cruel than banishment; the entire village severed relations with an offender against its norms, and in some cases even forced him to live at a distance. No one would greet him on the road or help him in any way except in the case of fire or death; he could not buy in the village store, the local doctor or midwife would not respond to his call, his children could not be members of the village youth group (*wakashū*). In the isolated settlements of the Tokugawa period the utter withdrawal of the sympathy of neighbors was more than most men could stand.

Once the village official was armed with the support of public opinion, therefore, his authority was very nearly absolute; he needed no help from the lord. His problem was rather to guide opinion to a desired consensus. In doing so he was aided by the urgent desire of the community to reach *some* consensus (a force that could also be dangerous) and by the opportunity his position gave him for influencing others. He was head or stood close to the head of a lineage whose support he could expect, and as a large holder he probably also had persons outside his lineage who were dependent on him as tenants, or for water or for the use of animals. These could be counted on to support him unless some stronger claim on their loyalties was exerted from another quarter. He was linked by marriage to other families similarly placed in the village since marriage generally occurred between families of equal status.[l]

[k] Thus, in village law codes listing a large number of prohibitions, many quite trivial, one frequently finds such statements as: "If anyone should violate these regulations he will most certainly be expelled from the village . . ."; or again, "If any violation occurs . . . the culprit's ears will be cut off and he will be driven from the village." (*Ibid.*, pp. 38, 42 of Appendix.)

[l] This is shown by the fact that the only circumstance recognized in most traditional villages for marrying outside the village was inability to find a marriage

Even with such advantages, however, the headman had to proceed cautiously; his object was to translate his views into the general will, not to impose them on an unwilling community. He therefore needed a reputation for virtue and impartiality, for putting the interests of the community before his own. "It is essential," a headman writes in 1813, "that a headman have wisdom, benevolence, bravery and integrity; if he lacks any one of these qualities he cannot perform his duties." Again and again the author of this treatise on village government warns that the headman must care for his good name, since if he were thought partial or corrupt he could not dispose of matters satisfactorily. He must therefore cultivate such tact and discretion—political virtues in all societies—that if a family in the village became impoverished, he could "speak to the relatives in such a way that they would agree to help the needy family to the extent of their ability without feeling imposed on"—tact indeed! Or, again, if someone in the village were misbehaving, the headman should speak to him in private and warn him of his conduct in a graceful way, saying: "This is not at all like you." The offender might then mend his ways; but if the headman made public threats and flourished his authority, the fellow might become stubborn and openly oppose him.

Above all, the headman must maintain a solid front with the other leaders of village opinion, taking full account of their views, dignity, and interests, always compromising with them rather than risking a breach. When an important issue in the village arose, he should consult his subordinates as to what course should be taken, listen carefully to their views, and express his agreement in such self-effacing terms as "Splendid! I had not thought of that." Only after he had heard the others should he announce his own opinion. Our informant does not say so, but it is clear that this consultation was intended to compromise privately all influential points of view before a public decision was taken. Abhorring dissonance, the village went to surprising lengths to avoid any open conflict of opinion; as recently as the postwar period, for instance, one village assembly was in the habit of meeting privately the

partner of equal family rank inside. (Ariga Kizaemon, *Nihon kon'in shi ron*, Tokyo, 1948, pp. 22–24.) A report by the headman of a Tosa village in 1857 tells us that in inquiring about a prospective bride from another village the first question asked was about her family's status. (Koseki Toyokichi, "Ansei 4-nen Kawakita-mura fūdo torishimari sashidashichō no kenkyū," *Tosa shidan*, 40 (1932), 149.) On changes in village marriage patterns, see Yamamoto Noboru, "Tsūkon kankei yori mita sanson kyōdōtai no fūsasei to byōdōsei," *Shakaigaku hyōron*, I, 3 (1950), 123–55.

day before its scheduled public meeting, in order that decisions on the latter occasion might be unanimous.[20] We see this same concern for public harmony in the advice of our headman about dealing with boundary disputes; he recommends that the disputing parties be brought together and persuaded to compromise their differences—significantly, nothing is said about discovering the right of the matter or seeing justice done. Only after a compromise had been reached— which is to say, after the matter had been settled—should the headman give an order![21]

It took tact, patience, and compromise to bring opinion to the desired consensus, but once that was achieved the headman spoke on behalf of all.[m] Consensus gave the headman enormous coercive power on special occasions and even in everyday life, but though such power became a habit with the most skillful headmen, so that it seemed almost a personal attribute or at least an attribute of office, in reality it was neither. The coercive power inhered in the community itself. But not everyone could act for the community. Those few who could were qualified to do so because they stood each at the apex of a system of farming, kinship, and property rights that knitted a group of families together in intricate interdependence.[n] The political power of the heads of these groups was merely one aspect, in practice undifferentiated from the others, of the paramountcy of each in his group. When these leading families were in agreement, their decision had behind it all the weight of their several groups, now acting as one. And such families did habitually act together, for uniting them were marriage ties, class interest, and a common concern in preserving the authority of the community.

[m] Miss Tsurumi emphasizes the importance of this point in discussing rural political bosses in postwar Japan. "The will of these bosses," she writes, "is imposed upon community members not as the decision of the individual bosses, but as the decision of the community as a whole, and the farmers vote as they are told even when they know it is against their interests." (Kazuko Tsurumi, "A Common Man's Philosophy in Postwar Japan" (typescript, 1952), p. 6.)

[n] The dependence of political power in the village on economic and social power —or rather the single identity of all three—is well illustrated by the fact that in at least some villages today there are in effect two different systems of offices. One is that prescribed by law and within whose competence all matters involving the village with higher administrative organs fall, and the other is a system of traditional offices with traditional titles which has authority over such internal matters as the law is not concerned with—for instance, quarrels between neighbors or within families, village festivals, and the morals of young people.

Part II

THE VILLAGE IN TRANSITION

6

THE GROWTH OF THE MARKET

There were scattered islands of commercial farming in Japan from very early times, but as late as 1600 peasants still typically produced to feed and clothe themselves, to pay taxes in kind, and to store whatever surplus there might be in good years against the certain crop failures of the future. But rural life changed rapidly after the Tokugawa conquest, as people became used to peace, transport improved, and the warrior class was removed from the fastness of the countryside to castle towns. The islands of commercial farming expanded, ran together, and began to fill in the surrounding sea of self-sufficient economy.

How great was the change in the two hundred years or so after 1600 is suggested by the pace of urban growth.[1] Town life dates from at least the eighth century in Japan. But as late as the second half of the sixteenth century, when overseas trade flourished as never before, there were no more than two or three population centers that justly deserved the name "city." One was Kyoto, the old capital, which had about a quarter of a million inhabitants; another was the nearby port of Sakai with upwards of 50,000; after that one could count perhaps only half a dozen towns with as many as 20,000. Edo did not yet exist as a city; Osaka, destined in another century to be the country's second largest city, according to Jesuit accounts still lagged behind Sakai. Despite urban fame and colorful town life other places were much smaller. For example, Yamaguchi, the seat of one of the most powerful lords of the time, and perhaps the largest administrative center outside the capital, cannot have had much more than 10,000 population; and Hakata, second only to Sakai as a port, was not much if any larger.

Then, in the two centuries after 1600, urban population grew with astonishing speed, increasing more than in the previous millennium. Edo, no more than a fishing village in 1590, grew into a vast and crowded city of more than half a million by 1731, when it was perhaps the world's largest city. Osaka and Kyoto grew less rapidly, but both had populations of 400,000 or more by 1800; together with neighboring Sakai and Fushimi they comprised an urban center of nearly a million people.

Nor were these the only considerable cities. Nagasaki, the terminus for what remained of Japan's foreign trade, and at least two provincial castle towns—Nagoya at the head of Ise Bay, and Kanazawa on the opposite coast facing the Japan Sea—had between 50,000 and 60,000 each. After that came perhaps 30 or 40 castle towns with over 10,000 population each, not to mention scores of posting stations, ports, and temple towns of 5,000 or more. Clearly a very large part of the population of the country was urban by the early nineteenth century. Professor Furushima's estimate is about 22 percent toward the middle of the eighteenth century. Though urban population was heavily concentrated in Edo and the Osaka-Kyoto area, castle towns were so widely scattered by virtue of administrative and strategic functions that there were few villages anywhere more than 20 miles from a town of fair size.[2]

Enormous quantities of grain, fish, timber, and fibers were required to feed, clothe, and shelter the growing population of the towns. Most of it came by way of local markets and merchants from Japanese farming and fishing villages, since foreign trade contributed almost nothing. What a task and what opportunities were set for villages which in the eighteenth century had produced little or nothing for sale! And what social adjustments were required to meet the challenge successfully! Not the least of these was to make farming far more specialized, for the country could no longer afford the gigantic waste of peasants all growing the same crops and therefore nearly everywhere growing some of them inefficiently.

The waste and inefficiency had been inevitable so long as urban population was inconsiderable and the opportunity to buy and sell was very limited. Then each region, village, and holding tended to produce what it needed, which was what all the others needed too. Everywhere rice and the lesser grains were the staples; they were supplemented only by a bit of fruit and vegetables grown for family consumption, a fiber crop for clothing, and perhaps some tobacco if soil and climate permitted. In the late Tokugawa period one still found villages with the characteristic subsistence pattern of cropping. But by the beginning of the nineteenth century this stage was long past. Except in notably backward places—wild and remote valleys, isolated promontories, areas cut off by poor soil from the main stream of economic development—peasants by then typically grew what soil, climate, and price favored, regardless of what they themselves happened to need. If a family were short of food or of critical raw materials as a result, it made no difference since nearly anything was available in the local market, supplied with commodities from places scores or even hundreds of miles away.

Most crops except grains, which to this day are grown nearly everywhere, gradually came to center in certain regions where growing conditions were especially favorable. Cultivation of mulberries and raising of silkworms eventually centered in the high, cool, and moist valleys of central Honshū; cotton centered chiefly in the Kinai, where Osaka provided an ample supply of commercial fertilizers and where the rainfall in many places was too meager and irrigation too difficult to grow rice; sugar cane was grown mainly in southern Kyūshū and the islands to the south, where the crop was favored by local soils, nearly tropical heat, and rainfall. It is impossible to follow the slow stages by which each of these crops came to center in the locality it did, but one can perceive how far the process of specialization had gone by 1877, not too late to reflect rather accurately the conditions of the late Tokugawa period. In that year, Kawachi, Owari, Settsu, Mikawa, and Hōki (five of Japan's 68 provinces) accounted for 34.4 percent of all the cotton produced; Ōmi, Mino, Echigo, Ise, and Kawachi accounted for 49.9 percent of all vegetables; Tamba, Shinano, Musashi, Kai, and Kōzuke for 52.2 percent of cocoons; and Chikuzen, Tamba, Settsu, Awa, and Musashi for 68.9 percent of indigo.

The same production figures for 1877 also show for each region the percentage of the total agricultural output represented by cash crops, thus bringing out very clearly—if roughly—the differential geographical development of commercial farming (Table III). At the one extreme were the Tōsan and Kinai regions, where cash crops accounted for 25.8 percent and 26.8 percent respectively of all crops. One crop in each of these regions—cotton in the Kinai and cocoons in Tōsan—was roughly as important as all other cash crops together. At the other extreme were Kyūshū, Shikoku, and the area along the Japan Sea, where cash crops accounted for less than 12 percent. In the Tōhoku region, for which there are unfortunately no data, commercial farming was probably even less developed.

One must be careful not to exaggerate the degree of commercial farming anywhere. It is clear from Professor Furushima's figures that as late as the early Meiji period one cannot speak of farming as predominantly commercial even in the Kinai. In that region, rice ac-

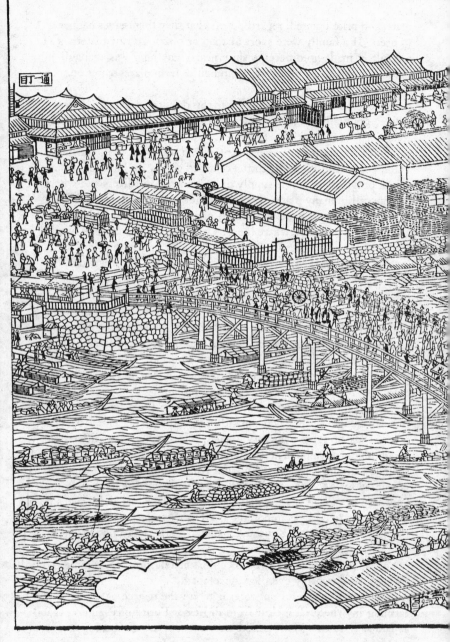

目丁一通

Looking west at Nihonbashi at the center of Edo. One
of two famous fish markets located on opposite sides of

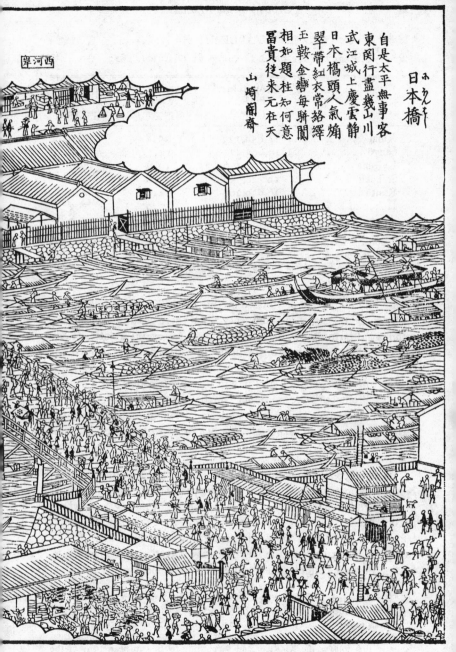

自是太平無事客
東関行盡幾山川
武江城上慶雲静
日本橋頭人氣烟
翠帯紅衣常絡繹
玉鞍金轡毎駢闐
相如題柱知何意
冨貴徒来元在天

山崎闇齋

日本橋

西河岸

the canal is in the right foreground; across the canal are
warehouses, and beyond them shops. (*Edo meisho zue.*)

TABLE III

PERASE OF CASH CROPS BY DISTRICT, 1877

	All Agricultural Products (in yen)	Cash Crops (percent)	Number One Cash Crop (percent)
Kinai	14,858,779	25.8	11.9
Sanyō	15,605,320	13.7	7.6
Kyūshū	23,800,176	10.2	3.5
Shikoku	19,426,756	12.0	3.0
Kantō	26,939,263	14.7	4.2
Hokuriku	18,999,313	12.0	3.3
Tōsan	35,463,319	26.8	14.8

Boundaries of these districts correspond generally, but not exactly, with those shown by the map on page xiv.

Adapted from Furushima Toshio, *Kinsei ni okeru shōgyōteki nōgyō no tenkai*, Tokyo, 1950, p. 10.

counted for 60 percent of all farm products in 1877—evidence of a still high degree of peasant self-sufficiency.[a] But there were enclaves where commercial farming was highly developed. In several counties of Kawachi and Settsu provinces, for instance, cotton alone accounted for between 40 and 50 percent of all farm products (by value), and in one county cotton, vegetables, and indigo together accounted for 61 percent.[3] Differences were no doubt equally great from one village to another, for here as elsewhere commercial farming mingled with the farming typical of an earlier era, the one often within a few miles of the other.[b]

As commercial farming spread, so of course did the use of money. Not that money was anything new to the peasant. A Korean ambassador in the fifteenth century marveled at the use of money everywhere in rural Japan: everyone would accept it, beggars and prostitutes would take nothing else, and the wayfarer need carry nothing more than a full purse.[4] But the ambassador must have stayed on the main roads, for in the back country he would have found money less common.

[a] Because a very high percentage of rice on most holdings went for taxes or was consumed at home—a condition still found in some places today; see Chapter 13.

[b] Even today one can pass quickly from villages where commercial farming is highly developed to villages where it is meager, for example by descending from the train that follows the Ki River and proceeding by bus up nearly any of the narrow valleys that run back into the mountains on either side.

Ogyū Sorai, with his keen eye for signs of social change, tells us that coins were a curiosity outside the towns until the Genroku period but since then had come into use everywhere, even in the loneliest mountain hamlets.[5] One suspects Sorai of exaggerating the suddenness of the change since he was writing only a few years after Genroku, but there can be no doubt that a momentous change, signified by the use of money, was taking place in the economy in the first half of the eighteenth century.

The very landscape testified to the change. New markets were springing up everywhere and established ones were growing to new size; by the late Tokugawa period these markets, usually held at ten-day intervals, were to be found even in remote and backward districts. There were a score or so of such markets in most provinces by the early eighteenth century, some dating back a century or more but the majority apparently of more recent origin. The peasant could buy everything he needed in them; a list of commodities regularly sold in a market established in Takada village (Aizu *han*) in 1665 included cloth, harnesses, cotton, paper, rice, soybeans, firewood, hoes, hoe handles, sickle handles, winnowing baskets, looms, tobacco, grain, vegetables, mortars, straw hats, and straw matting—in addition to items offered for sale only occasionally. It is significant that the regular commodities were all articles in daily use among the peasants; gone were the luxury goods commonly found in local markets before the Tokugawa period when warriors and their households had been a conspicuous feature of village life.[6]

Scattered about the country were hundreds of tiny markets like the one in Aizu, serving an area within a radius of perhaps four or five miles, selling a bit of everything. Less numerous, but perhaps more important in knitting the country together economically, were larger markets each dominated by a single commodity that drew buyers from all over. Such a place was the great silk market at Fukushima about 1818:[7]

The first great market of the year in Fukushima opens on the 14th of the sixth month. During the night of the 13th peasants gather with their silk from a distance of many miles around and wait for the market to open at dawn. Buying and selling begins on the 14th and continues for two watches. During this time, about one hundred horseloads of silk amounting to 3,600 *kan* weight are sold for fifteen or sixteen thousand *ryō*. . . . The sellers, who number several thousand, have their silk examined for quality and weighed and are paid accordingly. Nowhere in the country is there a market where so much money changes hands as here.

Fukushima may indeed have been the biggest silk market of the time, but it was by no means the only one. The country to the southwest that was later to make up Gumma Prefecture was dotted with silk markets; by 1868 there were 24 in the area, all open once a month or more during the marketing season. At Tomioka, the little mountain town where the Meiji government subsequently established one of the first modern silk-reeling mills in Japan, there was a market open nine days a month. Some of these Gumma markets dated back several centuries—the earliest to 1293—but significantly most originated during the Tokugawa period, seven in the nineteenth century.[8]

⌈One must not imagine that all buying and selling among peasants occurred in markets; much trading took place inside the village between peasants and local merchants.⌉Most villages where commercial crops were grown had one or two merchants who habitually bought up local produce and sold it in the nearest market. But not all of what the village exported first passed through the hands of these merchants; part was generally sold in the market by the peasants themselves.[c] When the position of the merchant was very strong, however, he might have a virtual monopoly on purchase in the village and his operations would link him not only to neighboring market towns but directly to wholesalers in Edo and Osaka as well. But whether the merchant's operations were on so large a scale or not, he was almost invariably one of the larger landholders in the village and counted moneylending among his regular activities.

Much of the petty retail trade was also in the hands of these wholesalers who, along with storage sheds, kept shops well stocked with sugar, candy, salt, paper, writing brushes, umbrellas, candles, and so on. But peddlers who took goods on consignment from merchants in the town or city and hawked them through the countryside were formidable competitors. According to Ogyū Sorai, they traveled with their packs and animals everywhere, finding their way up mountain valleys even to the last settlements on the edge of the wild.[9] Significantly Sorai regarded peddlers as a recent phenomenon, at least in such numbers as he attributed to them; and he thought them evidence of an unseemly style of life now spreading with the use of money among the common-

[c] A document of 1783 from the Kawachi-Settsu area tells us: "Most peasants of Ōtsuka village engage in petty trade in addition to farming." (Wakita Osamu, "Setsuka watasaku chitai ni okeru nōmin no dōkō," *Keizai ronsō*, LXXIV, 5 (1954), 51.)

folk, doing infinite harm. Nor was he the only one of this opinion. Ro Tōzan, a scholar living in Sendai—one of the most backward regions of the country—expressed a similar view in a memorial to his lord in 1726:[10]

For some years merchants have come here from other places, but those who do the most business and bring the greatest distress are from Ōmi. They put together medicines, cosmetics, and cotton and silk cloth, which they distribute to agents who go everywhere in this area selling on credit. . . . In recent years buying on credit has become quite common, and there are places where debts amount to very large sums. . . . If, as in earlier times, such fellows did not come, then the peasants would make their own clothing, or even if they bought it they would save up the money first; but because these fellows come selling fine things on easy terms, the peasants go into debt to buy quite useless things.

Industry no less than trade contributed to the mischief, as Tōzan admitted in another place.[11] Cottage industry was of course no new feature of village life; peasants had always made things for use in their homes, and over the centuries they had nurtured to maturity a tradition of skill that could sometimes be turned to account in the market place. Nobody objected to such industry; but Tōzan and nearly every other warrior objected fiercely to domestic industry that produced chiefly for the market, prospering (they thought) at the expense of agriculture. After all, there was just so much labor, and if it was used for industry, agriculture was bound to suffer: it was as simple as that.

Before 1600, industry of this allegedly destructive kind was confined mostly to the towns. Silk weaving, for instance, was very nearly a monopoly of the artisans who lived in the Nishijin district of Kyoto, for the demand for silk cloth was still primarily aristocratic and more importance was attached to quality and artistry than to price.[12] Then, too, the choicest yarn was imported from China through government customs at Nagasaki, which facilitated control of the essential raw material by the Kyoto guilds and therefore of the silk industry by the Shogunate, whose chief aim was to prevent its spread to the countryside.[13] But the urban monopoly could not last. With the growth of city population and the spread of money in the country the consumption of silk increased enormously, and along with other industries the silk industry jumped the neat channels decreed for it by guild organization and government statute, and moved increasingly from the town to the village. City artisans of course did not disappear and they even continued to monopolize some branches of production; but by the end of the Tokugawa period the industry as a whole was rurally based.[d] In the emerging mass market price made all the difference, giving rural producers a decisive advantage, for they were less encumbered than urban producers by guild restrictions and were nearer to raw materials and water power. Moreover their labor costs were far more elastic since they did not demand a livelihood from industry, merely part-time employment to fill the lulls in farming.

Even in industries where city workers were most deeply entrenched, the peasant producer eventually prevailed. In the early eighteenth century, the Nishijin weavers were already complaining of rural competition, though without much warrant. Now, a century and a half later, they were complaining without much hope.[e] Only 10 per cent (by value) of the silk cloth coming into Edo in 1859 was made in Kyoto—the remainder was "country stuff" (*inakamono*).[14] Government did its best to suppress rural industry for fear that agriculture would suffer and to protect urban workers, who spoke through powerful guilds. But all such efforts were woefully inadequate. After prohibiting silk weaving in rural areas, the Shogunate realistically recognized the futility of the measure and in addition forbade Kyoto merchants to go into the country to buy silk cloth. But cloth continued to be made and merchants continued to buy it in the country, because the price was right there, and the same prohibition had to be repeated in the years 1773, 1779, 1795, 1816, and 1855.[15]

Some industries, though predominantly rural from the beginning, were of no importance until the Tokugawa period. Cotton, for instance, was not much grown before the Muromachi period, and even then it seems to have been confined mainly to eastern Japan, where growing conditions were not especially favorable.[16] Toward the end of the sixteenth century, however, cotton found its natural habitat in

[d] Contemporary writers typically saw this as a threat to the towns generally rather than merely to some groups in the towns. Takemoto Ryūhei, for example, wrote: "In recent years, small shops and small merchants have greatly increased in rural areas, which is the reason for the luxury there and the impoverishment of the towns." ("Kannōsaku," *NKSS*, XX, 599.)

[e] Government officials were also pessimistic about rescuing urban industry from its plight. Writing to the Edo *Machi-bugyō* in 1859, the Kyoto *Bugyō* said: "The output of cloth in the provinces has recently been on the increase, throwing industry into confusion. The Kyoto weaving masters and a great many others connected with their trade have lost their living and face the cruelest hardships as a result. But for the time being there seems no way of helping them." (Quoted by Horie Eiichi, "Kinsei kinuorigyō no shijō kōzō," *Keizai ronsō*, LV, 3 (1942), 78.)

the Kinai; thereafter the production of raw cotton very rapidly increased, and the manufacture of cotton spread over the whole country. Ōkura Eijō, writing in 1834, tells us that cotton grown in the Kinai was shipped by local merchants to Osaka, whose wholesalers distributed the cotton (by now ginned) to provincial merchants everywhere; they in turn sold to peasants, who worked up the raw material into yarn and cloth.[17]

The hemp cloth industry of Uonuma county in Echigo Province provides an example of a different kind. This industry dated back at least to the Nara period, when taxes from Echigo were paid partly in the cloth. But the industry achieved no considerable growth until certain innovations in bleaching and weaving were made toward the end of the seventeenth century. After that the output of hemp cloth increased from about five thousand rolls to about two hundred thousand rolls annually at the end of the eighteenth century. By this time, local sources of raw material were no longer adequate to supply producers and hemp had to be imported from Aizu and Yonezawa. Such was the scale of production that marketing of the finished product was organized nationally. Peasant weavers, whose numbers in Uonuma county alone apparently ran to many thousands, sold their cloth in three local markets that drew buyers from as far away as Kyoto and Osaka. Toward the end of the eighteenth century certain wholesale merchants were given a monopoly of purchase in these markets by the local lord. This measure, as was intended by its authors, worked to depress the producer's price, and at length the peasant weavers began banding together into small companies (*nakama*) to circumvent the prescriptive monopoly and ship their cloth directly to Edo. Three times the licensed wholesalers brought suit against the new companies—with what result we do not know; but the episode shows that the weaving industry in Echigo was sufficiently strong to challenge political control.[18]

Echigo affords an excellent illustration of industry flourishing in a remote and isolated place. An alluvial plain facing into the cold blasts from the Japan Sea and rising in the hinterland to high mountains that cut off easy communication with the rest of the country, it was in addition snowbound during most of a long winter, which prevented double-cropping and forced farmers to concentrate on the cultivation of food-crops. Hence there were few places in the country inherently less hospitable to industry. But the peasants of Echigo had learned to use their harsh environment to advantage. Using native grasses as raw materials, they employed the long winter months for weaving; in time they perfected a technique suitable to the coarse fibers and learned to utilize the brightness and cold of the snow in bleaching.[19]

Not all areas were so fortunate. But, judging from surviving *mei-saichō*—a document in which the village reported on local conditions to the lord under certain stipulated headings, one of which was almost always by-employments—it would appear that by the late Tokugawa period most villages manufactured some article for sale. A document of 1803 from Hitachi Province, for example, stated: "As for by-employments, the men cut firewood and fodder; the women spin and weave cotton yarn for use by the family and for sale if any is left over."[20] Although this phrasing would hardly suggest a thriving local industry, it comes from an area where it is a surprise to learn of industry producing for sale at all, and one must remember that these reports tended to understate industrial production for fear of inviting new taxes and incurring the displeasure of the higher authorities.

Rarely if ever did industry displace agriculture in importance in the local economy, but sometimes it became equally important, giving rise to villages that might fairly be called semi-industrial. For instance, there was Hirano village, located near Osaka in the middle of one of the richest cotton-growing regions in the country. By 1706, a very early date in speaking of industry, 61.7 percent of all arable land and 32.1 percent of all paddy in Hirano were planted to cotton! This testifies not only to the extraordinary development of commercial farming in the village, but also to a thriving industry there, since the peasants ginned the cotton locally before shipping it to wholesalers in Osaka.[21] Most of the population of Hirano was employed at least part time in ginning. A document of 1773 tells us that 70 or 80 percent of the holders of the village "devote themselves primarily to farming but live in part by ginning the cotton they grow and what in addition they buy from neighboring villages."[*]

Hirano was but one of many semi-industrial villages in the area. In some counties of Kawachi and Settsu provinces, cotton accounted for between 40 and 50 percent of the value of all agricultural products, and where cotton was grown it was generally also ginned.[22] Nor was ginning the only important industry in the region around Osaka.

---

[*] This figure is confirmed by more exact data in 1837–38 showing 300 ginners (*kuriya*) among the 312 holders in the village. In addition to holders, however, there were 509 *mizunomi* who lived by tenant farming and by working for the ginners for wages by the day. (Takao Kazuhiko, "Settsu Hirano-gō ni okeru wata-saku no hatten," *Shirin*, XXXIV, 1/2 (1951), 4–5, 14.)

Cotton spinning and the manufacture of vegetable oil were nearly as important. In Yamato Province, for instance, there were 208 licensed oil makers in 1773, many of them using water power and producing up to 20 or 30 *koku* of oil annually. In addition there were a great many illicit producers, if we may judge from the complaints against them by those with licenses, and from the fact that the licensing system broke down toward the end of the Tokugawa period because it could no longer be enforced.[23]

Villages where industry mingled on equal terms with agriculture were not confined to the Kinai, either. Ōkubo, a village located in the rich sericulture region around Fukushima, had a population of 229 families in 1874 and a decade earlier a total of 411 silk looms. Clearly, much of the adult population of Ōkubo worked part time at weaving and its auxiliary processes. In 1876, the silk industry brought this village an income of about 10,000 *ryō*, or roughly 2,000 *koku* of rice, which exceeded the total agricultural output of many villages of similar size.[24] Although Ōkubo produced more silk cloth than most villages in the area, it was far surpassed by the smaller village of Tatsukoyama, which with 14 fewer families produced 40 percent more cloth in 1876.

The organization of local industry varied widely, many different historical stages being simultaneously spread over the countryside. There had been a time when peasants typically grew their own raw materials and worked them through numerous processes to a finished product ready for the consumer; but this early stage of organization was no longer characteristic of most regions, though it persisted everywhere to some degree. By the latter part of the eighteenth century, production was typically broken into separate operations performed by different families, so that each product ready for the consumer stood at the end of a rather long series of market transactions.[g] We have seen that raw material for the hemp cloth made in Echigo was imported by local merchants from other provinces; after twisting the raw material into yarn, the peasants put it out to specialists for dyeing, then wove the

---

[g] Contemporaries were quite aware of the changes that were taking place in the organization of industry. An edict of 1835 in the Kiryū fief described the growing division of labor in the silk industry as follows: "In former times the peasants and their wives and daughters raised silkworms, reeled silk yarn from the cocoons, and wove the yarn into cloth as an occupation in their spare time. But in recent times, industry having become more and more prosperous, there has developed a large class of silk-yarn wholesalers (*ton'ya*) who have quit raising cocoons and buy silk yarn from families in their own districts and others." (Quoted in Horie, "Kinsei kinuorigyō," p. 75.)

yarn into cloth which they sold to merchants who performed the final operation of removing the nap.[25] In Sanuki Province, peasant growers pressed the juice from sugar cane, crystallized it to eliminate some of the impurities, and then sent the semirefined sugar to village specialists (*shiboriya*) who completed the process.[h] If we may credit the description of a generally reliable witness, cotton in the early nineteenth century commonly passed through 14 or more hands from raw material to finished cloth.[26]

Professor Shōji's researches on the area around Fukushima suggest how far the division of labor had gone in the silk industry by the late Tokugawa period. Dividing the area into three regions with different types of farming—paddy, upland, and mixed—Professor Shōji compiled production data on the three main silk products of each region just after the Restoration. The results[i] showed that the silk industry had already become regionally specialized, and that it was integrated by a thriving trade among the various regions producing different silk products. Thus one region bought silkworm eggs from the others and sold cocoons; another bought cocoons and sold eggs and yarn; the third bought yarn and sold cloth. A similar though less pronounced division of labor existed among villages within a single region.[j]

The more a peasant family bought and sold, the larger the area of its economic life that was lifted out of the context of custom-bound social groups and subjected to the impersonal decrees of the market. How far economic activity had been transferred to the market place by the late Tokugawa period is difficult to say. The best indicators are

[h] There were said to have been about 5,500 peasant families growing cane and refining sugar and about a fifth that many *shiboriya* in Sanuki at the end of the Tokugawa period. (Adachi Ikutsune, "Bakumatsu ni okeru shōgyōteki nōgyō no hatten kōzō," *Jimbun gakuhō*, I (1950), 67–68.)

[i] The three regions contributed as follows to the output of various silk products in the entire Fukushima region (Shōji Kichinosuke, *Kawamata chihō habutae kigyō hattatsu shi*, Fukushima, 1953, pp. 2–3).

Region	Cocoons	Silk Yarn	Silk Cloth
I	18.03%	11.55%	99.93%
II	25.36	43.27	.....
III	56.61	45.18	.....

[j] For example, Ōkubo village produced 21.31 percent of the silk cloth of its region but only 5.31 percent of the yarn; and in the same region Takazawa village produced 24.47 percent of the yarn but only 0.57 percent of the silk cloth. (*Ibid.*, pp. 4–5.)

probably the family budgets cited by Tokugawa administrators to illustrate conditions among the peasantry. Though these were rarely actual
budgets, they were made up for illustrative purposes by persons who
knew their subject, and they therefore throw considerable light on the
economy of individual holdings.[27] Consider the example given below,
which purports to be the budget of a family on a rather large holding
in Settsu Province at the end of the eighteenth century.[k]

Farming on this holding was evidently less commercial than on
many holdings in the area; for one thing, the holding was planted less
heavily than most to cotton[l]—the prime cash crop throughout the
Kinai and of all crops the one requiring the heaviest applications of
fertilizer.[m] Second, this holding had an unusually high proportion of
paddy land planted exclusively to rice and wheat (as a winter crop).
The family was consequently not only self-sufficient in food but able
to pay the entire land tax in kind, even though in this area a large part
of this tax was commonly paid in money. It will be perceived, then,

[k] *Income*

    1. from 2.5 *chō* of paddy

	rice	51 *koku*
	wheat	28.5 *koku*
	straw	312 *momme* of silver

    2. from 4.5 *tan* of unirrigated fields

	cotton	120 *momme* of silver
	vegetables	462 *momme*

    3. from handicrafts

	cotton weaving, "straw work," straw matting	295 *momme*

Expenditures

	land tax	19.5 *koku* of rice
	miscellaneous	551 *momme* of silver
	fertilizer	2,077 *momme* of silver
	tools	491 *momme*
	wages of hired hands	730 *momme*
	food	16.5 *koku* of wheat
	food	3.33 *koku* of rice
Balance		Surplus of 250 *momme*

Toya Toshiyuki, *Kinsei nōgyō keiei shi ron*, Tokyo, 1949, pp. 59–60.

[l] In 1877, cotton accounted for 37.2 percent of the value of all crops in the
county where this holding was located; note that on this holding cotton brought
less than the straw from rice and wheat. (Furushima Toshio, *Kinsei ni okeru
shōgyōteki nōgyō no tenkai*, Tokyo, 1950, p. 47.)

[m] According to a contemporary treatise, cotton required approximately 100
percent more fertilizer than rice. (Furushima and Nagahara, *Shōhin seisan*, p. 34.)

that this holding was by no means an extreme example of involvement in money economy, but the contrary.

It is astonishing in view of this that the money expenditures of the holding totaled 3,849 *momme* for the year. This was a very large sum: translated into rice (at the average price in the accounts of a Settsu peasant for 1782–1802) it comes to approximately 50 *koku*, a sum nearly equal to the entire rice crop of the holding. Since, on the other hand, the money income of the holding was only 1,189 *momme*, a large part of the income shown in kind—chiefly rice and wheat—must actually have been ultimately sold. This is also suggested by the fact that the year-end surplus left after all expenditures is given in money.

The budget shows money expenditures under four headings—tools, fertilizer, labor, and miscellaneous. Tools were the smallest of the four, followed by "miscellaneous"—a category of unspecified content which, judging from the items commonly appearing in other budgets, probably included expenditures for social occasions, transport, animal rental, and articles of daily use such as salt, tea, vegetables, cooking oil, lamp oil, charcoal, firewood, pots and pans, soy sauce, fans, perfume, medicine, headgear, umbrellas, candles, dye, bedding, leather, rope.[28] Perhaps, just as the writers of the time contended, the peasant was less self-reliant than his grandfather had been, but life was manifestly easier for him, too.

Commercial fertilizer was the largest item of money expenditure, accounting for over half the total. At first glance this is a surprisingly high percentage, for the area planted to cotton was small; but the budget may have been intended to reflect the exhaustion of sources of natural fertilizer, since this condition was widespread in the Kinai." The enormous growth of population in the century and a half after 1600 had pushed terraces higher and higher up the hillsides; and this movement was further encouraged by the spread of cash crops, which on the whole were less dependent than rice on water. Since these crops generally required intensive fertilization, they not only helped destroy the sources of natural fertilizer but very seriously increased the demand on them. There was therefore a constellation of powerful forces drawing holdings into dependence on commercial fertilizers.

Our Settsu holding, then, was by no means untypical. Records of

" Many Kinai villages were totally without land for collecting leaves and cutting grass by the early Meiji period. (*Ibid.*, p. 4.) The exhaustion of sources of natural fertilizer was occurring elsewhere, judging from budgets from other areas which show nothing so consistently as relatively large sums spent for fertilizer.

the port of Osaka show that fertilizer was the third largest item (by value) of 119 imports in 1714.[29] Most of the fertilizer at this early date was probably destined for use in the Kinai, but by the early nineteenth century fertilizer was being shipped from Osaka and other centers to all parts of the country. Almost all periodic village reports on local conditions, whatever their provenance, mention the use of such fertilizers. Many also cite its cost per *tan* of land in the cultivation of various kinds of crops, from which it is evident not only that fertilizer entered significantly into costs[o]—a view confirmed by surviving peasant account books—but that by the late Tokugawa period peasants were acutely aware of the fact.

Labor ranked second in the Settsu budget as an item of money expenditure, and this was its position in most budgets of the time. Surplus labor was increasingly finding employment in trade, handicrafts, and transport. *Nago* and the older types of *genin* were accordingly disappearing, and less free forms of labor were being driven out by more free. This transformation was accompanied by a considerable increase in the price of labor (see Chapter 8). Local documents were crowded with references to wages, and district administrators were forever complaining of the high costs of labor, predicting the certain ruin of agriculture as a result. Nor did the complaints and forebodings come exclusively from areas where industry was expanding; they were also heard from such remote places as Tōhoku, whence it seems that labor was migrating seasonally and even permanently in search of employment.[30]

Some holdings employed an astonishing amount of wage labor. A case in point is the Satō family near Fukushima who specialized in the production of silkworm eggs. According to the Satō accounts for 1872, the family employed in the three weeks at the height of the silkworm season a total of 460 man-days of labor.[p] And even on this large scale

---

[o] The conviction was apparently widespread among the peasants that the price of fertilizer was too high, for there were many protests such as one from three Kinai villages in 1839 declaring that the peasants were being ruined by ". . . the high cost of fertilizers *in recent years.*" (*Ibid.,* p. 140.)

[p] Income of the family for 1872 was as follows (Shōji Kichinosuke, *Meiji ishin no keizai kōzō,* Tokyo, 1954, p. 174):

	Ryō
Silkworm eggs	20,340
Cotton	1,290
Cocoons	1,462
Raw silk	3,750
Trees (fruit?)	50

the enterprise was no recent one, since a document a century earlier speaks of 120 buyers, some from as far away as Shinshū, visiting the family in a single year to contract for silkworm eggs![31] The Satō were not of course a typical farm family, but the cases of labor employed on roughly this scale, especially in the brewing industry, are surprisingly numerous. Quantitatively more significant in the labor market, however, were a vast number of large and middling farmers who employed one or several hired hands from spring through fall, taking on still others at the peak periods of work. (See Chapter 8.)

Small holders of course rarely hired labor and then for no more than a day or two at a time, but such holders were scarcely less affected than the larger ones by the development of wage labor. It was now much easier than ever before to turn spare time and surplus family labor to immediate account. For many small holders wages earned by part-time work in the neighborhood were an important source of money income, and in some villages peasant families appeared who lived almost entirely by working for wages. Employment for wages clearly served the same economic function of complementing the income of small holdings that labor services had earlier, but the social results were strikingly different. This is a subject to which we shall return in a later chapter.

Valuable as budgets and village reports are for the history of agriculture, they yield only fragmentary data. To follow through time an individual holding we must turn to agricultural diaries. Most such diaries are too terse[q] or short to be of use, but in 1942 Professor Toya found in a village in Musashi Province a diary that was extraordinarily full and covered an exceptionally long period. At the time of discovery the diary had been kept continuously by successive heads of the same family since 1720—a period of 222 years—and in addition to daily entries it contained a continuous year-end record of yields!

Professor Toya published the daily entries for the four years 1728, 1804, 1840, and 1867, and the summary year-end data for every year during the period 1720–1899.[32] It is a pity the entire journal was not published, since the terse daily entries—"Overcast today; cut wood"—

---

[q] The peasant, to whom writing came hard, typically recorded in a diary only what he could not trust himself to remember. Thus if he were keeping a particularly full record, a man would probably note every year what crop he planted to each field, how much the field yielded at the harvest, the amount and variety of the seed he used—all significant facts he would soon forget. But rarely would he note the size of each field since that did not change from year to year, and without this datum the other figures must be used with extreme caution.

made with no thought but to record faithfully and economically what happened, give as complete a picture of life in a well-to-do farm family as might reasonably be desired. We read of the work done each day, of deaths, celebrations, village problems, contacts with district officials, and a multitude of lesser events. But if the four years for which we have daily entries give us no more than a tantalizing glimpse of peasant life during the last half of the Tokugawa period, the continuous year-end data during that time provide an exceptional record of the changing economy of a farm through several generations.

When the journal opens in 1720, the Ishikawa family was scarcely in touch with the market. It grew tobacco, beans, potatoes, cotton, and cocoons—all cash crops—but in very small quantities which were probably consumed at home rather than sold. For the rest the family grew grains clearly meant for food: chiefly rice, wheat, barley, and millet. The high degree of self-sufficiency this pattern of cropping suggests did not last out the century, however. A notable shift toward commercial farming occurred when silkworms began to be raised in quantity on the holding in the last decade of the century. Part of the worms were sold for cash, but part were kept for the production of cocoons and silk yarn. Since the Ishikawa lived very near Hachioji, one of the most important silk markets of the time, it is no wonder that they developed an interest in sericulture and silk reeling.

As the family devoted more and more of its land and labor to sericulture, certain of the old subsistence crops inevitably disappeared. Rice, wheat, barley, and millet continued to be cultivated in approximately the same amounts as in the early eighteenth century. But hemp, which replaced cotton as a fiber crop in 1769, was dropped in 1781, and after that date cloth was apparently bought with cash from the sale of cocoons and raw silk, instead of made at home as before. Tea disappeared as a crop in 1750, tobacco in 1827, and taro in 1868—all having first undergone a gradual restriction of acreage. These changes in cropping reflect a shift away from subsistence to commercial farming, and we are therefore not surprised to find that the journal recorded more and more trips to nearby markets as time passed—two in 1728, 17 in 1824, 24 in 1840, and 16 in 1867.

Changes in the use of labor and in methods of cultivation accompanied or followed changes in cropping. In 1728, 45 man-days were spent gathering firewood, but only eight were used in this work in 1804; by that time the family presumably bought most of its fuel. There was also a shift from natural to commercial fertilizers, dried fish replacing grass gathered on the mountainside. The labor saved by this shift was employed in new tasks; in the care of the cocoons and in silk reeling, of course, but also in more intensive cultivation. For instance, no weeding was recorded at all in 1728, but weeding was repeated several times in 1867, and the use of commercial fertilizers meant more intensive fertilization. These and other improvements that may be inferred brought a rise in yields. The greatest increase came as a result of a shift from dry to wet rice in the early eighteenth century, but increases in other major crops, though less dramatic, were considerable.[33]

This brief history of the Ishikawa holding illustrates how pervasive change was, once started. It started but never ended with closer relations to the market, for buying and selling were merely surface indications of changes that went to the very heart of peasant life. Crops, labor organization, farming techniques, even the view men took of such things as wealth, work, and neighbors changed with the altered relation to the market. We shall follow some of these changes in subsequent chapters.

7

AGRICULTURAL TECHNOLOGY

We often think of Japanese agriculture as having been static or nearly so until very recent times; many statements to this effect may be found in both Western and Japanese authorities. But the fact is that it underwent notable technological (though not mechanical) changes long before the modern period.[1] Between 1600 and 1850 a complex of such changes greatly increased the productivity of land, altered that of labor both in specific operations and over all, and contributed to lasting changes in agrarian institutions. The writers of the day gave no picture of order and permanence but one of incessant flux.

Few changes were the result of inventions; most resulted from the spread of known techniques from the localities in which they had been developed to areas where they were previously unknown or unused.[2] How the spread occurred is not known in detail although it is obvious that growth of the market played an important role, breaking down local barriers, transporting ideas and objects from place to place wherever merchants traveled. But never does the mere availability of a new technique assure its adoption; men must first be convinced of its value or at least persuaded to try it, and where there is no margin for failure and any departure from tradition seems to invite disaster, that requires a formidable intellectual leap. How there was created a state of mind that could contemplate the leap is impossible to say. True, trade with the outside world was continually diminishing the power of custom and magic in village life, breathing into farming a new spirit of enterprise: but that statement merely pushes the problem back one step.

There is ample evidence of the fact of a new attitude toward change, though the reason for it remains obscure. Receptivity to the new and tolerance of the unknown and untried are particularly noticeable in the agricultural treatises which, after about 1700, were ardently reformist and empirical.[3] Not that these remarkable works were free of older attitudes, but the anachronisms less and less often touched matters of substance. Frequently works opened with a statement of the cosmic

In other words - movement
away from agrarianism -
Shinto-Confucianism -
making money

meaning of agriculture in expressing man's essential harmony with
heaven and earth; but having done honor to this conventional and
harmless Confucian theme, the best authors abandoned it, sticking
thereafter strictly to the practical business at hand. This was the business of educating the peasant in better ways of farming: of explaining
the growth patterns of different crops, the proper planting and harvesting times, the characteristics of various soils, the effects of fertilization
and weeding—always with a view to increasing crop yields and cash
income. Let us illustrate.

The *Nōgyō zensho* was one of the earliest agricultural treatises,
completed in 1697 and published the following year when its author,
Miyazaki Antei, died.[4] It came to ten old-style volumes (one large
one in the modern edition). It was not, as the early date might suggest, a collection of old wives' tales, but a genuinely scientific treatise—
one of the first produced in Japan. The author tells us in his Introduction that after farming for 40 years he spent another 40 broadening his
knowledge, collecting and collating data. He read the Chinese authorities; then he traveled about the country testing the written word and
his own experience against observation and the experience of others.
Everywhere he went on foot through the villages noting local soils,
crops, and tools, relentlessly quizzing the older men and taking down
what they said. He had great respect for facts and (after his Introduction) no time for speculation: when he recommended a seed or a way
of treating the soil it was usually—though not always—because he had
observed the results and found them superior.

Having grown old collecting material, Miyazaki wrote his great
book, but before sending the manuscript to the printer he submitted it
for criticism to others skilled in both writing and farming. After that,
he says, he revised it so that it gradually came to have greater useful-
ness to the people. The remark is characteristic of the man: his ambi-
tion *was* to help the people—not, as earlier writers generally had done,
merely to show how to enrich the state. "I had lived and farmed for
forty years in a village," he wrote in another place, "and having learned
much, I deeply regretted the ignorance of the peasants. Thus it was
that I forgot my own stupidity and thought to write a book the peasants
could go by."

One must not take this self-effacement too seriously; Miyazaki had
a much higher estimate of his abilities than he would admit. And he
was always giving himself away: conscious that he was breaking new

ground, he simply could not refrain from saying as much. "This is the first book on agriculture in this country!" he announced in his Introduction. The statement is incorrect, but in a trivial sense only. There had been earlier works; the most famous was the *Seiryōki*, written in the preceding century, which Miyazaki must have read, but it was distinctly inferior to his own in organization, fullness, and accuracy. What he probably meant to say was that his was the first scientific work on farming—not a modest claim certainly, but factually permissible.[5]

He obviously intended his work as a handbook on farming, since it was organized for easy reference and any given topic could be found instantly under its appropriate heading. The book had no unifying theme or narrative thread, but that was because it was not supposed to be read straight through from beginning to end. This was one of its special virtues and original features; many books of the time on serious subjects took the form of rambling essays or travelogues in which useful information was indiscriminately mixed with gossip, folklore, and homilies. Miyazaki's book was free of these irrelevancies and of any moral except that good farming pays; moreover it brought all information on a particular subject together in a single chapter that could be read and understood separately. The topics he covered represented the entire range of Japanese agriculture; there was one chapter on each of 19 varieties of grain, 57 vegetables, 11 grasses, 36 trees, 22 herbs—in addition to separate essays on such subjects as planting, tillage, soils, fertilizers, irrigation, and the management of forest land.

Never was Miyazaki content merely to describe contemporary practice; he was always recommending and warning, advising what crops to plant in which soils and climates, which varieties were hardiest and how they ought to be cultivated. In giving advice he drew constantly on his knowledge of farming in various parts of the country, comparing methods in one region with those in another and not hesitating to pronounce on their relative merits. It is typical of him, for instance, that the chapter on *daikon* opened with the statement that the plant was cultivated with the best results in Owari and Yamashiro, and he advises anyone cultivating the crop to get seeds from one of those provinces. Then followed detailed instructions on the type of soil favored by *daikon*, how to prepare the ground for planting, how to protect the plant against insects, and a description of the plant's growth and maturation. Every sentence contained information; Miyazaki's spare, matter-of-fact style was like the practice of farming of which he

who read these books.

wrote: economy of means, which was a favorite theme with him, was its essence.[a]

Many general works on agriculture followed the publication of Miyazaki's classic, but none was so influential during the Tokugawa period. Of more importance were the specialized works which were produced in considerable number to meet the demand for fuller treatment of particular farming subjects. By the mid-nineteenth century there were few crops that did not have their authoritative treatises, and the same was true of such subjects as weather, soil science, irrigation. Ōkura Eijō's (1768–?) three-volume work published in the early nineteenth century, significantly entitled *Nōgu benri ron* (*On the Efficacy of Farm Implements*), is a good example of the genre.[6] In it Ōkura discusses what must have been every farm tool or device in use in Japan at the time — the hoe, spade, fork, harrow, weeder, ground leveler, fertilizer spreader, pile driver, devices for moving rocks, the field sled, and many others. Ōkura illustrated most of the implements he discussed with detailed drawings showing different views and stages of construction and giving specifications. The accompanying text exhorted the peasant to improve his tools and told him how and why— all in language he, or a literate neighbor, could understand.

How widely read in the village works on agriculture were it is difficult to say, but without doubt they *were* read.[b] In modern Aichi Prefecture in the eighteenth century, we find a peasant—no scholar, to judge from his style—setting down his observations on farming, perhaps for the benefit of his son. In discussing soy beans, millet, and tobacco—the chief crops on his holding (note the practical definition of subject matter)—this author followed the *Nōgyō zensho* too closely to allow of any doubt that he had made use of it or of some work based

---

[a] The harmony of style and subject matter in the *Nōgyō zensho* was not accident, as the author's Preface makes clear: "I have no literary gifts and therefore cannot adorn my prose with fine flourishes, but this book is intended for use by farmers and needs no literary embellishment." (Miyazaki Antei, *Nōgyō zensho*, edited by Tsuchiya Takao in the *Iwanami bunko*, Tokyo, 1949, p. 26.)

[b] And read critically, too. Thus, a farmer writing for the instruction of his family in northern Japan states: "The *Nōgyō zensho* recommends saving melted snow and then soaking the rice seeds in it before sowing them in the spring. This is supposed to bring out the power of cereals so that they may not be damaged by insects or drought. This piece of bad advice is probably because Miyazaki was born in Chikuzen [in Kyūshū] and consequently knew nothing of cold climates firsthand." ("Shika nōgyō dan," *KJKS*, edited by Ono Takeo, Tokyo, 1931, VII, 269.)

on it; and his introductory remarks in part follow Miyazaki's language word for word.[7] Admittedly this is an exceptional case; rarely in the short informal tracts we have from the hands of peasants can the influence of the teacher be so palpably perceived,[8] but many of these rustic works show the same spirit of reform and the same appetite for facts as better known books.[c]

One that has recently been published is particularly interesting because it seems to have been written a few years before the *Nōgyō zensho*.[9] That the author was a peasant is clear from internal evidence; he was also an unpretentious man who left his manuscript unsigned. Like Miyazaki he started (he said) with a practical knowledge of farming and then improved it by talking to the best farmers to be found in "various places"; and, again like Miyazaki, he wrote for the instruction of others, presumably friends and neighbors. In almost every respect his essay is inferior to the *Nōgyō zensho*; it is short, fragmentary, discursive, repetitious; but it is no whit less enthusiastic for the cause of reform, nor less insistent on the unique value of experience. Among passages on crops, soils, and seed selection the author scattered broadcast exhortations to better farming. Over and over again in different contexts and with different illustrations he told the reader that good farming is *not* a matter of luck but of intelligent effort. Neither poor soil nor natural calamity could keep the industrious, alert farmer from prospering; nor could luck save the slothful or ignorant from eventual ruin.

For those who would farm intelligently he had a single admonition which he repeated tirelessly: study and learn! Study and learn from personal experience and from that of others. How? One way he recommended was to keep a record of one's farming—of seeds, plants, soils, fertilizers, harvest and planting dates—so that the "turning of the front wheels may warn the rear." Then, for instance, if one variety did better than another in a particular soil, one knew it immediately,

---

[c] Not even the best of these works was wholly free of superstition. For example, an Etchū peasant who had the independence to criticize the great Miyazaki quite justly for talking of things of which he had no personal knowledge made the following comment: "In planting anything one must take special care of the effects of death and affliction (*hae-tomari hae-wazurau*). It goes without saying that a person who is ill or in mourning for his father or mother should never be permitted to sow grain; nor should he be allowed to plant vegetables, grasses, or trees. If perchance such a person plants rice, it will certainly not grow well." ("Shika nōgyō dan," p. 337.)

whereas one might not otherwise discover the fact until too late. It was also possible to learn from others by cross-examining and badgering peasants who excelled at farming until at last they revealed the secrets of their superiority.[d] Though so far few had taken the pains to try, there was no doubt one could learn about farming in this way, just as doctors learned medicine. [There were rich rewards for those who would do so: increased wealth, security, ease.] As the author exclaimed, "If on land yielding 10 *koku*, 11 can be harvested: that is the treasure of a family!"[10]

This exclamation perhaps brings us as close as we can hope to come to the psychological source of the impressive technical progress in agriculture during the Tokugawa period. The wellspring of incentive was the enrichment of the family, not individual gain—much less the welfare of society or the state. No innovation that failed to appeal to the interest of the family could win acceptance, nor could any that did appeal fail of acceptance in the long run. It is no accident, then, that the technical changes of this period tended to strengthen the solidarity of the nuclear family and its role in farming.

All of the important innovations in farming increased the productivity of either land or labor or both. Commercial fertilizers—chiefly dried fish, oil cakes, and night soil collected in towns and cities—were perhaps the most important of all innovations in raising yields. Not that these fertilizers were unknown before the Tokugawa period, but they were confined to villages located on the outskirts of towns or near the seacoast where the frontiers of farming and fishing met. It was only with the development of inland transport and the spread of local markets during the seventeenth and eighteenth centuries that commercial fertilizers penetrated the interior of the country and the deep hinterland of towns. Rarely did they entirely supplant manure, grass, leaves, and ashes gathered from waste and forest land, but we have

[d] The author of a manuscript treatise entitled "Nōgyō isho" (An Agricultural Testament), written by a kind of super village headman (Tomura) in the Kanazawa fief for the benefit of his son, likewise urges that farming be studied systematically, and he warns specifically against placing too much confidence in received aphoristic knowledge of the subject: "There are many sayings that are not to be trusted." This man had what his son may have thought an exaggerated idea of the economic value of scientific knowledge, since he says, "Some men hand down money to their posterity; I hand down this manuscript." (Shimizu Takahisa, "Genroku ni okeru Hokuriku nōgyō no shinshiryō ni tsuite," *Nihon rekishi*, 96 (1956), 59–61.)

seen that by the early nineteenth century they came to supplement them importantly almost everywhere.

The peasant must initially have had misgivings about exchanging hard-won cash for dried fish or night soil; but he did not have to be taught the value of fertilizer, only its new and unfamiliar forms. From the beginnings of rice culture, fields in all parts of the country had been planted year after year to the same crop without rest, and the peasant knew from oral tradition and personal experience that only the most intensive fertilization could sustain this exhausting regime. Besides, natural fertilizers were nearly everywhere perennially in short supply as a result of the intense demand for them.[e] Even in heavily wooded or mountainous country where the supply was more than ample, the peasants' ability to exploit this natural bounty was severely limited by the vast amount of labor that cutting and carrying grass and leaves required, particularly as such work fell mostly at the planting.[f] No wonder nearly everyone looked with favor on fertilizers that came ready to use in straw bags and were available in whatever quantity the purse could stand.

Of course the new fertilizers had to prove their worth, but they did that as soon as they were given a fair trial. How much they raised yields is impossible to say, but there can be no doubt that their contribution to this result was impressive.[g] At least contemporaries were impressed, and they would never have been mistaken about such a matter—after all, these fertilizers cost money! Writers on agriculture were unanimous in stressing the value of fertilizers and the peasants agreed.[11] The authors of a village report (*meisaichō*) of 1782 from the

[e] Since natural fertilizers all came ultimately from the same source, the supply of one could not be increased except at the expense of others: if a peasant cut more grass for compost, for instance, he necessarily reduced the supply of manure (and perhaps starved his work animal into the bargain).

[f] A village report (*meisaichō*) from Kōzuke Province in 1780 gives one an idea of the immense labor the use of natural fertilizers required, stating that between 70 and 80 horseloads of cut grass were required per *tan* of paddy and about 30 horseloads per *tan* of upland. Thus a holding of 10 *tan* divided equally between the two types of land would need about 525 horseloads! (*Mura meisaichō no kenkyū*, edited by Nomura Kanetarō, Tokyo, 1949, p. 684.)

[g] The significance of fertilization for yields (where there is sufficient water) is suggested by a project now getting under way in India; experiments on six representative farms in Uttar Pradesh suggest that an addition of Rs 321 cash expenditures per farm, mostly for fertilizer and seed, would add Rs 1,219 or 77 percent to the gross value of output per farm. (Book review by John D. Black in the *American Economic Review*, XLVII, 6 (1957), 1033–34.)

Kinai seemed almost to say that good farming was merely a function
of fertilization, stating that the average farmer spent from 50 to 60
momme per *tan* of land planted to cotton for fertilizer, but that the
more successful spent nearly twice as much.[12] Other documents[h] might
be cited making much the same point about other crops.

[The new fertilizers not only raised crop yields, but also permitted
more intensive use of the land.] Natural fertilizers were generally insufficient to sustain more than a single crop a year, but with the advent
of commercial fertilizers, double and even triple cropping became common wherever winters were not too harsh and soils were sufficiently
drained for a winter crop. Of course multiple cropping neither doubled nor trebled the yield of a holding; usually not all fields could be
sown to a second crop, and wheat and vegetables, the favorite winter
crops, did not yield as heavily as summer rice. On the other hand,
whatever they did yield (minus seed and fertilizer) was a net gain;
and in the event summer crops were already sufficient to provide food
and pay taxes in kind, the winter and spring crops could be sold. The
income could then be used to buy tools, animals, and more fertilizer,
giving a further impetus to productivity, or at least helping to sustain
it at the new level.]

A second technical development of great importance was the increase in the number of plant varieties. Professor Tōhata and his associates have calculated from the names of seeds appearing in literary
sources that the number of rice varieties increased from 177 in the early
seventeenth century to 2,363 by the middle of the nineteenth.[13] This
figure probably exaggerates the increase, since some varieties very likely
appeared under more than one name and others may have been used
for generations before being recorded in any surviving document. But

---

[h] The *Chōbō fudoki*, a work compiled in 1841 at the order of the lord of
Chōshū, gives some hint of the significance of commercial fertilizers. Its 395 volumes are packed with economic data on some three hundred Chōshū and Bōshū
villages, permitting a comparison of one with another in respect to population,
arable acreage, crops, income, and expenditures. Professor Toya, whose conclu-
sions have been confirmed by other studies (Oka Mitsuo, "Chōshūhan Setouchi ni
okeru shōhin seisan no keitai," *RGKK*, 159 (1952), 22–35), has shown that in general the more commercialized farming was in a village, the higher yields were. For
example, two villages which may be called A and B were similar in several important
respects: average family size, average size of holdings, percentage of paddy double-
cropped; in addition both raised vegetables for sale. But village A also grew cotton,
the prime cash crop of the area, and had a much larger cash income from by-employments—probably from processing the cotton. This village spent 20 percent more
on fertilizer per unit of arable land than village B and harvested 10 percent more
rice per *tan*.

it is obvious that even after making all possible allowances the increase was very great. And not only were the number of varieties increasing; existing varieties were becoming more widely known, as is shown by the increasing number of varieties with names indicating origins outside the locality of the recording documents.[4] The names of 12 percent of the rice varieties recorded by the end of the Tokugawa period reveal migration from place of origin.

Writers on agriculture were of course aware of the significance of plant varieties: witness Miyazaki's advice to obtain *daikon* seeds from Yamashiro and Owari. Nor was the knowledge esoteric; the peasants knew as well as the agronomists that with more varieties plants could be better adapted to the local peculiarities of soil and climate. Why should they have bothered to name individual varieties if not to keep them distinct and thus make possible discriminating use of them? Why should they have kept records of what varieties they planted to which fields? And, most significant, why should they have used several different varieties at once, continuously experimenting with new ones? Almost all of the detailed records of farming show the peasant planting four, five, or six varieties of rice each year, and almost every year some variety not planted before appeared and one of the old ones was dropped, sometimes with a notation that it had not done well.[14] Although the peasant had no word for it, perhaps, he was consciously experimenting to find the variety best suited to each of his fields. Occasionally the records give us information that points unmistakably to higher yields as a result of his efforts. An agricultural diary from Tōhoku, for example, shows a persistent testing, adopting, and discarding of varieties of rice between 1808 and 1866, and during this period the date at which the harvest was completed was pushed back from the sixth to the twenty-third day of the ninth month, lengthening the growing season in this northern country by 17 days![15]

One of the most impressive technical achievements of the Tokugawa period was the extension of irrigation.[5] Part of this vast work

---

[4] For example, a variety of rice named "*Bōshū*" (a province in Chiba Prefecture) is mentioned in an Aizu source (Shōji Kichinosuke, *Meiji ishin no keizai kōzō*, p. 38), "*Ise-saburō*" in a Chōshū source, and "*Saigoku*" or "Western Country" in a source from eastern Japan (Tōhata Seiichi, *Nihon nōgyō hattatsu shi*, Tokyo, 1953, I, 16–17).

[5] Two factors particularly contributed to the rapid development of irrigation in the Tokugawa period. One was the development of engineering, which enabled arable to be extended into the lower courses of great rivers subject to frequent flood. Another was the availability of private investment funds, especially during the last

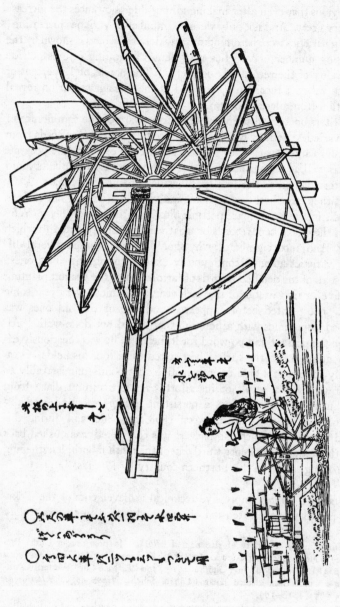

The tread wheel (*fumiguruma*), shown in operation here, was used for lifting water into a ditch or paddy field from a lower level. Its construction required expert carpentry. (*Nōgu benri ron.*)

consisted of the construction of thousands of small wells, ponds, ditches, and devices for lifting small amounts of water, but much of it was on a very large scale—great arterial ditches carrying water a score of miles or more, drainage and embankment works that for the first time made arable the rich alluvial soil along the lower courses of the larger rivers, and so on. How great was the increase in irrigated area for the country as a whole is difficult to say, but it was certainly enormous if land registers are a fair general index. These village documents give a strong impression of rapid growth, an impression further strengthened by such figures as we have for larger areas. Between the late sixteenth and late seventeenth centuries, for instance, a total of 398 new villages were founded in Musashi Province and the estimated yield of the province rose from 667,000 *koku* to 1,167,000.[16] We do not know how much of this increase may be attributed directly or indirectly to new irrigation, but assuredly some part of it can, since several large irrigation projects were completed in Musashi during this period.

The conversion of dry fields to paddy naturally brought a sizable gain in crop yields. Although the magnitude of the increase varied from place to place, it is worth recalling that rice yields on the Ishikawa holding eventually rose about 100 percent as a result of a shift from dry to wet rice, which suggests how great the increase might be at times. But higher yields were by no means the only result of new irrigation works, and not all of the results were beneficial. Sources of firewood, fertilizer, and fodder were progressively depleted as the cultivated area (with the aid of new irrigation works) encroached on meadow, forest, and waste. Peasants nearly everywhere complained of the loss in this way of valuable communal resources.[17] But though they complained of the loss, and individual peasants may have been ruined by it, on balance it was undoubtedly beneficial for farming, for the diminution of communal resources tended to weaken collective control over farming and to release new individualist energies.

The possibility of specialization—that is freedom from the necessity of cultivating uneconomic crops—was a major contribution of the market to productivity. An illustration: in Wakae county, Kawachi Province, growing conditions were generally unfavorable to rice; not

half of the period. How important the latter may have been is suggested by data from Ise Province, where most new irrigation works during the Tokugawa period were undertaken after 1700 and were financed mainly by merchants, landlords, and peasants who had presumably grown rich and adventurous on the profits of trade. (Tōhata, *Nihon nōgyō hattatsu shi*, pp. 45–46.)

only was summer rainfall in normal years light and water for irrigation scant, but the soils of the county tended to be light and sandy, quite
different from the heavy, sticky soil rice likes best. Nevertheless, at
the beginning of the Tokugawa period rice had been widely grown in
Wakae for food and to pay taxes in kind. But from the early seventeenth century, cotton, a relatively new crop to Japan, gradually dis-
placed rice until by 1877, 28 percent of paddy land and 58.8 percent
of upland in the county was planted to it. Cotton flourished under local
growing conditions; it was easily marketed in nearby Osaka and
brought a good price.[18] There can be no doubt therefore that this shift
in cropping was a net economic gain—for individual holders, for the
region, and for the country as a whole.

There were numerous other technical changes during the Tokugawa period that deserve at least passing mention. In the early decades
of the period, rice seedlings were commonly planted in the ground
more or less haphazardly, but by the nineteenth century care was being
taken to plant them in evenly spaced rows. This uniformity assured
the maximum number of plants to a field without crowding, and encouraged more intensive weeding by permitting a flat-bottomed weeder
to be run between the tidy rows without injury to plants. By the nineteenth century greater care was also being taken to level paddy fields
so the plants would stand in water at a uniform depth; this made irrigation far more effective and allowed water to be used to protect plants
against low temperatures. Also, as time passed, seeds were more commonly soaked in water to bring them to the sprout before planting,
thus lengthening the growing season; oil was more widely used as an
insecticide, and a crude rule-of-thumb crop rotation came to be commonly practiced on unirrigated fields.[19]

Although techniques of seed selection were known earlier, they
were much more widely used in the Tokugawa period than before. One
method of selection was to suspend seeds in a salt solution to separate
the heavier seed from the lighter; another (which could be combined
with the first) was to use as seed the grain produced by the hardiest
plants. In addition to increasing yields these techniques reduced the
amount of seed sown, probably between 20 and 50 percent.[k] But more

---

[k] An eighteenth-century treatise gives as normal two or three *shō* of seed per
tan of land for rice, but in 1809 we find a family in Aizu (incidentally, with rising
rice yields) sowing one *shō* per *tan*! (Shōji, *Meiji ishin*, p. 40.) A family in
Shinano achieved a 30 percent reduction in rice seed between 1796 and 1799 while
reducing the area planted to rice by only 8 percent. (Shimada Takashi, "Suwahan
nōgyō keiei no ichirei," *Keizaigaku*, 25 (1952), 41.)

important in the long run than economizing on seed was the contribution that seed selection made to the development of new plant varieties; in fact, until the beginning of scientific plant breeding, most new domestic varieties of rice must have been by-products of seed selection.

It is somewhat easier to get an impression of the magnitude of gains in crop yields than to know in a particular instance what factors were responsible in what degree for gains achieved. Even on the magnitude of gains one must be exceedingly cautious. The firmest figures come from records of output kept by individual peasants, who had no interest in misleading themselves (as the village always did the tax official) but who rarely recorded acreage for individual crops. The harvest figures in such records are no doubt generally accurate, but since we dare not estimate acreage from them—since the relationship of yields to acreage is precisely what we want to know—we had best leave them strictly alone. But a few records do not require guesswork. The journal of a family in Aki Province gives annual production data for five fields of constant size during the period 1787 to 1888. On all five fields yields rose significantly: on the three that were planted throughout the period to one crop (rice) the decennial average of production rose between 50 and 71 percent; on one of the other two fields the increase was even greater. This field was planted to rice continuously from 1787 through 1856; taking 1787–97 as the base period, the decennial average ran 100, 148, 168, 203, 212, 195, 195.[20] This was perhaps an exceptional holding but it certainly was not unique. According to the painstaking estimates of Professor Imai, yields on land planted to rice on a Kinai holding (for which exceptionally full records survive) increased approximately 75 percent between the early sixteenth and early seventeenth centuries.[21] One must remember, too, that there were very important gains in productivity that were not reflected in crop yields at all, such as those from crop substitutions and the more intensive use of land by double cropping. Such increases may have been greater than those visible in crop yields, but for obvious reasons they are nearly impossible to estimate. The figures cited above at least suggest the sort of visible increase in productivity that was possible; how widely it was achieved—or exceeded—is of course another question.

To get any useful notion we must turn to more general (and much less precise) indices. Though at first glance remote from the problem, one of the most impressive is the official complaints of inequities in the land tax; specifically the complaint that prosperous farmers—and perhaps more significantly, good land—were taxed at a lesser rate than poor, quite independently of corruption and favoritism, which also made for inequalities.[1] But why should there have been in the tax system an inherent bias in favor of good farmers and superior land? The land tax cannot have been intentionally regressive or officials would not have complained so much of the unfairness of that feature. There would seem but one answer: there was often a gap between the estimated yields upon which the land tax was based and actual yields, and this gap was greater and occurred more frequently on good land than poor—a difference caused by differential rates of increasing productivity. Let us see how.

Official estimates of yield, field by field, were the result of the periodic land surveys (*kenchi*) mentioned earlier. [Since *kenchi* were rarely made as often as every eight or ten years, and frequently not for a century or more,[m] they could not keep pace with actual yields in a period of rapidly rising productivity.] The result was that improved land was taxed at a lesser rate in relation to productivity than unimproved land.[n] The existence of this differential, to which there is ample

[1] The following passage from "Kannōsaku" by Takemoto Ryūhei (1769–1820) is typical: "Fields belonging to wealthy peasants bear a relatively light land tax, and they are consequently profitable. There are, however, usually but one or two such holders in a group of ten villages. As to the number of families that can live without borrowing, there are no more than ten in a hundred. The remainder are all poor. The fields of the latter pay a very heavy land tax without exception. On the other hand, the lands of wealthy peasants though yielding heavily are lightly taxed; hence they yield a surplus." For additional testimony on differential taxation, see Kan Kikutarō, "Matsuyamahan ni okeru jōmensei no kenkyū," *SKSG*, XI, 8 (1941), 54.

[m] A study by the author of tax records for 12 villages, extending in each case from the late seventeenth century into the nineteenth, shows that in ten villages there was either no change or negligible change from about 1700 on, and in the other two no change whatsoever from sometime before 1700. Startling as the realization is, it is evident that in these villages, which were scattered very widely over northern and central Honshū, land ceased to be periodically surveyed from about 1700 on; by the middle of the nineteenth century, therefore, taxes were based on assessments a century to a century and a half old! (Thomas C. Smith, "The Land Tax in the Tokugawa Period," *Journal of Asian Studies*, XVIII, 1 (1958), 3–19.)

[n] This differential in taxation incidentally suggests the solution to a difficult problem of considerable interest. The consensus of scholarly opinion holds that the land tax was so heavy during the Tokugawa period that agriculture generally yielded no surplus to the cultivator. Yet, there was manifestly capital for the improvement

contemporary testimony from widely scattered places, suggests therefore a widespread and significant increase in productivity.

Technical innovations during the Tokugawa period increased not only per-acre yields but per-acre labor requirements as well. Not that all innovations had the effect of intensifying the use of labor, but this was undoubtedly the over-all effect on most holdings. One important reason for this was that innovations rarely if ever came singly; they hung together in clusters by a kind of inner logic; one innovation brought others in its train, and often could not be adopted independently of them. For example: multiple cropping required more intensive fertilization, which in turn was facilitated by animal plowing to turn the soil more deeply than was possible with spading and so permit heavier applications of fertilizer without damage to plants; and animal plowing was exceedingly difficult without improved drainage, which made it possible to dry the ground in the spring so as to offer less resistance to the plow; and so on. Other "clusters" of innovations might be cited. Through such linkages of interdependence the ultimate effect of even individual labor-saving innovations was often to intensify the use of labor.

Commercial fertilizers are an illustration. Insofar as they replaced natural fertilizers they saved an enormous amount of labor. They drastically reduced and might entirely eliminate the work of cutting and hauling grass from the mountainside, then trampling it into the plowed and flooded fields; moreover, this labor was saved at the planting, when the work load reached its annual peak and time and human energy were most precious. How great was the potential for saving at this season may be judged from the fact that in the seventeenth century about ten man-days per *tan* of paddy were spent in cutting grass and composting fields prior to planting.[22] But this is only part of the story. Multiple cropping was a common result—indeed often the chief aim—of the adoption of commercial fertilizers; and insofar as it was,

of farming, and throughout the period wealthy peasants tended to invest in land. This would suggest that the land tax was actually less heavy than alleged; but if our conclusion about the differential in taxation is correct, the land tax would have been light for improving holders only. For other holders it may have been very heavy. Hence the paradox of oppressive taxation and peasant poverty on the one hand and rising yields and the investment in land on the other may be an apparent contradiction only; it is probable that the two parts of the statement apply to different groups of peasants.

the new fertilizers added more labor to farming than they saved, though it should be noted that the addition came mostly at a time when employment was otherwise slack.

Another illustration is the *semba-koki*, the only important mechanical innovation in farming during the Tokugawa period. Significantly this device first appeared about the Genroku period (1688–1703) in the area of commercial agriculture around Osaka and thereafter spread gradually to other parts of the country. It consisted of a wooden frame with a protruding row of long teeth at first made of bamboo but later of iron, between which the rice stalks were drawn to strip away the grain. This replaced the earlier technique of drawing the stalks with one hand between two large chopsticks (*koki-hashi*) held in the other. One contemporary source has it that the *semba-koki* was ten times as fast as the chopsticks. This may be an exaggeration, but it is evident that the new tool was the far more efficient, and moreover it could be used by hands that were not sufficiently strong or skilled to operate the clumsy chopsticks. Thus it not only saved labor at the harvest— another peak of labor demand—but made new sources of family labor available. Still, the end result was not always a saving of labor; for by releasing labor at this particular season the *semba-koki* often made it possible, for the first time, to plant a winter crop hard on the fall harvest.[23] (See page 142.)

More or less permanent changes in cropping occurred on thousands of holdings during the Tokugawa period, and they generally brought an increase in per-acre labor requirements. The changes were chiefly of two kinds: the substitution of rice for an unirrigated crop, and the substitution of a cash crop for a subsistence crop. With the expansion of irrigated acreage, low-yielding crops were commonly replaced by rice, which was the most labor-intensive of all food crops and when planted to a previously unirrigated field required the upkeep of new ditches, terraces, and embankments, thus adding appreciably to the labor load. The chief cash crops (cotton, tobacco, sugar cane, indigo) were all labor-intensive,[o] and they tended to supplant on upland fields crops that were notably less so.

Some technical changes during the Tokugawa period added wholly

[o] The only actual figures available on labor requirements of cash crops are for cotton and indigo, which required 40–60 and 75–100 man-days respectively per *tan* of land as compared with about 40 for rice, and rice was far more labor-intensive than the crops actually replaced on upland fields. (Toya, *Nōgyō keiei*, pp. 432–70; and *Meiji ishin to jinushisei*, edited by Rekishigaku Kenkyūkai, Tokyo, 1957, p. 129.)

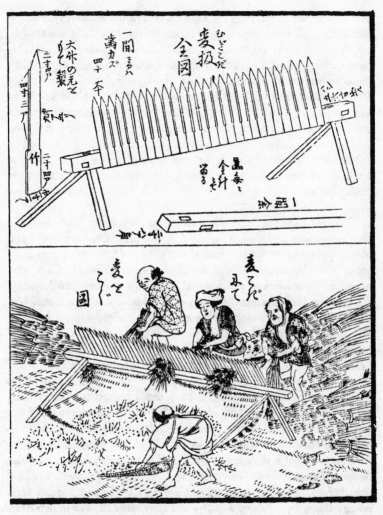

Peasants threshing wheat with the *semba-koki*; the upper illustration gives specifications for making the device. (*Nōgu benri ron.*) See page 138 for an illustration of the chopstick technique (*koki-hashi*) which the *semba-koki* replaced.

new operations to farming (at least on individual holdings), without eliminating others. New irrigation works are an excellent example, but there are many others. Seed selection, the treatment of seeds before planting, planting in evenly spaced rows, more intensive weeding, the adoption of insecticides, the use of irrigation as a protection for plants against frost—all were important changes of this kind. Some new crops had a similar effect. At least one that was rapidly spreading—mulberry—could be added to a holding without necessarily reducing or eliminating other work; for the trees might be planted on the borders between fields or on odd plots of ground not otherwise used; or, of course, leaves for feeding the silkworms could be bought from others.

Technical changes in production are never socially innocuous, and the innovations in farming sketched in the preceding sections of this chapter were no exception. But, though it would be difficult to exaggerate their importance, from one viewpoint their social effects were negative: they blocked other social effects of a more revolutionary kind. They are consequently often overlooked even though they contributed vitally to making Japanese agrarian society what it is today. We cannot fully explore this subject here, but a few words are appropriate as an introduction to the following chapters, which deal more explicitly with the social consequences of technical change.

The most radical effect of technical change, of which all others were in a sense merely functions, was a trend toward smaller farming units. This seems a natural and even inevitable development if one assumes for the moment that the small nuclear family was the unchanging, ultimate integer of peasant society. With the progress of agricultural technology, it took less and less land to support this family, which because of new labor-intensive techniques could anyway work less land than before. But this does not explain why given the state of technology the nuclear family actually was the decisive factor in determining the optimum size of the farming unit. Why was the labor force not expanded to create a *larger* farming unit, rather than the farming unit limited by the capabilities of the family labor force?

The most obvious factor—population increase—is also the most difficult to assess. This is not only because the increase in farming population was to some extent offset by an increase in arable, but because the increase in population did not correspond closely in time with the trend to smaller holdings. The bulk of population increase came before 1725, whereas the trend toward smaller holdings was most marked after that date. It must be remembered, of course, that there was considerable temporal overlapping locally. Still, the over-all separation of the two trends is sufficiently marked to suggest that population increase did not initiate the trend toward smaller holdings. It apparently had that effect only when two other factors came into play, which for the country as a whole was after 1700.

One of these was technical change of a kind that, on balance, made the operations of farming more intricate. Far from simplifying and making more uniform the multitude of tasks that confronted the labor force (as mechanical innovations presumably would have done), innovations actually increased the demands made on every farm worker. They demanded of him more specialized knowledge and skill, more attention to detail, the exercise of more initiative and judgment. Weeding, seed selection, planting in rows, the use of strong and costly fertilizers, the leveling of fields, the use of water as protection against frost—these and many other operations depended for their effectiveness on the alertness, effort, and skill of individual workers. To speak metaphorically, rather than impelling farming forward to a manufacturing stage of production these operations served to strengthen its handicraft character. The increasing emphasis in farming on just such operations put the larger labor force at an ever greater disadvantage in competing with the small one. The large labor force with its hereditary servants and *nago*, its part-time workers and degrees of family membership, was a loosely organized and relatively heterogeneous social group. By contrast the small labor force, which in most cases coincided precisely with the nuclear family, was tight, disciplined, and socially homogeneous. It consequently not only could supervise its members more successfully, but could rely on them to a far greater degree for spontaneous effort since it gave them stronger and more immediate incentives. Under the circumstances, technical innovations brought the opposite of the economies of scale we tend mistakenly to associate with *all* technological advance; that is, beyond a certain small size, the larger the farming unit the more inefficient it was likely to be.

The second factor, which increased the effect of the first, was a secular rise in the cost of labor. The continuously rising remuneration of labor outside the family acted as a distintegrative force on the large, heterogeneous labor force. Its social bonds were already relatively weak and now gave way before the pull of high wages outside. As this group consequently began to dissolve, it became even less competent than before to meet the challenge of an agriculture becoming steadily more individualized; so it slowly made way for a smaller unit of organization.

It must be understood that the trend to smaller units of farming, though exceedingly important, affected relatively few holdings. The vast majority of holdings were already family-size or smaller and could not be further reduced. Those that were affected, however, were the large holdings around which agriculture and in fact the entire village was organized. These holdings did not disappear as legal entities—as units of ownership—but they did gradually cease to be working farms; for very slowly they were broken up into a number of small tenant holdings, although the owners might and often did continue to work some land themselves.

The social counterpart of this development was the slow but steady dissolution of the extended family into its nuclear constituents. We shall give some attention to the details of this process later; but it will not be difficult to understand it in principle now if one keeps in mind that the extended family was a product of the older mode of cultivation. Just as that mode had required a large family organization, so the shift on large holdings to tenant cultivation now required a small labor force. With the trend to tenant cultivation in full tide, the *raison d'être* of the extended family disappeared.

The long-term significance of the trend to smaller units of farming will be more clearly understood, perhaps, if seen in a larger context. We must remember that it is by no means the only historical pattern of agrarian development. In some Western countries, indeed, the over-all trend during the past three or four centuries has been toward *larger* farming units. This trend has encouraged mechanization in farming; has increasingly divided the farm population into a few capitalist farmers on the one hand and many wage laborers on the other; has weakened the solidarity of the village community by increasingly differentiating its members as to status, role, and wealth; has largely deprived the family of significance in the organization of production; and has drastically altered the ratio of urban and rural population by increasing food output while simultaneously reducing the labor requirements of agriculture.

Inadequate as this series of statements patently is to describe the jigsaw of agrarian development in England and some other places, it at least suggests how remote that development was from the experience of Japan, despite the fact that the starting points in the two cases were similar in important respects. For in Japan the trend toward *smaller* units of farming made mechanization virtually impossible; it kept the agricultural population a relatively homogeneous class of small peasant farmers despite the presence of landlords and obvious differences of wealth; it preserved the organic unity of the village community despite the growth of a nonfarming population within it; it enhanced rather than diminished the role of the family in farming; and it maintained the farming population at a constant level, and so at a very high ratio to urban population despite industrialization.

It is not within the province of this book to weigh the question why technical development in Japanese agriculture was such as to turn development toward small rather than large farming units. But there can be no doubt of the importance of the fact that it did. Nor does its importance lie merely in blocking a different course of development. That view, which is all too common, has the perverse effect of giving a regressive look to technical innovations that greatly increased productivity and brought other equally significant results. The following chapters will show how far from regressive they actually were.

8

THE TRANSFORMATION OF LABOR

In an earlier chapter we saw that family organization and the organization of farming were intimately connected; a change in one was ultimately reflected by a change in the other. For instance, labor incorporated in a farming unit tended also to be incorporated in the family of the holder. But as the market developed this became less often true. [The family remained the unit of farming, but the market tended to separate labor from group membership and social obligations; labor lost much of its social significance and was treated increasingly as an economic entity.] Although the details of this long and complex process escape us, some of its broader features can be discerned. They show rather clearly how profound was the change in the social relations of farming during the latter half of the Tokugawa period.

Of all types of farm labor known to Tokugawa Japan, the *fudai* or hereditary servant was most completely assimilated in the master's family. Often he was adopted as a child[a] and treated in some respects like a son; but even when acquired as an adult he was often treated in some ways as a family member, and he or his son might in time be given a hut and established as a branch family. (See Chapter 2.) Hereditary servants were probably the oldest form of agricultural labor recruited outside the family, except slaves, with whom they had something in common and with whom they may even have been related in origin. They were still very numerous in the Tokugawa period, especially outside the Kinai, and there had probably been a time when they constituted the core of the labor force on most large holdings everywhere.

Hereditary servants could survive in large numbers, however, only so long as there was no other outlet for the surplus labor of poor peasant families, which in turn was only so long as the village remained effec-

[a] But sometimes also as an adult: a petition to some higher authority (which is not clear) from a Kinai village states in part: "I pray to make Matsunosuke, age 35, son of Heibei, who lives in Yashiro village, Kato county, Harima Province, in the domain of His Excellency Saitō Shinhachirō, my *genin and adopted son (yōshi)*." (Imai Rintarō and Yagi Akihiro, *Hōken shakai no nōson kōzō*, Tokyo, 1955, p. 126; my italics.)

tively cut off from an expanding outside economy. For as trade began
to knit the village first to the town and then to the city, new and freer
forms of employment became available in lumbering, transport, trade,
handicraft industry, and eventually agriculture. They tended to dry
up the sources of hereditary servants. After all, why should anyone
give up more of his freedom than was necessary in order to work? And
why should a family sell the persons of members when their labor could
be more profitably sold instead? Nor, as the economics of farming
changed, was the hereditary servant any longer necessarily the most
desirable type of labor from the viewpoint of the user. The newer types
of labor had the decided advantage of making it possible to acquire
labor when it was needed for short periods, without assuming far-reaching personal obligations toward its possessor. This was a decisive advantage as farming became more competitive and subject to sudden
market changes.

Hereditary servants did not of course disappear everywhere at the
same time, nor were they replaced immediately by types of labor free
of all hint of servitude. Aspects of *fudai* status clung for a long time to
the newer types of labor, in some places even to the present time. By
the end of the Tokugawa period, however, hereditary servants were
no longer the dominant type of farm labor. Far more numerous, now,
were persons hired for a fixed period and payment. Such persons were
often called "*hōkōnin*," a term which seems at least to have been used
consistently to distinguish them from hereditary servants, and which
we shall use in that sense in any case. Among *hōkōnin*, as indeed among
fudai, nago, or any other broad class, there were numerous differences
of status, but two stand out. One concerned the period of employment,
which ranged from one or two days to many years; the other concerned
the time when payment for the labor was given. In some cases payment
was made upon completion of the employment period or at regular
intervals during it if the period were long; but in others it was made
in advance and had thus the character of a loan binding the worker to
the employer. Payment in advance was usually restricted to cases
where the employment period was a year or more, the other form of
payment normally being adopted for shorter periods. There were consequently two main types of *hōkōnin:* those bound by debt for a relatively long time and those hired for short periods at wages. To distinguish them we shall call the former "*hōkōnin*" and the latter "wage
labor."

Occasionally the population registers of a village reveal the gradual

could *fudai* really be regarded as sold slaves; in the western sense of the words now were they anymore slaves than the rest of local disappearance of hereditary servants[b] and the emergence of *hōkō-nin* in their place. Kamikawarabayashi village, located a few miles west of Osaka, is a good example.[c] Cotton was grown in this village from the late seventeenth century through the first third of the eighteenth,[d] bringing a period of exceptional prosperity during which even very small holders farmed at a profit. Significantly, it was during just this period that the transition from hereditary servants to *hōkōnin* occurred. In 1659, before cotton had become an important crop, there were 31 hereditary servants and six *hōkōnin* in the village; and even the latter bore strong marks of hereditary status since employment periods ranged up to ten years. As the area planted to cotton expanded, however, hereditary servants declined in number and finally disappeared altogether, while the number of *hōkōnin* steadily increased—rising from six in 1659 to 14 in 1689, 26 in 1695, 31 in 1710, and 43 in 1728.[1]

The transformation of agricultural labor illustrated by Kamikawa-rabayashi was more or less typical, and other cases of the kind might be cited.[2] Generally, there is little evidence of hereditary servants by the late Tokugawa period, and at the same time ample proof of an agricultural labor shortage, which explains why. Covering most of the latter half of the Tokugawa period and affecting all parts of the country, the shortage of labor was no temporary or local phenomenon. Everywhere there were complaints of it from scholars, officials, and villages; and it was severe enough to cause serious trouble for holders who depended on any form of hired labor. "In recent times," stated a petition for relief from a village in Musashi in 1802, " '*hōkōnin*' have become exceedingly short, and wages (*kyūkin*) are consequently so

[b] Reference here may be made back to a certain Hachisuke mentioned in Chapter 2, page 14. He was a hereditary servant and he or his descendants may be traced in the family of the master for three generations through population registers for 1721, 1744, and 1764. Then evidence of the group disappears; no trace of it is to be found in the registers for 1784 and 1794. Of three other hereditary servants held by the same master in 1764, two had disappeared by 1784 and the last one by 1794. The disappearance of hereditary servants from this family cannot be explained by a reduction in demand for labor, since according to the family accounts it used a total of 965.5 man-days in farming in 1799, of which family members supplied only 185.5. A more likely explanation for the disappearance of hereditary servants is to be found in the destructive effects on this type of labor of industrial development, which was notable in this area during the latter part of the eighteenth century. (Shimada, "Suwahan nōgyō keiei no ichirei," pp. 34–37, 45–46.)

[c] Another example is a village in Shinshū where hereditary servants declined from 36 in 1656 to six in 1746, while *hōkōnin* increased from 29 to 47 in the same period. (Miyagawa, "Taikō kenchi" (4), pp. 43–44.)

[d] After that time cotton growing declined owing to the seepage of water from the Muko River. (Imai and Yagi, *Hōken shakai*, p. 1.)

high that . . . large holders have recently been unable to make a living from farming alone."[3]

This was typical: the same complaint was heard fifty years earlier, and it was echoed later from Kyūshū in the far south and Tōhoku in the far north,[4] regions mostly distantly removed from the centers of economic growth. Labor was in short supply after about 1700 because capital in trade and industry was growing faster than the population. Despite all the artificial checks attempted, therefore, labor was drawn off from agriculture into the more rapidly expanding sectors of the economy. This drain was partly reflected by the movement of population from the village to the city—but only partly, since trade and industry were by no means exclusively urban phenomena. Even so the population registers testify to the village loss of labor,[e] and so of course does the growth of urban population during the last three-quarters of the eighteenth century, when the population of the country as a whole was static.

The Shogunate and the baronial governments (*han*) were both alarmed by the labor shortage in agriculture, which proved one of the most acute and intractable economic problems of the latter half of the Tokugawa period. The alarm is understandable. Not only was the warrior class sensitive to any threat to land revenues or the stability of the peasant class, but they rightly sensed in trade and industry new social forces subversive of the warrior's style of life, perhaps ultimately even of his political supremacy.[f] Drastic steps were therefore taken to relieve or soften the effects of the labor shortage in agriculture. Government attempted to stop immigration to Edo and even to return recent immigrants to their villages; to prohibit the migration of labor from one lord's jurisdiction to another; to prevent labor in the village from following occupations other than farming; to stimulate the birth

[e] For example, a population register of 1698 from a village in Shinshū shows a total population of 272; of this number 25 persons—roughly 10 percent of the population of the village—were listed as working outside the village as *hōkōnin*, and of these, 16 were in the city of Edo. (Ichikawa Yūichirō, "Edo jidai no nōka no jinteki kōsei no henka—shūmon aratamechō kara mita Shinano Sakuchihō," *RGKK*, 147 (1950), 33.)

[f] Not merely for economic reasons, as is sometimes thought, but for cultural and social reasons as well and perhaps even mainly; for not only was the rising merchant class wealthy, but—what was far worse—their most important activity, commerce, was based on profit maximization, whereas the warriors took for granted a highly personal structure of loyalties and obligations. The resulting conflict of values gave rise to a vast warrior literature in condemnation of merchants and mercantile ethics. Many examples of such tracts may be found in any collection of economic writings from the period, such as *NKSS*.

rate, to fix wages, and much else.[5] It was all to no avail: despite every-thing, labor would go where material rewards and freedom were great-est—and if that was not always off the farm, at least it was not in the fields.

We must be careful not to suggest that the labor shortage came suddenly or brought an abrupt transformation of farm labor. The transformation of hereditary servants into *hōkōnin* extended not only over many centuries but through many types of *hōkōnin* as well. Al-though precision is out of place in tracing the course of this develop-ment with its infinite regional variety, one can discern in the jigsaw three broad types of *hōkōnin*. Each was characterized by a significantly different degree of freedom and represents a different stage in the development of wage labor. It would be a serious mistake, however, to imagine this as a neat development from one type to another, without much overlapping and the presence of many hybrid types.

Least free of the three types was a *hōkōnin* given to someone by his family for an indefinite period in return for a loan. He served as a kind of security on the loan and was compelled to work for the person with no compensation but his keep until the loan was repaid.[9] Such *hōkōnin* were not far removed from *fudai* status, and in fact readily reverted to it. Having assumed indentured status involuntarily at the behest of family, they were dependent on family for recovering their freedom, since they were paid nothing themselves and so could contribute nothing to that result. Debts contracted on such unfavorable terms sprang from poverty, not enterprise, and whatever was borrowed had in most cases to be used to pay taxes or to buy food rather than to im-prove farming. Debts therefore often went so long unpaid the *hōkō-nin* came to be considered bound to his master indefinitely, with no hope of redemption. Sometimes this outcome may have been foreseen by all parties from the beginning, the fiction of a loan being adopted merely to avoid the Tokugawa prohibition on the sale of human beings.[h]

[9] The *hōkōnin* was commonly said by the loan agreement to have been "placed in pawn" (*shichimotsu ni sashioki*).

[h] In repeating the prohibition in 1625, the Tokugawa, with a bow to reality, specifically legalized pledging *hōkōnin* for periods up to ten years—but no longer; this probably accounts for the great number of *hōkōnin* we find with terms of service of precisely ten years. (Furushima Toshio, *Nihon hōken nōgyō shi*, Tokyo, 1942, p. 141.)

Still, the *hōkōnin* bound by debt was different from the hereditary servant in principle: his freedom could be redeemed, while the *fudai* could be freed only by the generosity of the master. And sometimes this distinction had practical significance, most notably with a second type of *hōkōnin*. He was identical with the first except that his labor received *some* compensation. A certain agreed value was assigned in advance to his labor during the term of the loan, and the sum agreed on (which was less than the amount of the loan) was then deducted from the debt outstanding at the end of the loan period. The following loan agreement illustrates this arrangement.[5a]

> My son, Takezō, age 19, I hereby put in pawn for a money-secured-by-person loan from you. Takezō is to work for you for three full years, from the twelfth moon of this year to the twelfth moon of the Year of the Rabbit. If during this time he serves you well, it is agreed that 15 *kan* of the total debt of 35 *kan* will be canceled.

With time this second type of *hōkōnin* became more common and the first less so.[6] This shows clearly that labor was taking on an economic value of its own—as labor, independent of any value attached to it in securing the loan. Its value was now so closely calculated, in fact, that in some cases the loan agreement stipulated that so much a day be deducted from the *hōkōnin's* total "pay" for every day he was ill and unable to work in excess of a certain allowable minimum.[‡] One might almost say that this calculation of the value of labor in daily units foreshadowed day labor. In any case, the impersonal businesslike denial of pay in the absence of work was merely a corollary of the principle of pay *for* work, at a stipulated rate however low.

That principle was of the utmost importance: it meant that the *hōkōnin* could not be held indefinitely against his will. His labor must eventually free him if only there were no interest charge on the loan. Sometimes there was such a charge, however, and then he might be no better off than the hereditary servant. As a directive to district magistrates issued in the Aizu barony (*han*) pointed out, interest in such cases often accumulated faster than the principal could be paid off, with the result that the *hōkōnin* lost his freedom permanently just as surely as if he had been sold.[7]

‡ This excerpt from a pledge of 1789 is typical: "If Mantarō (the *hōkōnin*) falls sick and cannot work, he may be excused for three days, but after that 32 *mon* will be charged for each day he is unable to work. In case of a long illness, Unosuke [his brother?] will be made to come and work in his place." (Mori, *Nago seido*, p. 53.)

There was still a third type of *hōkōnin,* whose appearance marked a great stride toward the development of free labor. Like other *hōkōnin* he was bound by debt for the duration of the loan, but his labor during that time constituted repayment of it in full: at the end of the stipulated period neither any part of the principal of the debt nor unpaid interest remained to hold him. Loan agreements of this type often contained a change in legal terminology that underscores the important new degree of freedom for the *hōkōnin* they represent. In the previous types of agreement the money loan to the borrower was called *shindaisen,* meaning a loan of money secured by someone's person; in the new type of agreement the loan was sometimes called *kyūkin*—a term with no connotation of unfreedom, and one which may be translated as "monetary compensation" or perhaps even as "wage."

One must not exaggerate the degree of freedom afforded by even the new type of employment, however. The "wage" was still paid in advance and bound the *hōkōnin* for a certain period no less firmly than when the loan was called by a more ominous name; moreover, no less frequently in this case than in others the debt agreement contained a promise on the part of the borrowing family and its guarantors' to replace the *hōkōnin* if during the loan period he proved intractable, absconded, or fell ill. Often, too, the agreement fixed the rate at which the loan (or "wages") was to be worked off, setting it in such a way that the bulk of the debt was not worked off until a short time before the end of the loan period. Thus the binding force of the debt was not reduced uniformly, becoming less and less with each month and year the *hōkōnin* worked, but remained virtually undiminished until near

---

¹ Sometimes the obligation fell primarily on the guarantors: "We, the guarantors (*ukenin*) undertake to send to work for you, for 20 days each month, from the first month of this year until the twelfth month of next, a two-year period, Seisuke, age 30, the son of Seizaemon, of this village. You have already given Seizaemon the wages of Seisuke, amounting to 200 *me.* Thus, Seisuke shall work for you during the agreed period. If he does not, the guarantors undertake to provide someone in his place, so there will be not the slightest inconvenience to you. It is so agreed.

February 1829

Seizaemon (seal)	Father of *hōkōnin,* Mitsue village
Seisuke (seal)	*hōkōnin*
Kurobei (seal)	guarantor, Mitsue village
Zembei (seal)	guarantor, Mitsue village

To the Honorable Yosuke of the same village."
(Furushima and Nagahara, *Shōhin seisan,* p. 175.)

the very end. One surviving loan agreement, for instance, shows that a loan amounting to 11 *kan* was advanced for a promise of three years of the labor of one man; the sum was to be worked off at the rate of one *kan* the first year, two the second, and eight the third. This shows that the coercive element of debt was still present and that it was reflected in the valuation of the *hōkōnin's* labor; otherwise the "wage" would have been approximately the same in all three years.[8] Put another way, the value of the *hōkōnin's* labor was acknowledged to increase as the coercive character of the debt diminished with the passage of time.

Another feature of this type of *hōkōnin* was reminiscent of earlier types: the loan (or "wage") was not made paid to the *hōkōnin* himself but to a third person, almost invariably the *hōkōnin's* family head. In fact the *hōkōnin* himself was usually not even a party to the loan agreement;[k] his cooperation was of course necessary to the agreement but the family head was apparently thought to be able to guarantee that. One might imagine that the power of the family head thus to dispose of the *hōkōnin's* labor was rooted in parental control over the very young rather than in the authority of the family headship. But the texts of loan agreements, which usually give the *hōkōnin's* age and relationship to the family head, suggest nothing of the sort. *Hōkōnin* were rarely under 20 years of age and frequently as old as 35 or 40; and they included wives, younger brothers, sisters, aunts, grandchildren, and daughters-in-law of the family head in about the same numbers in aggregate as sons and daughters. One even finds instances of members of branch families being put out by the heads of main families.[9] This serves as a reminder of the enormous power of the peasant family over its members, and warns against concluding hastily that increasingly free terms of employment meant a corresponding increase in *individual* freedom.

Loan agreements survive in scant number and only in a few localities, and one consequently rarely knows which of the three types any particular *hōkōnin* was. On the other hand, it is frequently possible to find out for what period a *hōkōnin* was held by his master since such information was usually noted in the population registers. From these

---

[k] There are occasional exceptions in which the *hōkōnin*, though obviously not the main party to the agreement, at least appears as a signator along with the main party. This would suggest a slight loosening of the family head's control, a fact that the expanding labor market makes entirely understandable.

documents it is evident that there was a tendency for the term of *hōkō-nin* service (or employment period?) to become shorter with time. Several stages in the shortening may be noted. First the period of indefinite duration (*fudai* or the first type of *hōkōnin*) gives way to a fixed but still very long term of ten or 15 years; then the term gradually shortens until in most cases it is no more than two or three years; finally, the period is commonly shortened to one year or even to a single season.

This drastic shortening of the employment period reflects the fact that labor was being slowly lifted out of the context of the social group and recognized as having an economic value independent of social relations. The farm worker, who as hereditary servant had once been compensated chiefly by assimilation to the family, was now increasingly regarded merely as a hired hand to be employed only so long as he was needed: the valuation of his labor was more economic, less social. This is confirmed by the fact that *hōkōnin* burdened with the longer employment periods received lower annual rates of "pay" (that is the sum advanced against the labor or person of the worker) than those with shorter periods.

The tendency of the employment period to become shorter may be illustrated in Kamikawarabayashi village, where, as we have already seen, hereditary servants were generally replaced by *hōkōnin* toward the end of the seventeenth century; fixed periods of employment had thus replaced periods of indefinite length. During the next 50 years, the majority of *hōkōnin* were bound for periods of ten years or longer and the single commonest period was exactly ten years. But, after 1760, such long terms became noticeably less common, and by the decade 1800–1810 they had entirely disappeared. At the same time the number of *hōkōnin* was declining. This was in part because a change in crops had reduced the demand for labor in the village, but also in part because *hōkōnin* were being replaced by wage labor hired by the day.[10]

With the emergence of day labor the long evolution of farm labor from hereditary servants to wage earners, from family members to free agents, was complete. We have however overlooked at least one stage in this evolution. Between the freest type of *hōkōnin* and wage labor there was one common transitional type that deserves mention. This was the man whose labor like the *hōkōnin's* was pledged to an employer for a stipulated period; but the period was relatively short and during it the man worked for the employer part time only and did not live with him; further, his pay was reckoned by the day. Such men were often small holders who eked out an inadequate farm income by thus working part time for wages. Although many were destined to lose their land and in the end to become full-time day laborers, they had for the moment a high degree of economic independence by comparison to any type of *hōkōnin*. Often they worked for different employers in successive years or for several employers concurrently, evidence of slight constraint put on them by any one employer.[l] Even so, their relations with the employer were not always free of an element of personal obligation, and in some cases at least it would seem to have been the result of a long-standing relationship of subordination and patronage. An illustration may be taken from a village in Shinshū.

The Imai family, which had either given its surname to Imai village or taken it from it, was the head of the largest lineage group and probably also the oldest family in that village. A certain Ichirōzaemon worked part time for this family in the years 1796, 1797, and 1798. What his relationship to the Imai was is difficult to say, but the accounts of the family for the year 1799 give some hint, since they list Ichirōzaemon as doing one day's *tetsudai* at the rice planting. This was the term commonly used in this area for *nago* labor services, and it was probably used in this sense here, for care was taken throughout the accounts to distinguish *tetsudai* from both labor to which something was paid and labor given as exchange labor.[l] It is by no means certain that Ichirōzaemon was or had been a *nago* of the Imai, but he was clearly beholden to the family by the vestiges of some such relationship: otherwise why in addition to working for them for wages did he perform *tetsudai*?

Another person who worked for the Imai in 1799 was Nagasuke. He contracted to work 20 days a month for the Imai and five days for a man named Kampei; the remaining five he was to work "at home," so evidently he held land of his own under some tenure or other. The Imai accounts during the year show the family lending Nagasuke[m] tools, work animals, and even labor—clearly for use on land he worked for himself. What lay behind this paternalistic help is uncertain, but

[l] The accounts call hired labor either *hiyatoi* or *meshitsukai*, depending on whether hired by the day or a longer period; labor exchanged for other labor was called *tema-gaeshi*. (Shimada, "Suwahan nōgyō keiei no ichirei," pp. 48–53.)
[m] "Lent a horse to Nagasuke to harvest his barley." (*Ibid.*, p. 58.)

it suggests a relationship to the Imai similar to that of Ichirōzaemon. But whatever the relationship it did not dominate Nagasuke's every action, as the following amusing entry in the Imai accounts shows:[12] "Nagasuke said he was behind workdays for Kampei, and he therefore asked for the day off to work for Kampei. So I gave him the day off, but he did not go to Kampei's." Apparently he went home instead.

Wage labor probably first appeared in industry and trade, for these sectors of the economy were expanding more rapidly than agriculture. Besides, production in them was more easily separated from consumption—which is to say, labor was not so deeply embedded in social production groups. Also, the value of a day's labor was easier to reckon because a larger share of productive resources was priced and less time elapsed between investment and return. But wherever day labor appeared first, it tended to spread from one place or sector of the economy to others. When a document from a village some 40 miles from Edo tells us "As to by-employments, the men in this village gather firewood on the mountainside *or go to work in the vicinity of Edo by the day (hiyatoi)* . . . ," we may be sure that day labor was known inside the village as well as outside. Why, after all, should anyone take less free and remunerative employment in a village than could be found just outside?[n]

This is not to say that wage labor had universally replaced earlier types of labor by the late Tokugawa period, for it has not done so to this day; but it had at least become very common. We find villages in which large numbers of families lived entirely or mainly by working for others at wages,[o] and hear commonly of migrant workers (though

[n] In some places, of course, wage labor came into the village with industry; this was apparently the case in Hirano village, where in the early nineteenth century the larger cotton ginners in the village each employed several day laborers. (Takao Kazuhiko, "Settsu Hirano-gō," p. 729.) Or to cite a case outside the Kinai: in the late eighteenth century a certain wealthy farmer in Echigo is said to have had 20 looms and employed some 30 workers in making fine hemp cloth which he shipped to Kyoto and Osaka for sale. (Kitajima Masamoto, "Kōshinchi ni okeru nōminteki shukōgyō no seikaku," *NSKK*, 12 (1950), 19.)

[o] The author of *Saizōki (ca.* 1700) writes: "Out of a village of 100 families, 50 are cultivators and 50 work for others by the day (*hiyatoi*)." (Cited by Furushima, *Kinsei Nihon nōgyō no kōzō*, II, 586.) This was an exaggeration if taken to apply to most villages, but it undoubtedly applied to some. For example, a village in Tosa with a population of 495 (including nonworkers) in 1857 contained 80 persons whom a local document described as "persons who work by the day (*hiyatoi*) in other villages or in the castle town." (Koseki, "Ansei 4-nen," p. 133.)

not families) who wandered about the country working only a short time in one place.[p] It is perhaps not surprising to find day wage labor commonly in the Kinai, or in the rich sericulture region stretching from Shinshū to Fukushima, or in the Kantō, or indeed in any region marked by important cities or commercial farming. But when one finds complaints of a shortage of "labor by the day and month" at the end of the eighteenth century in Tōhoku,[13] or comes upon references that make day labor seem a commonplace even in Kyūshū,[14] one must be prepared to believe that wage labor was at least known everywhere.

It was of course not equally important everywhere, and nowhere was it the only kind of labor. The overlapping of different forms of employment occurred in all parts of the country and even on individual holdings. Not only that: one man sometimes worked for another under more than one form of employment simultaneously; for instance, a *nago* might do so many days' labor services annually for his *oyakata* and work the rest of the time for him for wages. But despite all the overlapping the tangle of diverse forms was slowly being unraveled, suggesting that in an expanding labor market freer forms of employment inevitably tend to drive out less free.

The diary for the year 1846 of a village headman named Hara concretely illustrates the tendency.[15] Hara, who lived in present-day Kanagawa Prefecture, was a wealthy peasant working about three *chō* of land himself and letting out additional land to tenants. Although his farm was not intensely commercial judging from the crops mentioned in the diary,[q] it was enough so to be directly affected by outside influences. The diary records frequent trips during the year to the towns of Odawara and Atsuki to sell wheat, and presumably to buy the dried fish and oil cakes which were used as fertilizers on the holding. Hara also hired labor by the day from time to time.

Most of his labor, however, was provided by two female and three male *hōkōnin* who were hired by the year; family members apparently did no farm work, but confined themselves to supervising. We are not told the terms on which the five *hōkōnin* were employed, but the diary gives ample evidence that in this area *hōkōnin* were difficult to find

[p] The term *tabi-hiyatoi*, meaning literally "traveling day labor," was common in Kyūshū in the late Tokugawa period. (*Fukuoka-ken nōchi*, I, 425; also Fujita Gorō, "Kinsei ni okeru nōminsō no kaikyū bunka," in *Shakai kōsei shi taikei*, Tokyo, 1949, XIII, 71–72.)

[q] Also, frequent references in the diary to certain types of work suggest a rather high degree of self sufficiency—such as making barrels or buckets, rope, and straw mats.

and keep on almost any terms. Hara spent six days at the beginning of the year trying to find *hōkōnin* to employ; and having found the five he actually hired his troubles began in earnest. The two women and one of the men turned out to be reliable workers—at least the diary records no complaint against them—but two of the men, Seijirō and Otomatsu by name, kept Hara constantly on tenterhooks and put him to great expense. The trouble was that he never knew when they were going to be available to work and when they might be absent without leave. On numerous occasions during the year both simply disappeared (*kakeochi, ketsuraku*), staying away for several days at a time. Finally, the two went off together in the ninth month, just at the busiest season of the year when the harvest was beginning; Otomatsu returned after eight days but Seijirō did not come back at all, and Hara had to replace him for the rest of the year by workers hired by the day.

The astonishing thing, however, is not the unreliability of the *hōkōnin* but that each time Seijirō and Otomatsu ran away, Hara took them back without penalty—except once when Otomatsu was made to work on a holiday. Both he and they apparently knew that although new *hōkōnin* could not easily be found new employment could; but one wonders how long an employer could afford to farm with such labor. Indeed, there would come a time when no matter how cheap *hōkōnin* labor was it was more expensive, because less efficient, than higher-priced day labor; already at the end of the year Hara seems to have been making an involuntary shift from the one to the other.

The shortage of labor not only freed it increasingly of restraints but also drove up its price relentlessly. The rising cost of labor was a trend that lasted throughout the last half of the Tokugawa period and beyond, drawing complaints all the while from those who found the rise painful. Administrative officials and village headmen, both speaking on the whole for the larger holders, variously claimed that the rising cost of labor was ruining, had ruined, or would soon ruin agriculture. Looking beyond the immediate economic impact of rising wages to their effect on national character, Confucianists insisted that easy money for the mass of working people was breeding luxurious tastes and indolence among them.[16] But, although contemporary writers were agreed that wages were rising dangerously, they give us a very inadequate idea of how great the rise actually was. Fujii Naojirō, writing in 1787, tells us that farm wages had nearly quadrupled in the past 20 years,' but he cites no figures for other prices, so that we may infer nothing about the movement of real wages.¹⁷]

The fullest available price data for the period are those compiled by Professor Imai from materials in and around Kamikawarabayashi village. They permit us to follow locally the trend in real wages in considerable detail over a period of nearly a century. To appreciate how steep the rise was one must keep in mind three factors relevant to any estimate. First, there was an increase in the annual pay rate of all *hōkōnin* regardless of the length of the employment period. Second, the annual pay rate was decidedly higher for *hōkōnin* with short employment periods than with long. Third, short-term *hōkōnin* tended to replace long-term as time passed. Let us consider each of these points in turn.

TABLE IV*

AVERAGE ANNUAL WAGE OF HŌKŌNIN CLASSIFIED BY LENGTH OF EMPLOYMENT PERIOD

(Figures in *momme* of silver)

Employment Period (years)	1718–40	1741–60	1761–79	1782–1800	1801–20
1	76.0	113.0	138.0	163.0	163.0
2	....	43.5	....	110.5	110.0
3	22.6	53.3	....	122.0	55.0
4	13.1	27.5	....	96.7	87.0
5	....	....	7.6	46.0	71.6
6	....	....	....	42.3	....
7	5.8	....	21.4	....	44.8
8	2.7	3.7	11.6	18.2	18.2
9	....	....	10.8	11.8	....
10	4.0	2.8	8.9	10.6	22.5
11	2.6	....	....	10.9	39.8
12	....	1.7	....	....	12.5
13	....	2.3	....	....	15.3
14	....	....	....	15.6	....
15	1.0	1.3	....	....	....

* Adapted from Imai and Yagi, *Hōken shakai*, p. 149.

' By this time the upward trend in wages was at least half a century old. Tanaka Kyūgu, writing about 50 years earlier, stated that in the past 30 years the annual wages of male *hōkōnin* had risen from 3 *bu* to two or three *ryō*—that is, had trebled or quadrupled. ("Minkan shōyō," *NKSS*, I, 327.)

Table IV shows that the annual wage rate of all classes of *hōkōnin* rose during the eighteenth century. Although most other prices were rising too, wages apparently rose much faster than prices in general. Rice affords a good comparison since it reflects the general price level more accurately than other commodities. The index price for rice in Kamikawarabayashi from 1718 to 1820 by 20-year periods was 100, 111, 111, 129, and 99. Compare this gently sloping curve with the much sharper one described by the wages of one-year *hōkōnin*, which in the same period were 100, 149, 182, 214, and 214.[18] It should be noted, moreover, that the annual wages of one-year *hōkōnin* rose more slowly than the annual rate of any other class of *hōkōnin*. For one-year *hōkōnin* the rise between 1718 and 1810 was just over 100 percent; but for seven-year *hōkōnin*, for instance, it was about 700 percent and for eleven-year *hōkōnin* it was 1,500 percent!

Second, *hōkōnin* were paid at notably different annual rates according to the length of the employment period. Although, in general, wages were increasing more rapidly for the longer periods, the annual wage rate was at all times far higher for the shorter periods than for the long. To cite a few examples: in 1718–40, the average annual wage rate for 15-year *hōkōnin* was 1.0 *momme*, for ten-year *hōkōnin* 4.0 *momme*, for three-year *hōkōnin* 22.6 *momme*, and for one-year *hōkōnin* 76.0 *momme*. No wonder the changing structure of the labor force in terms of these classes had an important bearing on real wages!

This brings us to the third factor. As already noted in an earlier section of this chapter, there was a very marked tendency in Kamikawarabayashi toward shorter employment periods: *hōkōnin* with long terms gradually give way to those with short. Thus, in the period 1688–1758, 75 percent of all *hōkōnin* in the village were held for periods of ten years or more, but only 22 percent were held for that long in the period 1760–1810. Nor was this all; *hōkōnin* were being replaced during the latter half of the eighteenth century by day labor, which although not shown in the table was paid at about double the rate of the highest-paid *hōkōnin*.[8]

No village is typical of course; but Kamikawarabayashi illustrates two developments that were taking place everywhere, though at differ-

---

[8] The decline may be traced through the population registers; these show a total of 107 *hōkōnin* in 1708–28, 20 in 1760–79, and 15 in 1780–99. The evidence for the use of day labor (which of course is not reflected in the population registers) comes from the account books of the largest holder in the village. (Imai and Yagi, *Hōken shakai*, pp. 156–57.)

ent rates. One was the sustained and precipitous rise in the cost of labor. The other, closely connected with the first, was the dissolution of the group-bound obligations of farm labor; the successive stages of this process were marked by the transformation of the typical farm worker from hereditary servant to *hōkōnin*, then from long-term *hōkōnin* to short, and finally from short-term *hōkōnin* to wage laborer. These two developments struck powerfully and destructively at the bases of the traditional mode of farming on large holdings. Together with technical changes in farming and the growth of industrial by-employments, they forced a shift from *tezukuri* to tenant farming on large holdings—with important results for the entire farming community.

land worked by family

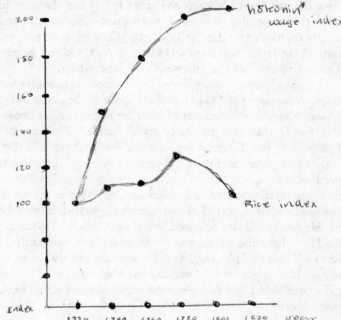

hōkōnin* wage index

Rice index

200
180
160
140
120
100

index

1720   1740   1760   1780   1800   1820   year

* 1 year hōkōnin

9

THE TRANSFORMATIONS OF *NAGO*

The rising cost and greater freedom of labor had equally important, but in general quite different, effects on large and small holdings. Since the one type of holding was prone to buy and the other to sell labor, the competitive positions of the two as farming units, though not exactly reversed, were drastically altered. [Circumstances now strongly favored the family-size farm and severely penalized any larger unit.] The consequences of this fact were very far-reaching.

Large holders at times suffered heavy economic losses for want of labor. A document of 1844 from Kaga spoke of the plight of holders who were forced by the scarcity of labor for hire to cultivate more land with family than they profitably could handle.[a] The records of a holder living in a Tottori village noted a similar situation in that area in the late eighteenth century. "There are villages," according to the words of the records, "where hardships are experienced every year because the planting cannot be finished on time owing to the scarcity of *hōkōnin*"—a claim that does not seem exaggerated in view of the trouble headman Hara described in finding *hōkōnin* in 1846. Nor, as the Hara diary also shows, was the labor problem necessarily solved when *hōkōnin* could be employed, for they did not always work well and might disappear without warning just when most needed. The Tottori source claims that *hōkōnin* were even known to refuse to obey a master's orders.[1]

[a] "*Hōkōnin* in farming have been steadily diminishing in number in the villages . . . and as a result holders who work large holdings have been unable to cultivate their land properly for lack of labor. This alarming situation is owing entirely to the fact that in recent years people in the country have willfully become merchants or artisans, or have gone to the towns as *hōkōnin* or taken work in other provinces. Naturally, therefore, the cultivating population has decreased."

But this was not because the countryside was being depopulated, for later on the document states: "While the population of villages increases year by year, at the same time there are places where *hōkōnin* are so short that the cultivation of the land is impaired." Clearly, part of the rural population was being drawn into other occupations in the village. (*Kagahan nōsei shi kō*, edited by Oda Kichinojō, Tokyo, 1929, p. 578.)

In this unsatisfactory state of affairs, apparently widespread, Fujita Yūkoku saw evidence of a profound change in class relations. Hereditary servants who served in the same family for a lifetime, Fujita said, were being replaced by *hōkōnin* employed by the year. Since the latter constantly moved from one household to another, quite naturally they did not know the true meaning of "master," cared only for their own comfort, and were ever eager to avoid hard work. This, Fujita thought, was the reason farm labor was short[2]—forgetting that if this were indeed the explanation of the shortage, nonfarm labor should on the contrary have been plentiful, which it was not.[b]

Not only was labor scarce and unreliable; it was also ruinously expensive. Everybody who bought it said so, and though there is obvious reason for treating the testimony of such witnesses skeptically, one is impressed by the frequency of the testimony and the fact that it came from all parts of the country.[3] Besides, scattered figures tend to confirm the assertion that the burden of labor costs on large holdings was very heavy indeed.

Hōkōnin pay varied with the length of the employment period, and no doubt also to some extent with sex, skill, and locality. Despite this, however, there is remarkable agreement among contemporary writers during the first half of the nineteenth century that one year's labor cost between 2.5 and 4.0 *ryō*.[4] We have insufficient price data to say exactly what that was worth in other commodities, but Professor Tsuchiya's estimate is probably not far off, that throughout the late Tokugawa period the value of 1 *ryō* was equal to about 1 *koku* of hulled rice.[5] A male *hōkōnin* then would earn, in addition to food and shelter and often clothing, about 3 *koku* of rice a year, which was enough to feed three adults for the same period of time. At first glance this seems an improbably high wage but there is firm evidence in surviving account books that it was commonly paid.

At this rate of pay a male *hōkōnin*, for instance, could very nearly support a small family from his earnings. Or—perhaps more impres-

[b] Others also found moral reasons for the scarcity of labor (for example, laziness), but it is evident even from their statements that the real reason was expanding opportunities for employment: "Men and women who will work as *hōkōnin* are scarce. This is especially true of those employed [in the towns] by warriors, but there is a scarcity of such people even in the country. One wonders why. Is not the most important reason the extravagance of the times? Recently money has been easy to come by; since it can be made without effort, people leave their inherited occupations, yet easily managed to live." (Tanaka Kyūgu, "Minkan shōyō" (1721), *NKSS*, I, 324.)

sive—he would earn about the same amount most holding families earned from farming alone, since few holdings yielded more than ten *koku* before taxes and production costs. From these comparisons it is evident that wages must have been a serious problem for holders who were obliged to keep several *hōkōnin*.

Let us illustrate. Assuming that the 3 *chō* of arable land farmed by the Hara family yielded a uniformly high return of 1.5 *koku* per *tan* of land, the gross income from the holding would have been 45 *koku*. If the wages of the five *hōkōnin* employed on the holding averaged 3.5 *koku* each (including keep), which is probably too low a figure for the Kantō in 1846, the aggregate wage bill would have been 17.5 *koku*: 39 percent of gross income. When one adds to this the wages paid to the day laborers who were hired from time to time and the cost of fertilizer and taxes amounting to no less than 30 percent of gross product, it is impossible to believe that the Hara farm was operating at a profit.[c] No wonder Ōishi Kyūkei (1721–94) fastened upon differential labor costs—owing to some holdings being worked entirely with family labor and others in part only?—to explain why some holdings were profitable and others were not![d]

In the long run rising labor costs proved an insupportable burden to large holders. Government of course did its best to reduce wages but all efforts were ineffectual; and at last, despairing of relief, large holders took the only course open to them and reduced the amount of labor they used. There was only one way of doing this without selling land, which went against the grain, or without working the same amount of land with less labor, which was uneconomic. It is not surprising therefore that it was adopted everywhere sooner or later. This solution was for the holder himself to farm less of his holding and to turn more of it over to tenants for a rent. A headman from Shinshū wrote early in the nineteenth century that all large holders were being

[c] On the Hara holding, see Chapter 6; for additional wage data, see *Fukuoka-ken nōchi kaikaku*, edited by Fukuoka-ken . . . iinkai, pp. 423–24.

[d] ("*Jikata hanreiroku*," NKSS, XXXI, 367–68.) Nor was he the only one. An agricultural treatise from Sado Island states: "Those whom we call superior farmers have a surplus at year's end, because they have enough family members of working age to cultivate properly and therefore get high yields. Those whom we call inferior farmers have no surplus at year's end, chiefly because they have too few family members of working age to farm satisfactorily and therefore get poor yields." ("Nōsho shūryaku," NKSS, IV, 445.) This same treatise quotes the *Nōgyō zensho* approvingly (p. 383): "The desire to cultivate more and more land is the sickness of the peasantry. If a person acquires too much land, he will be unable to cultivate it properly even if he knows how, owing to a scarcity of labor."

forced to adopt this measure to avoid ruin since, he said, wages now
exactly equaled the return on labor, so on every *hōkōnin* employed
there was a loss equal to the cost of his keep.[6] Headmen from other
parts of the country gave similar testimony.[6]

Although the need to cut labor costs was the main reason for adopting tenant farming, another was the desire to shift to tenants the burden
of other costs, which were also rising. Writing in 1721, Tanaka Kyūgu
tells us that one *ryo* used to buy 50 or 60 bales of dried fish for fertilizer
but would now buy no more than seven or eight, and as a result the
cost of fertilizer had soared to two *ryō* per *tan* of land! A spade which
once cost 300 *mon* now sold for nearly 900; horses that some years
back had brought one or two *ryō* per head now cost ten or more; and
so it was with straw, fodder, rope, leather, farm implements. Everything the farmer used was up in price,[7] and up considerably more than
the things he sold. This was perhaps in part due to the strength of
merchant guilds with their many ways of controlling prices; at any
rate the scissors movement of prices was a fact, widely complained of
by the peasants.[7]

But if the large holder could not support the burden of rising
production costs, one wonders how the small holder—especially the
tenant—managed. The answer to this question has several parts. For
one thing the small holder was far more willing, if need be, to absorb
higher costs at the expense of his standard of life. [Poverty was his
usual condition; but the large holder had a position to maintain, and a
taste for good living that he was tempted to indulge rather than curb
in this period of expanding wealth and luxury.] Unable to resist the
temptation, many wealthy peasants took concubines, frequented inns

---

[6] For instance, the headman of a Kantō village wrote in 1799 that ten years
earlier there were about 40 *hōkōnin* in his village, but now there were no more
than eight or ten. Families that had once kept eight or nine *hōkōnin* now had only
two or three. No wonder: the wages of *hōkōnin* varied from 3.5 to 4.0 *ryō* a
year, in addition to keep and clothing. Therefore a large holder, if he were now
to work his land exclusively with *hōkōnin*, would need between 30 and 40 *ryō*
annually for cash wages alone! No one could raise so large a sum without borrowing
at exorbitant interest, and hence tenant farming was the only recourse. (Nagahara
Keiji and Nagakura Tamotsu, "Kōshin-jikyūteki nōgyō chitai ni okeru murakata
jinushi no tenkai" (2), *SGZS*, LXIV, 2 (1955), 42–43; also Wakita, "Sekka
watasaku chitai," p. 48.)

[7] A typical complaint on this score, from a village in the Kinai: "In recent years,
the price of fertilizer has been high and that of grain very low; hence the farmers
are oppressed." (Imai and Yagi, *Hōken shakai no nōson*, p. 63.)

and hot springs, collected books and art objects, built fine houses, studied poetry, painting, and even the military arts.[9] In describing these
activities, contemporary writers may have exaggerated, but there can
be no doubt that spending among wealthy peasants made the survival
of large farming units more difficult.

Second, the small holder (or tenant) could substitute his own and
his family's labor for many of the high-cost factors that large holders
were obliged to buy because they worked with hired labor. This is one
of the points an Etchū writer at the end of the eighteenth century was
making in comparing holder cultivation (*tezukuri*) to tenant farming:[8]

> If one compares the advantage to the large holder of working his land with
> hired labor or entrusting it to tenants, the advantages of the latter method
> are obvious. Adoption of the former may even result in losses. Hence all
> large holders have adopted tenant cultivation. The reason for this is that the
> tenant by extraordinary diligence will cultivate twice as much land as hired
> labor, and he will provide his own fertilizer by the bitter work of gathering it.
> Thus he can make a bare living from a very small plot, even though he has
> no additional land of his own and no income from work outside his home.

If this solves one problem, however, it raises another more acute
one. Tenancy, it appears, did *not* reduce the amount of labor used in
farming but actually increased it. Why, then, did it ease rather than
aggravate the labor shortage in agriculture? The answer cannot be
that the tenant worked with family labor which, unlike hired labor,
could be held without paying it a competitive wage. [Family labor
(whether used or not) was compensated in food, clothing, shelter, sustenance in childhood, protection in sickness, provision for marriage,
security in old age. The value of these compensations, though impossible to express in terms of an annual wage, nevertheless had to total
roughly the equivalent of the *hōkōnin's* wages. If they did not, no
sense of obligation could have kept family members from becoming
hōkōnin; and, in fact, the family would have been quick to employ its
members in that way rather than at home.]So the question might be
rephrased: how was it that labor could be paid at a rate on small holdings that was prohibitive on large?

Part of the answer is that the technical changes taking place in farming were such as to favor small units over large. As already noted,

---

[9] See the vivid description of the style of life of this class of peasants in the
"Seji kemmon roku," pp. 48–49. (Translation in Thomas C. Smith, *Political
Change and Industrial Development in Japan*, Stanford, 1955, pp. 17–18.)

seed selection, commercial fertilizers, and many other innovations required a patience and devotion to the minutiae of cultivation that the nuclear family could provide but the large, unwieldy, and socially heterogeneous labor force could not. Owing to a certain congenital inefficiency, therefore, the labor costs of the larger unit were higher while its crop yields were lower. The disadvantage with respect to yields comes out clearly in the journal kept by a large holding family in the Kinai during the 1830's and 1840's. Time and again the author of the journal notes that crop yields were higher on the small holdings in the neighborhood than on his, which was worked partly with *hōkō-nin* and partly with labor hired by the day. No wonder that about this time he sharply reduced the amount of land he worked and turned more and more land over to tenants.[h]

In the ultimate triumph of the small farming unit over the large, however, technical efficiency in farming operations was probably less important than another factor. That was the unique ability of the family labor force to combine farming with other occupations: to supplement farm income with earnings from by-employments. In the early Tokugawa period this had been a negligible advantage because opportunities for nonfarm employment were scant. On *all* holdings, therefore, there was a prodigious waste of labor. Only for a few brief periods during the year could the labor force be fully employed; the rest of the time it was underemployed in varying degrees. How great was the resulting waste of labor is illustrated by a holding in Kōzuke Province which required only 185 man-days a year to work, although the holding family had available for work 900 man-days annually! Nor was this because the holding in question was smaller than family-size since, after all production costs and the family's food for the year were deducted, the holding showed a deficit of only one *ryō*.[g] Since there was underemployment of this order on all holdings in the seventeenth century, one understands the extent of the advantage that any class of holdings would enjoy that permitted this waste to be substantially reduced.[i]

[h] The proportion of the land worked by the holder himself dropped from 66.6 percent in 1821 to 27.7 percent in 1830, and to 19.7 percent in 1844! Such was the swiftness of adjustment once the fact was recognized that the small farming unit was more efficient. (Imai and Yagi, *Hōken shakai no nōson*, pp. 170–71.)

[i] Rural underemployment in this degree is characteristic of underdeveloped economies. Professor Tawney states that in the 1930's in some areas of China farm employment provided only about 100 days' work a year. The average cultivator in the Punjab in recent times worked no more than 150 days a year. Defoe de-

As trade and industry developed, providing new employment in rural areas, it became possible to reduce the waste of labor on family-size holdings. And this was possible on this class of holdings only: because the family was the only labor force that could work at the new employments and at the same time maintain its integrity as a farming unit. One does not have to look far for the reasons. The family alone could claim for the use of the farming unit the income of individual members of the labor force from nonagricultural sources—individual earnings from by-employments belonging to the family no less than the income of the group from farming. The large labor force had no such control over the individual earnings of many of its members, at least not in comparable degree. In fact, the large holder dared not even let *hōkōnin*, who in many cases were the most important element in his labor force, take temporary employment off the holding for fear of losing them permanently. Nor could he keep *hōkōnin* fully employed at home by combining agriculture with handicraft employment; most handicrafts resisted organization on a scale that would keep ten or a dozen persons employed at the same time; moreover they required a tradition of skill that could be nurtured in the family but not in a labor force whose members changed from year to year.[j]

Although the family was not able to achieve full employment, it greatly reduced underemployment and gained a decisive advantage over the larger farm unit. As a result, its per capita earnings were significantly greater; or, to put it differently, its agricultural labor costs were significantly lower, as can be seen by comparing the use of labor on small holdings and large. Writing in the early nineteenth century Ōkura Eijō illustrates how on small holdings the slack in farm employment was taken up by industrial employment in the paper-making areas:[k]

---

scribed those regions of England in his day where the only source of livelihood was farming as "unemployed counties." D. C. Coleman, "Labour in the English Economy of the Seventeenth Century," *Economic History Review*, VIII, 3, (1956), 288–89.

[j] The Robbaku family in Kyūshū, for example, employed five or six *hōkōnin* every year from 1858 to 1868. Ordinarily about half of the *hōkōnin* employed in any one year were new; although some *hōkōnin* served the family for several years in a row, none served throughout the 10-year period. (Fujimoto Takashi, "Bakumatsu Buzen ni okeru kisei jinushi no seikaku," *Keizaigaku kenkyū*, XIX, 2 (1953), 154.)

[k] The importance of industrial employments to the small holdings occasionally had disadvantages: "In recent years the prices [of raw materials] have so increased

Immediately after the winter wheat is planted between the 10th month and the year's end, paper making begins, and continues through the winter until the harvest begins in the spring. After that the new rice crop is planted and during the following months there are periodic weedings. Then, in the eighth month, paper making is started again and continues until the middle of the following month when it is time to commence the fall harvest.[10]

How different was the situation on the Hara holding about the same time! Despite the fact that the holding was located where various handicraft industries connected with sericulture flourished, Hara employed five *hōkōnin* but had no handicrafts to keep them busy during the lulls in farm work; as a result the diary records 370 man-days, not counting family members, spent in idleness during the year, merely for lack of work.[11] On each of these days a *hōkōnin* had of course to be paid and fed. What better illustration could there be of the inefficiency of the large holding? The real trouble with large holdings was not the high cost of labor they entailed, but inability to keep the labor force employed fully enough to pay competitive wages.

Although small-scale farming offered certain decisive advantages, small-scale ownership was not necessary to achieve them. Even large holders could avail themselves of the benefits of small-scale farming by letting land out to tenants. That this recourse saved large holders as a class can hardly be doubted; one has only to note the prior plight of such holders and their subsequent recovery. Far from liquidating their landed holdings, as they had threatened to do when the labor-cost problem first became acute, they greatly expanded them *after* discovering the solution to the problem in tenant cultivation. The accounts of one large holder in the Kinai reveal that he was losing money on that part of the holding he himself worked but was making a profit on that cultivated by tenants.[12]

Change in the mode of exploiting large holdings did not come suddenly; at first it did not even come as a result of conscious policy. There had always been some inconveniently located or infertile fields that were given over to tenant cultivation simply because the holder did not want to bother with them himself. Consequently, when he gave a

that paper cannot be made at a profit. The paper makers have suffered so that over half have been ruined, and as a result out of more than 265 *koku*'s worth of land [in this village] nearly half has fallen into the hands of merchants." (Kajinishi Mitsuhaya, "Kindai Echizen seishigyō to ryūtsū," *SKSG*, XIX, 1 (1953), 13.)

new field to a tenant in order to overcome a seemingly temporary labor shortage, he was not aware of making any significant change in the organization of his holding. In fact he had made none yet; this was merely a minor adjustment similar to ones made many times in the past—for instance when a horse died, or a son fell ill and could not work. And he made the adjustment now, tentatively, ready to retrace his steps if it proved disadvantageous. But as the labor shortage became more acute and took on the look of a permanent condition, he began dimly to sense that what he had at first thought a temporary measure in fact pointed the way to his long-run salvation.[l] Growing awareness of this under the unrelenting pressure of rising costs prompted him to transfer more and more fields to tenant cultivation, eventually with no thought of cultivating them again himself. The transfer continued bit by bit until, at last, the land he worked himself was reduced to an economic family-size unit and the rest of his holding was in rents.[m]

Existing historical materials do not give us a close enough view of this process to follow the transfer of land field by field, but they do reveal the general tendency on individual holdings. We find a family in Shinshū expanding its holdings from 5 to over 13 *chō* between 1590 and 1809, but in the same period reducing the amount of land it cultivated itself from 3.3258 to 2.337 *chō*. If, in shifting increasingly to tenant cultivation, the main aim was to reduce labor costs, the desired effect was achieved: the number of "*genin*" held by the family was reduced from 17 in 1665, to 12 in 1672, to 6 in 1682, and to 0 in 1814.[18] A holding in Kyūshū expanded from 3 *chō* in 1774 to 13 *chō* in 1854, but income from land worked by the holding family itself declined in

[l] As early as the latter part of the seventeenth century, some writers were aware of the comparative advantages of the family-size holding. Miyazaki Antei, author of the *Nōgyō zensho*, called the desire constantly to add to the size of holdings the sickness of the peasantry, arguing that large holdings could not be properly cultivated owing to the shortage of labor. Suyama Don'ō (1657–1732) made the same point in "Nōsho shūryaku," *NKSS*, IV, 445.

[m] It was critical to individual holders that they not be too slow in grasping the situation and making the shift to tenant cultivation. There is a strong hint of this in figures on farm management from a village in Tajima Province. Of four large holdings in this village in 1728, three were cultivated mainly by their respective holders and one was cultivated mainly by tenants (80 percent tenant cultivation). By 1783, of the first three, one had totally disappeared and its holder had become a tenant, and two had dwindled to insignificant size; whereas the one worked mainly by tenants had increased from 8.3 *chō* of arable to 10.1 *chō*. (Miyagawa Mitsuru, Mizokawa Kiichi, and Tanaka Yutaka, "Tajima ni okeru daitochi shoyū no keisei to hensen" (1), *Kyōtō jimbun kagaku kenkyūjo chōsa hōkoku*, 1 (1952), 11–14.)

every year for which we have data except one." And in Tōtōmi Province, the income of a family from rents increased between 1776 and 1871 from 181 to 335 bales of grain, while income from the land worked by the family itself dropped from 90 to 47 bales and its tenants increased in number from 22 to 62 (1788–1864).[14] Note that in all these cases the holding was being expanded while the shift to tenant cultivation proceeded: proof that the shift had striking economic advantages.

Repeated on many thousands of large holdings the country over, this slow silent revolution in farming left few aspects of village life untouched. No group felt the effects of the revolution more quickly or profoundly than the *nago* population, which was thus increasingly freed of labor services at the very time labor was becoming more and more valuable. Each field the *oyakata* transferred to tenant cultivation, the less need he had for labor services; the lighter labor services became as a consequence, the greater freedom the *nago* had to dispose of his own now valuable labor for his own benefit.

On one holding where a gradual shift to tenant cultivation was being made, for instance, total *nago* work-days declined from 208 in 1767 to 188 in 1783, a rather rapid reduction of about 1 percent a year.[15] It is impossible of course to trace the decline in the labor services of individual *nago*. But in the seventeenth century *nago* commonly did 40 or 50 work-days a year, while few did more than four or five by the mid-nineteenth century. There is no reason for thinking that such a decline did not take place in the labor services of individual *nago* families, though perhaps not in one generation.

Declining labor services would have brought few benefits to the *nago* had the decline been accompanied by a corresponding decline in farm employment for him. Trade and industry were expanding, but not rapidly enough to have compensated fully for such a loss, since the benefits that could be expected from the *oyakata* declined roughly in proportion with labor services. But *nago* in general suffered no drop in farm employment since much of the land transferred to tenant cultivation was transferred to them.

" The income from land worked by the family declined from 33.93 *koku* of grain in 1839 to 21.53 *koku* in 1864. It is not difficult to account for this drastic reduction when one sees the wage bill shown in the accounts of this family. The total annual wages paid to *hōkōnin* between 1858 and 1863 varied between 11.8 and 13.6 *koku* of grain (wages on this holding were paid entirely in kind)—or approximately one-half of the gross annual yield of the land worked by the family in these years! (Fujimoto, "Bakumatsu Buzen," pp. 136–38.)

Even before the shift to tenant cultivation began in earnest, many *nago* held a small amount of land in tenancy, usually because the quality or location of the fields in question made it unprofitable for the *oyakata* to work them himself.[16] Consequently the *oyakata* had no sense of novelty or fear of disturbing established relationships in assigning *nago* still more tenant land, especially since the individual plots were small and the assignments were at first temporary. But even as it became clear that they were to be permanent and that they *were* disruptive of existing relationships, the fact that a man was a *nago* did not disqualify him as a tenant in the *oyakata's* eyes. On the contrary, who would make a better one? The *oyakata* knew intimately the *nago's* abilities as a farmer, he lived in close proximity to him, and he had certain very powerful claims on his loyalty. Besides, the *oyakata* was ultimately responsible for the *nago's* livelihood: and if he were going to lighten that burden proportionately as he reduced labor services, it was essential that he give the *nago* additional means of support.

So both labor and land were transferred to the *nago*. The result was to alter the *nago's* relation to the land as well as to maintain his employment upon it. The land was now under his *management*. Although he was a tenant rather than a holder, he himself made many of the critical decisions of farming—what and when to plant, what seed to use, how much to spend on fertilizer, when to harvest. More important, despite receiving in some measure the *oyakata's* continued protection in adversity, he took many of the risks a holder did in the same hope of rewards. (See Chapter 10.)

And this was a favorable time to assume such risks. With crop yields and prices both rising, expectations in average years were better than ever before, and windfalls when good growing years coincided with high prices were possible. On the other hand improved farming methods and an expanding market made crop failures and unfavorable prices less frequent. Besides, farming was not the only source of *nago* income. In this period of labor scarcity and rising wages a family might earn a considerable sum annually from by-employments; to get a notion of how much, one has only to recall that in the last half-century of the Tokugawa period *hōkōnin*, by no means the highest paid labor of the time, earned as much as four *ryō* a year plus keep.

With the development of trade and industry and the opening of new opportunities to *nago* by the management of land as tenants, the *nago* class—as a legal category—disappeared over much of the country.

That is, *nago* disappeared from the various village registers as a separate group.° In all cases the underlying reason for this was that *nago* were achieving an impressive degree of economic and social autonomy; but the particular way *nago* came to be removed from the registers differed from one case to another. It occurred in at least three ways.

1. We have seen (Chapter 1) that in some areas the lord took account of the growing competence of *nago* by raising those who were most advanced in this respect into the holder class. This was done simply by registering as holdings the allotments to which the *nago* had strong customary claims anyway. The land thereafter belonged (so far as the lord was concerned) to the *nago* rather than being held by him from the *oyakata*. This had the advantage of bringing *nago* directly under the lord's administrative control, rather than leaving the *oyakata* to mediate between *nago* and the higher organs of government. This change was enforced sufficiently widely and over a long enough period of time to leave little doubt that it reflected a general institutional development and was not due merely to local or temporary conditions. It is probable, however, that only a small fraction of all *nago* were subject to this kind of change in registration.

2. The second method was somewhat rarer, but it is nonetheless important to notice since it testifies to a surprising ability on the part of *nago* to accumulate wealth under favoring circumstances. It consisted of the *nago* buying his allotment and personal freedom from the *oyakata*. Records survive of nine *nago* making such purchases from a single family in Shinshū in 1797–99,[17] and six of the group made individual payments of 20 *ryō* or more—a sum of money equivalent to about 56 bales of rice at the current price.[18] We do not know how these *nago* came into the possession of such large sums, but it is at least suggestive that a large part of this *oyakata's* holding was cultivated by tenants, and that it was located in the Ina valley, an area where silk

---

° Occasionally one can follow the decline in number of *nago* through village population registers. In a village in Chikuzen Province, Kyūshū, for instance, there was a decline from 27 families in 1846, to 21 in 1846, to 9 in 1860. (*Fukuoka nōchi kaikaku*, pp. 4–8.) In a Shinshū village, in central Honshū, the decline was already well under way in the eighteenth century, the number of *nago* families falling from 25 in 1755 to 2 in 1807; but then for some reason the number increased to 4 in 1847. (Furushima, *Kinsei Nihon nōgyō*, p. 489.) To the northeast, in Echigo Province, a tiny hamlet composed of 2 holdings and 3 *nago* families in 1680 had grown by 1812 to 7 holdings and 1 *nago* family. (Kitajima Masamoto, "Echigo sankan chitai ni okeru junsui hōkensei no kōzō," *SGZS*, LIX, 6 (1950), 16–17.)

reeling, cotton ginning, and the transport industry afforded exceptional opportunities for by-employment. As to the purpose of the payments, the surviving documents recording the purchase leave no doubt: each payment gave the *nago* title to his allotment and made him "a holder like all other holders in the village."

Before considering still another way that *nago* escaped the confines of their class, we must repeat a distinction mentioned much earlier. *Nago* status and social status were not identical; legally either a person was a *nago* or he was not, whereas socially there was no such clear dividing line but rather a continuum of varying degrees of dependence on (or independence of) an *oyakata*. One therefore could cross the legal boundary into the holder class but continue to stand at a place on the scale of dependence-independence that made one socially a *nago*.

Nago status in this sense—as a social, psychological, and economic fact—often continued to be recognized in the village long after the corresponding legal status had disappeared. Earlier we noted that there were numerous and widely scattered cases of persons who were listed as holders in the land registers but as "*nago*" in less official documents.[p] We must not imagine this indicated nothing more than the survival of a name; the name survived precisely because the reality of personal subordination to the *oyakata* persisted. This is eloquently illustrated by the following document from Shinshū, which is addressed to "Tomosaemon, our ancient master," and signed by three *nago* who had become holders in the legal sense:[19]

For generations past we have been your hereditary *kerai* [*nago*]. Previously a payment for land and person [freedom] was made to your ancestor, and we became like other holders in the village. For this we are deeply grateful. Our parents sincerely served you in all respects; but we three for 13 years past, having misunderstood things, were willful on numerous occasions, and therefore have been brought to account by you [as village headman]. Although we have no excuse for our behavior as regards our past misdeeds, we appealed to you through the honorable one in retirement [the headman's father?], and you granted forgiveness. For this we are very grateful. As was done in generations past, we will henceforth present a slight thing as a gift on the second day of the first month, and we will in no wise violate

[p] For example, a document of 1846 from the village just cited, in which nine *nago* bought their freedom in 1797–99, states that 60 holders in the village at that date were descended from *nago*. Thus *nago* origins were not soon forgotten. And in a neighboring village holders who descended from *nago* were not known simply as "holders" (*hyakushō*), but as "freed holders" (*ukebyakushō*). (Furushima Toshio and Sekijima Hisao, *Yōeki rōdōsei no hōkai katei*, Tokyo, 1938, p. 232.)

propriety toward you in the slightest detail. The foregoing is to make sure
for the future.
12th month 1807

Despite being holders, the three signators were clearly very far from
being free of obligations to an *oyakata*.

3. It is probable that relatively few *nago* actually attained holder
status at all. Yet *nago* did generally disappear in both the legal and
social senses, and by the late nineteenth century only vestiges of the
class remained in a few scattered places. This suggests that there was
a way of escaping *nago* legal status that did not entail becoming a
holder first: that is, by attaining such a degree of economic and social
autonomy as a tenant farmer that the notion of *nago* legal status became
essentially meaningless and fell eventually into complete disuse.

Professor Ariga seems to me to have traced the broad outlines
of this process through surviving forms of labor service.[20] He has
argued most convincingly that the three major forms of labor service represent successive stages in the evolution of *oyakata-nago* relations from dependence to autonomy. They are as follows: (1) indefinite or unlimited labor services; (2) fixed labor services limited
to so many work-days a year; (3) labor services compensated by de-
ducting the value of each work-day from rent paid on tenant land. As
we saw in Chapter 3, unlimited labor services represented a stage
when the *nago* was scarcely more than an extension of the *oyakata*
family; no clear dividing line was then drawn between his and the
oyakata's economies, and resources flowed continuously from one to the
other without close accounting or specified limits. This relationship
changed under the influence of an expanding money economy.

The first notable change in labor services took the form of limiting
them to a specified number of work-days a year, a change reflecting
the gradual shift to tenant cultivation on the *oyakata* holding, and the
simultaneous emergence of the *nago* as a tenant farmer. The shift to
tenant cultivation had the effect of reducing the *oyakata's* labor requirements and increasing the *nago's*; this made it not only possible but im-
perative to limit labor services, for there was no other way of protect-
ing the *nago* against excessive or untimely demands on his labor by
the *oyakata* that might seriously interfere with his farming.[q] The *oya-*

---

[q] Another reason for the limitation from the viewpoint of the *nago*, of course,
was that by-employments were increasingly available, and consequently every work-
day he did for the *oyakata* at certain times meant the loss of a day's wages.

Peasant women threshing grain. One woman on the right is stripping away grain from the stalk with a *semba-koki* while the woman behind her is using the chopstick technique (*koki-hashi*) for the same purpose. (*Hyakunin jorō shinasadame.*)

kata, whose income now came increasingly from rents, was as interested in avoiding this event as the *nago* himself. The limitation therefore came about painlessly, in most cases probably even without any specific agreement: when year after year the *oyakata* asked for no more than a certain number of work-days during the year, an understanding eventually grew up that he would ask for no more. This understanding reflected the increasing separateness of the respective economies of *oyakata* and *nago,* since with it the flow of resources back and forth between them was no longer unrestricted, but limited to specified quantities.

Another result of the increasing shift of the *oyakata* to tenant cultivation was to interpose a new and potentially explosive issue between *oyakata* and *nago* in the form of rent. Since the *oyakata's* income now came increasingly from rent, and the *nago's* increasingly from the land he rented, the most direct way either could expand his income was by altering the rent to the disadvantage of the other. At this stage of the evolving relationship there was little overt conflict over this issue; the obligation to solidarity was still too strong, the respective economies were still too closely integrated, and relations between the two were too unequal to permit an open breach. An indication of this is that labor services, though now limited, were not yet regarded as an economic payment but still as the expression of a binding system of reciprocity.

The way was now prepared, however, for labor services to *become* a rent. Such services being now determinate, they could and did tend to be more and more thought of as constituting a payment for the allotment and dwelling the *oyakata* provided, a notion that was quite impossible so long as labor services were unlimited as to amount. Still, the notion of payment was exceedingly general, and no attempt was made to change the number of work-days from the level set by custom to a number corresponding to the market value of the *nago's* dwelling and allotment. Labor services finally became a rent when (just as on the land held as a tenant) the *nago* was obliged to pay a rent in money or kind on his dwelling and allotment, and in return his work-days were compensated at the prevailing wage rate, their value being deducted from rent at the end of the year.

When this occurred we can no longer properly speak of labor services. For labor services had now lost their social meaning and become mere substitutes for payments in money or kind. This of course was much more than a change in the character of labor services: it bespoke as well a transformation of the relations of the persons who received and gave them. No longer were these persons bound to one another by powerful mutual obligations rooted in cooperative farming. Cooperation on anything like the old scale had disappeared, and the two parties now stood in a relationship impersonal to such a degree that one would no longer give the other so much as a day's labor without specific compensation.

By this time *nago* in the social sense had ceased to exist, and the term must simply have lapsed in all usages for lack of a referent. For although *nago* social status might persist after the legal status had disappeared, the reverse case was hardly possible. Once the *nago* had become economically and socially an autonomous agent, it was impossible to treat him legally any longer as a *nago*—that is as the *oyakata's* ward.

10

THE DECLINE OF THE COOPERATIVE GROUP

In Chapter 4 it was said that, except from a legal viewpoint, *oyakata-nago* relations differed in degree but not in kind from those between large and small holders. Before the market began to perform any important function in most communities, agriculture was organized through cooperative groups. Each group consisted of a number of farming units of different size, some composed entirely of holdings but many of both holdings and *nago* allotments. In either case cooperation within the group was mainly between the largest unit, which stood at the center and integrated the functions of the group, and the small units whose individual and collective economies were complementary to it. The chief differences between one small unit and another were size and closeness of integration with the main unit, not whether the holding families were *nago* or holders. *Nago* generally represented the extreme of both smallness and closeness, but they were not sharply distinguished from many holders in either respect.

The changes traced in the previous chapter in the character of *oyakata-nago* relations are but one instance, though admittedly the most striking one, of the general weakening of the role of cooperation and obligation in farming. For one thing, the cooperative group as a whole generally could not survive in full vigor the disintegration of the *oyakata-nago* relations at its core. But, equally important, economic relations between large and small holders were being altered at the same time as those between *oyakata* and *nago*. In this chapter we shall first note some of the most important reasons for this, and then some of the new economic relations that were growing up in place of cooperation; finally we shall consider evidence of the decline of cooperative groups as units.

The shift to tenant cultivation on large holdings altered their economic relations with small holders scarcely less radically than with *nago*. Some large holders who had no *nago* turned tenant land over to small holders exclusively; but even those with *nago* usually surrendered some land to dependent holders. The same qualities recommended both dependent holders and *nago* as tenants, for in a society in which the sense of legal right was exceedingly weak, kinlike obligations were the best possible guarantee of good faith in any transaction. Besides, a main family was bound to help its branches when possible, and there was no doubt usually some desire to keep the use of land in the lineage insofar as possible. If the branch became increasingly independent as a result of the addition to the land it managed, no loss was suffered by the main family. Quite the opposite: it was thereby relieved of some of its responsibilities toward the branch at a time when it needed less and less labor from it.

As more and more land was given over to tenants, the largest farming units—as distinct from units of ownership—became smaller and the smallest ones were steadily enlarged, tending to reduce the scope of cooperation among farming units, since cooperation depended very much on differences of scale: on the different ratios at which factors were combined on holdings of different size, especially on those at opposite ends of the scale.[1] These differences had once been very great, with farms of three or four *chō* alongside others a tenth or twentieth that size. But by the late Tokugawa period, when working farms of more than one and a half *chō* were becoming rare in the most advanced areas, differences of scale were much less significant.[2] Farms (though *not* holdings, if the latter term may be used here to indicate the ownership as opposed to the management of land) were approaching something like uniform family size, and there was consequently about the same amount of land and capital per adult worker on each. The uniformity can be exaggerated, of course, but the leveling tendency was unmistakable, and to a far greater extent than in the past farms tended to have the same kind of resources in roughly the same ratios.

Take labor, for instance. The more land the small holder brought under his management by adding tenant land to what he already had, the less surplus labor he had from farming to give the large holder; and he had even less if he also worked part time for wages. Any labor he nevertheless gave he was likely now to resent since the resulting loss to him was calculable. But since at the same time the large holder needed less labor, there was unlikely to be serious trouble over the matter; by tacit agreement the help given dwindled to one or two days at both planting and harvest, and even that was often more for form's sake than anything else.

A similar development occurred with respect to capital. As the large holder gradually divested himself of the burden of cultivation, his stock of capital equipment naturally dwindled. By selling off items of capital he no longer needed, or merely by failing to replace items as they wore out, he in time found himself with only the equipment required for the small-scale farming he now practiced. In the meanwhile he continued to loan such animals and implements to dependents as he could; but the time came when he could no longer perform this important service, and his productive function in the cooperative grouping lapsed. Small farming units, however, had been adding capital as the amount of land under their management increased, and they stood less and less in need of such assistance.

Statistics on the ownership of draught animals in the late Tokugawa period give some hint of the growing equality in the distribution of capital. Animals were still far from equally distributed since there were fewer animals than families in most villages, and the difference between having one animal and none was enormous. But there was far greater equality than there had been earlier when one or two families in a village had commonly owned three or four animals each and together accounted for a large proportion of all the animals in the village; now a family rarely owned more than one animal.[3]

It was not only the transfer of the management of land that reduced cooperation between large and small holders; contemporaneous technical changes in farming tended to produce this same result. On balance technical innovations spread labor demand in farming over the year more evenly than before, not only reducing somewhat the annual peaks but also raising the intervening troughs. This had the effect of reducing the labor shortage on the large holding, and of making it more difficult for the small holder to give labor during the peak periods by postponing his own work to a slack season.

Four technical innovations, all previously mentioned (Chapter 7), altered the annual curve of labor demand most significantly. Commercial fertilizers were perhaps the most important of the four, since they made it possible to eliminate (or reduce) the work of gathering grass and leaves on the mountainside and carrying them to the fields to trample into the soil, thus saving an enormous amount of labor at the planting. A second innovation took the form of a new thrasher called the *semba-koki* which effected a similar saving of labor at the harvest. The two highest annual peaks of labor demand were therefore notably flattened out. At the same time other innovations were filling the intervening labor troughs with productive employment. Multiple cropping, which was itself the result of a series of other innovations, was probably the most important in this respect since it for

LABOR DEMAND ON A HOLDING IN SHINSHŪ IN 1823

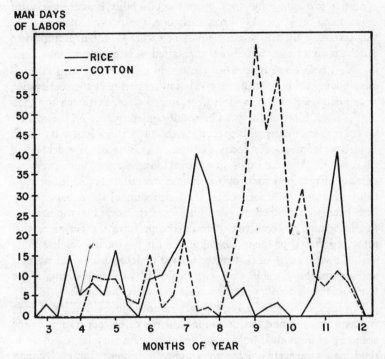

Data from Furushima and Nagahara, *Shōhin seisan to kisei jinushi*, p. 82.

the first time provided farm employment during the winter months. Almost as important, however, was the increasing range of choice in crop patterns that development of the market made possible by relieving the peasant of the necessity of selecting crops by reference to his own immediate needs. Since the peaks of labor demand of individual crops fell at different times, the peasant could now dovetail the peaks and troughs. The graph shows how this was done with rice and cotton on a Kinai holding in 1823, illustrating how effective a device it could be for smoothing out the curve of labor demand.

For a variety of reasons, therefore, the area of possible cooperation among families became narrower as time passed; at the same time, owing to increasing specialization, most holdings were less and less nearly self-sufficient. New needs were being created that could not be met as some of the older ones still could, within the narrow circle of a group of families or even of a village. As the market developed, therefore, it usurped more and more of the economic functions of the co-operative grouping; and even when the possibility remained open of overcoming shortages by direct exchange, the peasant, now that he was becoming used to another mode of exchange, often preferred to purchase what he needed since that entailed no later obligation in kind.

Well before the nineteenth century in many areas, farm families were buying all or part of the goods and services that the cooperative group had once provided—fertilizer, firewood, labor, thatch for roofing, lumber, food, clothing. The resulting dependence on the market was of course a matter of degree, not an absolute condition, and though far from complete even today (Chapter 13), it is steadily deepening everywhere. A recent example is the rapid replacement in the past few decades of thatched roofs by tile in many rural areas. As it happens, this is also an illustration of how the functioning of the group, having first been undermined by declining opportunities for cooperation, finally became so weak that it could not perform the functions that remained to it. For the increasing use of tile for roofing has less to do with the superiority of that material over thatch, which is far warmer and surprisingly durable, than with the inability of families any longer to mobilize sufficient cooperative labor to replace the thatch.[a]

Occasionally some maverick fact come upon by accident seems suddenly to illumine the declining importance of cooperation in the economy of individual holdings. The diary of a very large holder in the Kinai in the early nineteenth century, for instance, contains numerous entries recording the rental of work animals whose hire he paid in money.[4] That so large a holder should have been obliged regularly to hire animals suggests, first, how drastically capital had been reduced on large holdings in some places, and, second, how restricted cooperative exchange had become as a result, since apparently no neighbor came forward on these occasions to loan him an animal.

One must be careful, however, not to read into such indications the complete denial of cooperation. An illustration of the danger of such a conclusion is provided by the account books of a large holder in Aki Province. The accounts reveal unmistakably that wage labor hired by the day was replacing cooperative labor on the holding,[b] and one might

[a] It is at least partly for this reason that thatch is especially common in areas such as Tōhoku where cooperative groups are strongest, and comparatively rare in areas where cooperation is weak, such for example as the Kinai.

[b] The accounts show three kinds of labor in addition to family labor used on the holding: labor services (*tema*), labor exchanged equally for other labor (*gōriki*), and wage labor hired by the day (*hiyatoi*). The first two, both cooperative forms

conclude that the spirit of cooperation in the village was dead. Then
the following entry in 1856 occurs:[5] "Since my bullock died this year,
the October planting of wheat was delayed 13 days, when members of
the group (*kōchū*) came to help me." This is a useful reminder that
cooperation did not utterly disappear, however autonomous and self-
interested peasant families seemed to have become.[c] It continued to
be essential to maintenance of the irrigation system, the allocation of
water, the management of common land, and the upkeep of roads and
other village property. But it had ceased to provide the social framework for tillage and was no longer an everyday experience.

It is difficult to follow the decline of cooperation among holders
in satisfactory detail. Having no administrative significance, the facts
of cooperation were not recorded in any systematic way; but a number of institutions closely tied to cooperation changed form as cooperation declined, leaving a record of the process. One of these was the
large family that stood at the center of a cluster of cooperating peasant
families.

Some attention was given in Chapter 1 to the character of such
families in the seventeenth century. Reflecting the labor requirements
of large farming units under conditions approaching self-sufficiency,
these groups were often extended families composed not only of affines
and cognates but also of persons unrelated to the family head by either
blood or marriage. Numbering between ten and forty members and
three to six or so married couples, these large families overflowed by
conjugal groups from a main dwelling into a complex of buildings
disposed around a central compound.

At different times in different places as cooperative farming declined these great families disappeared, except as occasional and tran-
sient survivals. They did so by breaking up into the nuclear families
immanent in them. The immediate cause of this was that the extended
family, periodically forced to check its growth by extruding conjugal
groups then established as branch families, found itself obliged to re-

---

of labor, were increasingly replaced by day labor with the passage of time. In view
of this evidence of development, it is not surprising that rice yields on the holding
were rising and that cash crops were grown, including tea, cotton, and indigo—
from all of which it is evident that the holder was a progressive farmer and that his
farming was highly commercialized. (Gotō Yōichi, "Jūkuseiki San'yōsuji nōson
ni okeru funō keiei no seikaku," *SGZS*, LXIII, 7 (1954), 49, 52, 54–55.)

[c] Another reminder is encountered in the report of a headman from a village in
Tosa in 1857. (Koseki, "Ansei 4-nen," pp. 123–24.)

peat this process more rapidly than new conjugal groups formed within it. More basic, however, were the circumstances that forced such rapid segmentation.

Three circumstances were mainly responsible for this. Chief of these was the shift on large holdings to tenant cultivation; as that occurred, the amount of land worked by the family and, accordingly, its labor requirements were drastically reduced. It consequently became an advantage also to reduce the size of the family, to eliminate members whose labor was no longer required. This could be done only by establishing new branch families, which required that the branch be given the minimum means of support lest there be public criticism of the main family for niggardliness and lack of proper feeling.[d] The branch was therefore given land in ownership or tenancy or both, but the amount of land given in ownership was very limited indeed, since otherwise the advantages to the main family of founding the branch would largely be lost.

The other two circumstances explain why the grant of land in ownership could be kept so small and still serve the purpose of making the new branch family self-supporting. One was the steadily increasing productivity of the soil as the result of improved methods of farming. How rapid this increase was generally is difficult to say, but it was as great as 1 percent per annum over very long periods on some holdings (Chapter 7); during a century this rate would reduce by one-half the amount of land required to support a family of constant size. The second factor was the growth of by-employments.[e] Although

[d] The result was not only an increase in the number of families and a diminution of their average size (as is noted later in the text), but also an increase in the number of holdings and a diminution of their average size. Thus, holdings in a village in Shinshū increased from 42 in 1595 to 113 in 1870, with the increase being almost entirely in holdings under five *koku* yield. (Aoki Takahisa, "Kita Shinano ni okeru Bunroku kenchi," *SGZS*, LXIII, 1 (1954), 66.) And in a village in Izumi Province, holdings increased from 19 in 1597 to 50 in 1693, but average size declined from 13.20 to 6.23 *tan*. (Miyagawa, "Taikō kenchi" (4), p. 34.) Many other illustrations might be cited.

[e] In a study of four widely scattered villages (*buraku*) in 1951, Professor Fukutake found: "In every area [Akita, Ibaraki, Okayama, and Saga Prefectures], the percentage of non-specialist farmers [farm households combining farming with other occupations] is larger among non-inherited farm families than among inherited farm families. . . . This reflects the practice followed in the establishment of new families; i.e., to give very small property to new families." "Non-inherited" farm family here means one founded by its present head, as opposed to those founded in an earlier generation and inherited by their present heads. (Fukutake Tadashi, *Family System and Population of Farming Communities in Japan*, The Population Problems Research Council, Mainichi Newspapers, Tokyo, 1952, pp. 8–9.)

their importance varied greatly from one place to another, in some areas they contributed no less than higher yields to reducing the size of the minimum farm. Still another factor might be mentioned: the assignment of land in tenancy to the branch. This obviously added to the branch family's income without diminishing the main family's resources in land or even very much its income; but this factor may be considered as implicit in the other two—by-employments and high yields—because, without them, no tenant could have paid the prevailing high rent.

The breakup of the large extended family may be followed in some places in considerable detail through the population registers. This is illustrated by comparing the population registers of a Shinshū village for 1755 and 1830. The comparison reveals three striking changes in the village between the two dates. First, the total number of families in the village increased from 30 to 83; second, the average family size declined from 12.3 to 3.8 members; third, the average number of married couples per family declined from 3.3 to 1.20. All of these changes, moreover, were effected primarily by changes in the largest families.[1] Other illustration's might be cited showing that the extended family in all parts of the country was breaking up into a number of small nuclear families.[2] Everywhere the process was similar—only the pace was notably different from one place to another.

One infers that the breakup of the extended family mirrors the declining coherence and importance of the group of cooperating families: the same disintegrative forces were at work on both groups, but even more destructively on the larger one since it was looser to begin with. Occasionally, however, one glimpses directly the disintegration of the larger group (or a part of it). This is possible because in some

[1] In 1755, 19 families, or 63 percent of all families, had 10 or more members and the largest family in the village had 24 members; in 1830, the largest family had 8 members. (Tōdai kokushi kenkyūshitsu . . . chōsakai, "Shinshū Ochiai chōsa hōkoku," *SGZS*, LX, 2 (1951), 64.)

[2] For instance, the number of families in a village in Higo Province increased from 23 to 81 between 1663 and 1856, the average size declining from 8.6 to 4.2 members. In 1663, 9 families had 9 or more members and 3 had as many as 13, but in 1856 only 2 families had as many as 8 members. (Harada Toshimaru, "Higohan nōson ni okeru kazoku no kōsei," *Ōita daigaku keizai ronshū*, II, 2 (1951), 130.)

Or to give an example showing that the same trend was to be found in the Kinai, only earlier: in a village in Ōmi Province, the number of families containing married couples not in direct line of descent declined from 20 percent of all families to zero between 1654 and 1689. (Miyagawa Mitsuru, "Taikō kenchi to kazoku kōsei" (3), *Hisutoria*, 10 (1954), 39.)

places a group of cooperating families was registered as a single large family in the population register: that is, as a result of successive partitionings several actual families had appeared where there had been one before, but instead of being registered separately they continued to be listed as one family. They were therefore actually a cooperative grouping of families, or at least part of such a grouping. As the frequency and importance of cooperation among the constituent families declined, however, it became increasingly unrealistic to group them together as one family in the population registers; and at some point this fact was abruptly recognized and the families in the group were separately registered. The change in the average size of registered families was then very sudden. The *average* size in a certain Shinshū village, for instance, ran consistently between 12 and 14 persons from 1783 to 1823; but in the two years between 1823 and 1825 it dropped from 12.7 to 5.3, and it remained at about the latter figure down to the last available register in 1865. Here we see reflected the belated administrative recognition of the dissolution of cooperative groups, and not merely the breakup of a number of extended families as appears on the surface.[6]

The decline of cooperation was but one reason for the decline of the cooperative group; another was that new types of economic relationships were growing up, often between members of the same cooperative group. At least two characteristics made these new relationships difficult to reconcile with the old ones. First, they were not relationships of indefinite term expected to go on and on, but relations entered into for the convenience of the moment, so that instead of being the guide lines of a way of life, they were episodes that passed and were quickly forgotten. Second, they were market transactions whose central concern—short-term personal advantage—tended to push all other considerations into the background.

It is significant that these new economic relationships grew up especially between members of different economic classes, which was precisely the special province of the old relationships. Just as with *oyakata-nago* relations, wage relations, for instance, never (or rarely ever) occurred between members of the same economic class. One must therefore envisage the new relationships as overlapping, rather than merely supplementing or supplanting, older relations based on mutuality. In the overlapping, however, they touched the older relations with destructive effect.

An excellent example is the industrial wage relationship. In rural areas this relationship developed early and perhaps most extensively in the brewing industry. A highly competitive industry producing mainly for urban consumption, and further requiring heavy and expensive equipment and a large labor force, it was among the most capital-intensive of the time, and size of individual firms was relatively large. Although the relations of workers and owners in the industry were certainly not utterly devoid of the personal element, they had more of self-seeking than mutuality about them, although they often occurred between people who were already bound in other activities by an older type of relationship.

Owners were typically large landholders as well as industrialists, perhaps in order to assure an adequate supply of rice for *sake* making. They usually exploited most of their land by tenant cultivation; and since *sake* making was confined to the winter months, they often recruited at least part of their industrial labor force from local people, including their own tenants. Landlord-tenant relations, which still carried much of the sentimental freight of *oyakata-nago* relations, must have suffered some loss of the old feeling as a result. Wage disputes often occurred in the industry, and some of the bitterness engendered during them could scarcely have failed to carry over into agrarian relations. No doubt both parties could compartmentalize their behavior to some extent, acting differently in their different relationships, but there was a limit to this since the relationships themselves were not completely separable. For instance, mutuality required that a landlord reduce or waive the tenant's rent in especially bad growing years; but to do so was exceedingly difficult in this case because the tenant's wage for industrial work during the winter took the form of a reduction in his rent in kind as a tenant the following summer. Therefore if the brewer-landlord reduced rent, he might not have enough income left to pay wages in kind; and even if he did, he might not have enough also to serve as raw materials for his brewing operations the following winter.[7]

Commercial relations were also growing up alongside the older relations between large and small holders. Generally, the larger landholders were the merchants of the village, and in this role they advanced the peasant credit against his crop, bought up his surplus for shipment to the nearest market, imported the goods he needed from the outside, and sold them in the village. There were innumerable variants on these relationships, but perhaps one example will illustrate the spirit of a great many of them.

The oil industry, which pressed oil from vegetables and cotton seed in great quantities for cooking and lighting in the Tokugawa period, centered in the Kinai. It was favored in this region by the importance of cotton as a crop, by the opportunity the area afforded of planting vegetables in the winter following a summer rice crop, and by the presence of a large urban market nearby in Osaka and Kyoto. Large presses, many of them operated by water power, were scattered through the villages of the Kinai, and they were generally owned by large holders who produced oil on a scale requiring the purchase of raw materials from the smaller holders of their own and neighboring villages. Between the buyers and the sellers there were sometimes landlord-tenant relations or other types of older cooperative relations. Whatever remained of such relations must have been severely damaged by the aggressive spirit of the newer relationship. As illustration: the oil maker would often advance a sum of money to the small holder (or tenant) against the latter's crop, virtually assuring delivery of it into his own hands by interest charges that ran as high as 10 percent per month.[h] This was with a vengeance taxing the market what it would bear!

Economic relationships based on undisguised self-interest were not limited to trade and industry; in time they appeared in agriculture itself. As we have seen, wage labor was slowly supplanting in agriculture other types of labor that were less free but more personal. Often the two types of labor existed side by side: and not only were they found at the same time and place—in the same village and even on the same holding—but frequently the same persons were at the same time parties to both.

An especially vivid instance of this has recently been brought to light by the researches of a group of scholars on Kemuyama village in Iwate Prefecture.[8] A group of five families in this village constituted the inner nucleus of at least one surviving cooperative group there. One of the five was a large landlord family which nevertheless continued to work considerable land itself (3.3 *chō* of the 5.95 of arable it owned), and the other four were tenants of this family. Two

---

[h] An undated document which today would be called a mortgage agreement illustrates the spirit of at least many of these loans: "The loan is to be repaid without fail and in its entirety by the coming July. All my household possessions and the vegetables now under cultivation, I pledge without exception as surety to guarantee repayment. In the event that the vegetables are insufficient for the purpose, my household possessions may be sold and the money they bring applied to payment of the loan." (Quoted by Furushima Toshio, "Edo jidai ni okeru Kinai nōgyō to kisei jinushi—Yamashiro no kuni Otokuni-gun Kuga-mura ni okeru kosakuryō no seikaku," *RGKK*, 144 (1950), 10.)

of the tenants were also consanguine branches of the first family; and the other two held dwellings as well as land from it—a fact hinting strongly at *nago* status. All four received various though somewhat different benefits from their relationship with the landlord family. The list included the loan of farm tools from time to time, the provision of rice seedlings from the landlord's beds, the loan of money or rice in case of need, lower rent in bad growing years, gifts in the form of cast-off clothing, compost from the landlord's mountain land, and irrigation rights.

All four families performed labor for the landlord—an average of 13 man-days and one horse-day each in 1925. The work-days, however, were not all functions of the same relationship. The landlord's records for 1925 show that each of the four families did three different types of labor for him. Quantitatively most important was *suke*, or labor services; and it was presumably because this type of labor was limited to so many work-days a year that the other two types were required. One of these was *yui*—labor given in exactly equal exchange, day for day, for other labor. Clearly, the limits of labor services having been reached, recourse was had to this egalitarian though still traditional type of cooperation, showing that the hierarchical structure of cooperation between the families in question was weakening. The last type of labor was apparently used only when the potentialities of equal exchange were also exhausted, either because the four families needed no more labor from the landlord or because the landlord could give no more in exchange. This last type was wage labor, for the landlord paid the four families wages for every day they worked for him after he had used up the first two types of labor. Thus wage labor developed at the very heart of a group of families, linking as employer and employees individuals still joined in cooperative relations.

New market-type relationships, then, were overlying as well as supplanting the older relations based on solidarity and mutuality, infusing them with a divisive spirit of egoism and even strife. Or at least one may suppose so, if the quality of one social experience affects a person's attitude toward other experiences. Admittedly it is difficult to understand how the transference is made, but it is at least possible to observe the results of it. The transfer was so slow and subtle few could even have been aware it was taking place; but the change left its mark on at least one very important agrarian institution which recorded its stages.

The institution was tenancy: a halfway house between cooperative and individualistic farming. Developing very gradually out of the traditional mode of cultivation based on group effort (*tezukuri*), tenancy transformed *oyakata* and *nago* into landlord and tenant, and in doing so carried along some of the modes and sentiments of cooperation. But, as market values penetrated ever more deeply into the complex network of agrarian relations, the spirit and forms of tenancy changed; mutuality between landlord and tenant increasingly gave way to competition.

This change is reflected, in its several stages, in the complex of customs and agreements that governed the many issues between landlord and tenant—such as water rights, improvement of the soil, seed, fertilizer, buildings, tools, tenure, and social relations. No group of customs concerning any one aspect of tenancy reflected fully the changing character of the institution as a whole, but those customs governing rent—its form, amount, and manner of payment—probably revealed the essential changes more fully than others, since they were undoubtedly the most important, and certainly the most sensitive to changes in economic attitudes.

A massive government survey of tenancy practices originally published in 1921 revealed five distinct types of rent extant at that time.[9] Buried in this mass of data concerning diverse practices relating to tenancy, these variations were looked upon as representing little more than intriguing local idiosyncrasies until Professor Ariga, who on other occasions also has turned his ethnological interests to the aims of history, brilliantly showed that at least the first three types represented successive evolutionary stages. Although instances of the last two were rare at the time of the survey, which perhaps caused Professor Ariga to give them but little attention, they clearly represent further stages just then emerging.[10]

The five types of rent were: (1) *kariwake*, or sharecropping, under which rent was a percentage of the tenant's crop; (2) *kemmi*, under which rent was paid in kind, but instead of being a fixed percentage of the crop, the percentage was fixed annually after an estimate of the coming harvest was made; (3) *jōmen*, which was a stipulated payment in kind rather than a percentage of the harvest and was fixed for a period of about five years at a time instead of annually; (4) *daikin*, a pseudo-money rent fixed in kind (for a number of years, like *jōmen*), but actually paid in money; (5) a real money rent that was fixed as well as paid in money. Let us now trace the evolution of landlord-tenant relations through these five types of rent, in order to glimpse the shift to individualistic values *within* a cooperative relationship.

Kariwake, or sharecropping, was the most primitive type of rent; it occurred mainly in relatively backward areas, where crop yields were low and farm income could not be significantly supplemented by earnings from other employments. Under this form of rent the landlord shared the risks of farming with the tenant inasmuch as his share of the crop declined in proportion to any drop in crop yields; but the average rent for this reason was about 20 or 30 percent higher (in relation to crop yields) than other types of rent. *Kariwake* thus not only was a product of impoverished and backward farming but also tended to keep the tenant and his farming poor.

Since the landlord shared with the tenant the risks of farming to a greater extent than under other types of rent, he naturally exercised a firmer and more detailed supervision over the tenant's farming decisions and even his daily routine of work, advising him what crops to sow, what fertilizers to use, when to plant and harvest. He also contributed capital from time to time to improve the tenant's yields—after all, yields were shared—and he might even contribute labor if that was necessary to avoid a drop in yields. These functions obviously required that the landlord himself be an active farmer. Otherwise he would not have equipment to loan, knowledge to supervise the tenant intelligently, or the skill or labor to cut, transport, and thresh his own share of the crop after it was divided, according to common *kariwake* practice, as it stood ripening in the fields; and he would not be able to make use of the straw and chaff that were the chief reasons for dividing the crop at this time rather than after the harvest. Virtually every distinctive feature of *kariwake*—poverty, technical backwardness, dearth of accompanying by-employments, and the active role of the landlord—suggests therefore that it represented the first stage of the evolution of tenancy from cultivation by the holder (*tezukuri*).

Kemmi marked a considerable advance over *kariwake,* and its adoption was both a stimulus to better farming and a sign of it. Because it meant lower rents in relation to yields, *kemmi* strengthened the tenant's incentive to invest and left him more to invest with. For yet another reason it signified a more advanced agriculture than *kariwake.* Although admitting of a reduction of rent in especially bad growing years, the reduction was not automatic as in the case of *kariwake,* nor was it necessarily in proportion to yields; hence *kemmi* could be practiced only where yields were relatively high and stable, or earnings from by-employments unusually reliable. Since *kemmi* rents were usually not lowered at all until yields fell more than 10 percent below normal, the landlord shared considerably less in the risks of farming than under *kariwake*. As a result he had less to say about how the tenant farmed, and he contributed capital less frequently and labor almost never. Since, in addition, the tenant paid the rent in threshed grain rather than in crops as they stood in the field, it was unnecessary that the landlord be a farmer himself. It is possible that the spread of *kemmi* to some extent reflected the withdrawal of large holders from cultivation, tending of course to reduce the supervisory role of the landlord. Nevertheless, the landlord's paternal role toward the tenant did not entirely disappear. Rent was fixed annually, rather than for longer periods, explicitly to permit a closer adjustment to fluctuations in crop yields—for the tenant's sake as much as for the landlord's; *kemmi* in this respect as in others seems to have stood midway between *kariwake* and *jōmen*, incorporating features of both.

Jōmen fixed rent for a period of years; it permitted adjustments in the meantime but only when yields fell drastically—by custom 20 to 30 percent below normal. The entire loss from all but the most severe annual fluctuations therefore was placed on the tenant, so that it was only in areas where agriculture was especially productive that *jōmen* was feasible. At the same time, by guaranteeing to the tenant the whole of any increase in productivity during a period for which the rent was set, *jōmen* provided a powerful incentive to progressive farming. Like *kemmi*, *jōmen* represented a restriction of the role of the landlord in farming since he had less reason than ever to contribute to the tenant's efforts and less grounds for interfering with them. Indeed, *jōmen* was compatible with a complete withdrawal of the landlord from farming, even eliminating the need present under *kemmi* of inspecting the tenant's crop annually in order to set rent.

Some responsibility remained to the landlord for the tenant's welfare, however. The landlord was still expected, when a harvest was exceptionally bad, to make an adjustment in rent—to revert temporarily, as it were, to the practice of *kemmi*.[11] Admittedly his concern for the tenant was self-interested: in the long run his losses would be smaller if he made concessions than if he forced the tenant into failure by stubbornly demanding rent in full. This is another way of saying that the landlord was not purely a rentier, but was in a position that obliged him to contribute periodically, though somewhat passively, to the tenant's farming success. It is significant, however, that the size of his contribution, in the form of reductions of rent, could not always be based exclusively on crop yields. The tenant's family and farm economies were so closely meshed that, in deciding whether and how much to reduce rent, the landlord was obliged also to consider the state of the tenant's health and capital equipment, the condition of his finances, and numerous other factors that lay at the very heart of his family life. Adjustments in rent by the landlord therefore often had something—or appeared to have something—personal about them.

From *jōmen* it was but a short step to the *pseudo-money* rent, since it was natural under certain circumstances to commute rent levied in kind into a money payment. This helped both landlord and tenant. The landlord need not market the commodities after receiving them and the tenant need not transport them to him, tasks that were especially onerous when the landlord lived in town or in another village. Commutation was possible, however, only if the tenant could market a very much larger share of the harvest than he had been accustomed to, and if the landlord were not interested in rent in its original form of commodities. These two conditions could not be satisfied unless there were an extensively developed market and both parties were deeply involved in it. When one adds to these conditions that payment in money was especially advantageous when the landlord had withdrawn entirely from farming, particularly if he no longer even lived on the land, it is not surprising that with this type of rent landlord-tenant relations became quite businesslike. This was evinced above all in the fact that landlord-tenant relations, hitherto based on oral agreements, tended to be reduced to detailed, written contracts.[4] These documents left less to chance or good will, attempting to stipulate rights and obligations as fully and precisely as possible. Despite all this the sense of mutuality did not utterly disappear. So long as rent was levied in kind, the question of its amount could not be completely separated from the question of crop yields, so that in exceptionally bad years the landlord was still bound to make some concession and the tenant was beholden for it.

[4] The tendency to reduce tenancy agreements to written contracts and to shorten the rental period was evident as early as the first half of the eighteenth century. The author of the "Jikata yōshūroku" states: "Land is at present generally let to tenants for a period of five or seven years; written contracts are revised at the end of the rental period, which is sometimes made shorter." (Quoted by Furushima, *Kinsei ni okeru shōgyōteki nōgyō*, p. 63.)

(5)   The *true money* rent appeared when rents were not only paid but also *fixed* in money. Because this severed any direct link between rent and crop yields money rents tended to be more rigid than other types. This meant of course that the tenant accepted more, if still not quite all, of the risks of farming. An even more significant change was that the tenant was now fully exposed for the first time to the vicissitudes of the market. So long as rent was levied in kind, the landlord shared the risk of loss from unfavorable price movements by accepting rent in kind (or its monetary equivalent at current prices). But with the true money rent the entire risk of adverse prices was assumed by the tenant, who undertook to pay the landlord a certain sum of money whatever the state of the market. Added to the eternal danger to the tenant of crop failure, therefore, were the hazards (and opportunities) of the businessman betting on price. The tenant could venture such grave risks only when an expanding economy gave him reasonable hope of gain and some margin for loss, and further when he had learned to think of himself as an autonomous economic unit whose fate was divorced from others'. It would be foolish to say that there were then *no* traces left in tenancy of cooperative relations, but whatever traces were left were mere vestiges and clearly did not characterize the institution as a whole.

A word of explanation is perhaps required at this point lest the impression be given that this stage of development had been widely attained even in 1921 when the government survey of tenancy was made. Actually it was to be found only here and there as a faint beginning. It must be remembered that the various types of tenancy, or more strictly speaking rent, did not follow one another in simple sequence anywhere. All five types existed in 1921 and no doubt they had much earlier, too. Nor were the diverse types regionally distinct; on the contrary they were intricately mingled within regions and even to some extent within villages and on individual estates. Evolution therefore consisted of no simultaneous movement over the country from one type of tenancy to another, but of the continuous development, at different rates, of particular instances of tenancy from more personal to less personal forms. This had the effect of continuously altering the proportions of the various types of tenancy, but so slowly and in such complex ways that the changes cannot be followed. All that can be discerned is the general drift.

11

NEW CLASS RELATIONS

An important function of cooperative agriculture was to submerge individual and class interests, or rather to prevent consciousness of them from arising. Individual interests were mingled in those of the group and there hidden in social relationships, which made them still harder to perceive. But, as cooperation languished and social groups lost their cohesiveness, individual interests came out of hiding, and the market defined them more clearly by pitting one against another.

A conspicuous indication of this kind of change during the last half of the Tokugawa period was the steady concentration of landownership. This, a nearly universal phenomenon, bespoke a new attitude toward both farming and property—especially the property of others. So long as land was thought of primarily as a means of subsistence rather than a source of profit, the urge to acquire it was relatively weak; or at least there was no strong motive to acquire more than was needed for subsistence since land generally produced no considerable surplus and any surplus it might produce was difficult to sell. Besides, on land being worked by family labor of one sort or another, any increase in the size of the holding meant a roughly proportionate increase in the size and complexity of the family and its immediate extensions, and the family could not be indefinitely expanded: so there was also a social check on the growth of individual holdings.

All of these checks were either removed or considerably softened after about 1700. The growth of urban population and the improvement of commercial organization and transportation made it increasingly easy for the peasant to market his produce so that he could dispose of any surplus produced. But this fact alone did not assure a surplus, though it undoubtedly helped do so by stimulating the desire for one. Two other new factors, in part the result of this desire, were necessary to produce a significant and more or less consistent surplus from farming. One was the steady improvement in farming methods, with the resulting increase in crop yields, and the other was the growth of in-

means of subsistence →
means of profit

come from by-employments. And, while these developments were under way, the growth of tenant cultivation was at the same time removing the previously effective social check on the expansion of holdings. With a growing market, an expanding surplus, and a means of exploiting land through family groups other than one's own, the only check on the desire to acquire more and more land was the lure of consumption and the attractiveness of competing forms of investment.

There were three ways of acquiring land: one was to bring it newly under cultivation, the second was to buy it from someone else, and the third was to foreclose a loan for which land was pledged as security. Purchase and foreclosure obviously had the sharpest impact on class relations because both, in different ways, added to one holding while diminishing another. Foreclosure was the more common and socially disruptive of these two.[a] It was by no means easy to buy land; the peasant's feeling for the soil, especially what had come down to him from ancestors, and his ability always to secure an heir by adoption if progeny failed him, ordinarily kept land from coming on the market. But if the peasant were loath to sell land he would borrow on it to avoid selling, and in the end he often lost his land anyway.

Surviving mortgage documents tell all too plainly a dreary story of the dispossession of small men. They show that borrowing by peasants usually originated in poverty rather than enterprise, that loans were typically for trifling amounts made to men to whom a few pieces of money meant everything.[1] And interest rates were exceedingly high; 20 percent per annum was the most usual rate appearing in loan agreements, but as it was also the legal maximum even this figure may have been fictitiously low. Moneylending[b]—not to use the Christian term "usury," for there was apparently no moral scruple against taking interest—was an exceedingly old profession in rural Japan, and peasants were quite alive to its dangers for the borrower. Yet they did borrow— and lose—their land; in some places more frequently than in others, but

[a] According to surviving bills of sale and mortgage documents, a wealthy Settsu family acquired a total of 17.5695 *chō* of land by forfeiture between 1820 and 1870, as compared with a total of 5.1673 by purchase. (Kashida Seiji, "Futari no kisei jinushi," *Nihon rekishi*, 96 (1956), 52.)

[b] Moneylending was undoubtedly a cheap way to acquire land, as is shown by comparing the amounts paid for land in purchases and those loaned against land as security; for example, a family in a Musashi village bought outright a half *tan* of low-grade paddy for five *ryō* in 1710, but three years later loaned this same sum against a whole *tan* of paddy of the same grade. (Shimazaki Takao, "Musashi nokuni Kodama-gun, Bojidō-mura," *Mita gakkai zasshi*, XLIV, 2 (1953), 42.)

nearly everywhere after 1700 in such numbers as to alter significantly the pattern of landholding.

Some writers take this as proof that the peasantry was being increasingly exploited by the warrior class through taxation and illegal exactions of various kinds. [But at least as regards the tax burden it has yet to be shown that there was any absolute increase, let alone an increase relative to crop yields; and there is even some recent evidence suggesting a relative decline. Indications then point to a stable or perhaps falling level of taxation. But, if so, how account for the concentration of landownership? Why did so many frugal and industrious peasants lose their land through debt?

Almost certainly the answer lies in the variability of farm income combined with an inelastic cost structure. The major source of the instability of income was the inevitable and frequently violent fluctuations in crop yields from one year to the next.[c] Not that such fluctuations were anything new; but they were considerably more serious on holdings where cropping in response to market demand had become more rather than less specialized: where the loss of a single crop might mean an almost total failure of the harvest. An equally volatile factor in farm income was the state of the market, a factor that had been immaterial so long as the peasant had had little or nothing to sell. By the late Tokugawa period, however, holdings were often heavily planted to cash crops, even to a single cash crop which the farm family could not itself consume: cotton, tobacco, indigo, mulberry, and sugar cane, among others. In a village in Izumi Province in 1773, for example, there were holders with 100, 90, 76, and 57 percent of their land planted to cotton.[8] It was no longer enough, then, that the harvest be good. Prices had to be favorable also, for a man could be ruined despite bumper crops. When, as was not uncommon, he had no cushion of savings, even a slight dip in farm prices was serious.[d]

Although farm income was highly variable costs were relatively rigid. The prices of the commodities the peasant bought were con-

[c] Some records kept by peasants, recording little else than the size of the harvest each year, read like chronicles of disaster: "poor harvest," "crop failure," "harvest reduced by one-half," and so on appear as entries every few years. See especially the records kept by a farm family in Nambu barony between 1689 and 1824, a copy of which is in the *Shiryō hensanjo* at Tokyo University.

[d] The variability of farm prices is illustrated by the following price indices for rice and cotton beginning in 1835 in the Osaka area: rice in successive years was 120, 192, 294, 184, 127; cotton was 154, 208, 225, 262, 172. For both commodities the year 1817 is 100. (Furushima and Nagahara, *Shōhin seisan*, p. 140.)

trolled, within certain limits, by powerful merchant guilds that exercised local monopolies with government sanction.[4] Since the peasant
sold either in a free market, or in one positively rigged against him and
in favor of monopoly merchants to whom he was required by law to
sell, he was periodically caught in a cost-price squeeze.[5] The squeeze
was more frequent and tighter, moreover, by virtue of the fact that a
single item, fertilizer, accounted for a very high percentage of his total
cash expenditures; for one item could be more easily controlled than
several, and this particular item was one for which the peasant could
not reduce his purchases without suffering an immediate and sharp decline in income.

Taxes were another major factor in the rigidity of costs. While
rarely taking less than 30 percent of gross yield, they became less and
less responsive to variations in income. Traditionally the land tax had
been assessed annually on the basis of crop yields; but as yields became
somewhat more stable, the peasantry more prosperous, and the warrior
class more deeply implicated in the money economy, the land tax was
more and more commonly fixed for several years at a time. This had
the advantage of stabilizing the lord's revenues and at the same time
eliminating the vast administrative expense of assessing productivity
annually; it even had an advantage for the good farmer, since it gave
him the whole of any increment in productivity achieved during a tax
period.[6] But for the poor or marginal farmer, of whom there were a
great many, the rigidity introduced into his taxes was a constant threat
to solvency.

Income and cost factors added greatly to the insecurity of the individual holder, but they were not alone in contributing to the concentration of landownership. To these economic factors must be added
a predominantly social one: the decline of the cooperative group. At
its peak of effectiveness this group had given every member a large
measure of security of tenure and even protection against adversity.
Since all members alike had depended on mutual help, and were in addition bound together by a network of real or putative kinship, one
family's fate had seemed the genuine concern and responsibility of all
the group. So, if a family were short of food or seed, the group as a
whole or its head was bound to see the unfortunate family over to the
next harvest; or if a house were destroyed by a fire or fields by a flood
the group would mobilize labor to repair the damage. The market
changed this. Dissolving cooperative ties and disentangling one man's
fate from another, it replaced the group with the individual farming

unit as the focus of prime concern. The shift in focus was not sudden and certainly not complete; but though the disposition to help a kinsman or neighbor in need undoubtedly lingered,[7] it was now increasingly mixed with an impulse to take advantage of him.

So land, once an inert thing relatively secure to its possessor, became volatile and changed ownership quickly. As a result holdings were unstable in places where trade had made heavy inroads on cooperative farming. To get some notion of the degree of instability one need only look at a series of late Tokugawa land registers from almost any village where such documents are to be found. It was a rare holding that remained for a generation the same size, and many holdings changed almost from year to year;[8] thus if one plots the size of all holdings in a village on a single piece of paper, one soon produces a maze of criss-crossing lines leaving no doubt of the keen competition for land by the latter half of the Tokugawa period.[9] Or perhaps it would be more accurate to say that there was a general economic competition among peasant families, with changes in landownership merely the most sensitive index of individual success and failure.

In the competition no two families started as equals except that each might lose whatever property it had through neglect or mismanagement. Every holding was different as regarded size, soils, location, drainage, capital, rights to waste and common; every family different as to size, health, age and sex composition; every man as to wit, scruples, physical strength, and much else. The very differences that had once tended to make holdings complementary now made them unequal competitively. Even when differences in respect to individual factors were not great, their combined effect was often enormous, and it was the combined effect that in the end determined whether a family acquired or lost land, went up or down the economic ladder in the village. This is an exceedingly important point: that no one factor was decisive, not even the initial size of the holding, explains why large holdings sometimes dwindled into insignificance and some small holdings became very large. This is a subject to which we must return later.

Turning to the over-all pattern of landholding, without regard for how individual holdings fared, three trends are apparent from the land registers. The size of the largest holdings (though not necessarily the same large holdings) became larger; the number of middling holdings declined; and the number of very small holdings increased. Table V illustrates these trends concretely using data from a village in Shin-

162 New Class Relations

Northeastern

TABLE V
CLASS DIFFERENTIATION IN A SHINSHŪ VILLAGE*

Koku	1595	1663	1714	1771	1835	1870
Under 1	16 } 59%	0	1	9	43	43 } 72%
1– 5	9	1	1	30	35	38
5–10	5	4	7	12	18	15 } 20.3%
10–20	6	21	22	7	7	8
20–30	5	14	4	5	2	4
30–40	1	1	2	2	2	0
40–50	0	0	1	1	0	2
50–60	0	1	1	0	1	2
60–70	0	0	0	0	1	0
70–80	0	0	0	1	0	0
80–90	0	0	0	0	0	0
90–100	0	0	0	0	1	1
Over 100 ...	0	0	1	1	0	0
Total	42	42	40	68	110	113

holdings

* Aoki Takahisa, "Kita Shinano ni okeru Bunroku kenchi," SGZS, LXIII, 1 (1954), 66.

shū.[10] Between 1595 and 1870 (1) the largest holding in this village increased from 30–40 *koku* yield to over 100 *koku* yield, then fell off slightly to 90–100 *koku*; (2) middling holdings (10 to 30 *koku*) decreased from 26 percent to 10.6 percent of all holdings; and (3) small holdings (under 5 *koku* yield) increased from 59 percent to 72 percent. The precise pattern of concentration in any given place was of course unique—the result of a combination of many factors in respect to which no two villages were ever quite alike, such as climate, location, crops, tax rate, water supply, political structure, amount and quality of common land, by-employments, and marketing facilities. But the Shinshū village cited above may be taken as typical in the sense that it illustrates the general trend toward concentration without being an extreme case.[e]

[e] An example of extreme concentration is a village in Tōtōmi Province where a single holder, incidentally a hereditary village headman, held 70 percent of the total cultivated area of the village in 1868.

On the other hand there were some villages, also exceptional, in which land became somewhat more rather than less equally distributed. In a village in Aizu Province, between 1755 and 1870, for instance, the proportion of holdings under five *koku* declined from 10 percent to zero, while holdings between 10 and 15 *koku* yield increased from 37 to 60 percent. (Ōishi, "Tochi shoyū," p. 90. Shōji, *Meiji ishin no keizai*, pp. 30–31. See also Sumi Tōyō, "Bakuhan kōki Sennan kigyō chitai nōmin no tōsō," *Hisutoria*, 14 (1956), 13.)

There were regional as well as local differences in the degree of concentration. Since there was greater concentration in the more urbanized regions, these differences almost certainly reveal the influence of the growth of trade and industry on landholding. The first reliable land statistics, in 1883, show for instance in the Kinai, still notably in advance of the rest of the country commercially and industrially, that 37.5 percent of all arable land was worked by tenants, as compared to 27.3 percent in Tōhoku, perhaps the most backward part of the country. Moreover, the incidence of tenancy remained notably higher in the Kinai than in Tōhoku down to the end of World War II.[11]

One of the most important consequences of the concentration of landownership was the creation of a class of landless families, usually called *mutaka*, literally meaning persons without yield or *taka*. The appearance of *mutaka* introduced an entirely new social element to the village; for in the traditional village, owing to the mode of owner cultivation (*tezukuri*) on the one hand and the scarcity of nonagricultural employment on the other, a married couple without land could survive only as part of a larger kinship group with land, and it was this group that lived and was registered as the family. If a family lost its land yet remained in the village, its members would be assimilated as *genin* or *nago* by some other family that was in need of labor, thus disappearing from the registers as a separate group.[12] The appearance of *mutaka* therefore signifies, in the first instance, the dissolution of the large extended family, which we have already seen was breaking up under the impact of changes in the mode of cultivation.

The dissolution of such families did not give rise directly to *mutaka* since dissolution was accomplished by repeated segmentation into main and branch families, with the holding partitioned each time between main and branch lines.[g] A number of holding families were therefore ordinarily created by the breakup of each extended family; but some of

---

[f] In the Osaka metropolitan district, 42.5 percent of all farm families were tenants (not counting tenant-owners) in 1887; it is significant that this was 10 percent more than in any prefecture for which there are data at that time and far higher than in backward prefectures such as Yamagata, Yamaguchi, and Kagoshima, where the figures were 14.7, 15.7, and 7.2 percent respectively. (Furushima, *Kinsei ni okeru shōgyōteki nōgyō*, p. 172; also see Kinoshita Akira, *Nihon nōgyō ron*, Tokyo, 1949, p. 340.)

[g] We have records of branch families in the Kinai being established without any land whatever, but such cases were confined to very small holdings in regions of intense commercial farming—in other words, this situation obtained *after* the extended family on the large holding had been broken up, not before.

the holdings, especially those of the branch families, were small and lacked capital. Since moreover they were founded at a time when group protection of the weak was fast disappearing, many of these marginal holdings quickly fell victim to competition: the families on them borrowed against them, lost their land, and became *mutaka*.

By the late Tokugawa period, this process of dispossession of the weak had gone far enough that *mutaka* constituted a significant group in many villages. Of course differences from one village to another were enormous; the percentage of families who were landless ranged from 1 percent in some Kyūshū villages to 50 percent and even 70 percent in the Kinai. These Kinai figures are exceptionally high even for that area since they come from villages located in one of the country's richest cotton-growing provinces, on the main road between Osaka and Kyoto. Even in the Kinai there were mountain villages isolated by distance and terrain from commercial influences where the proportion of landless was no higher than in some Kyūshū villages.[h]

A few landless families may have lived entirely from nonagricultural employment,[i] but most managed to subsist in much the same way the smallest holders did, partly by tenant farming and partly by working at other occupations. Occupations varied greatly from one place to another, though everywhere traditional village crafts such as carpentry offered employment for a few. In mountain villages mining, lumber, and charcoal provided employment; along the main routes of overland travel work was to be had with the pack trains carrying local produce to market; near the seacoast there was work on fishing boats or at net fishing from the shore. Many occupations were open to villagers who lived within walking distance of a town,[18] and nearly everywhere petty trade was an important source of income for some.[j]

---

[h] In backward Buzen Province in Kyūshū, the percentage of all families that were landless in a cluster of 11 villages in 1835 was, respectively, 28, 15, 14, 14, 10, 10, 8, 7, 5, 1, and 1 percent. (Fujimoto, "Bakumatsu Buzen ni okeru kisei jinushi," pp. 136–37.) Comparable figures from six villages in Kitakawachi County in the Kinai a century earlier (1720) were 50, 65, 70, 18, 25, and 28 percent. However, in this same county were the two mountain villages mentioned in the text; they had 5 percent and 7 percent landless respectively. (Furushima, *Kinsei ni okeru shōgyō·eki nōgyō*, pp. 157–59.)

[i] There were also individuals, though probably not whole families, called *tabi-hiyatoi* who traveled about the country following the crops and taking work by the day wherever they could find it.

[j] This trade was exceedingly important to the peasant economy in some places. Writing of Okayama fief, Takemoto Ryūhei (1769–1820) tells us: "In recent years the number of small shops and merchants in country districts has greatly increased, and there are now a great many of them. This is the source of the eco-

Taking the country as a whole, however, village handicrafts were the most important source of employment, and significantly the greatest number of landless families was to be found where handicraft industry flourished.[k] This was also true of families who though not landless had little more than gardens. A distinguishing feature of relatively industrial villages therefore was that the average size of holdings was comparatively small.[l] And because the location of handicraft industry was as much determined by the distribution of raw materials and water power as by urban population such villages were widely scattered, despite an especially heavy concentration in the vicinity of towns and cities.

Not even landless families ordinarily lived exclusively from non-agricultural employments; most of them farmed at least a small piece of tenant land, although frequently the income of such families from agriculture was considerably less than from other sources. This must have been the case, for instance, in a cotton-weaving village near Nagoya where holdings in 1844 averaged only 1.588 *koku* yield:[14] where there was so little commitment to agriculture as this on the part of holders, the commitment on the part of the landless must have been at least as slight. The presence of any considerable number of such families weakened the authority of a community over its members. Removed from the network of cooperative ties that despite everything persisted among the farming families, and in addition no longer dependent on communal resources in the form of common land and water, such families were dangerously free of group pressure to conform. In some places moreover they were being joined by town workers spilling over into neighboring villages in search of housing and cheap rent. This introduced a leaven of strangers into the village who had no connection

---

nomic difficulties of the city and of the extravagance of the countryside. Even in remote mountain villages there are people who sell clothing and small articles, and some people spend their spare cash on these goods. . . . It is possible to forbid people living in the village from becoming merchants, but at the present time for many peasants it is impossible to make a living from cultivation alone; hence they must spend part of their time in trade." "Kannōsaku," pp. 599–600.)

[k] For instance, in Hirano village in Settsu Province, one of the most "industrialized" villages in the country, there were in 1837 a total of 673 landless families compared to 325 holding families! (Takao, "Settsu Hirano-gō," p. 13.)

[l] In Ōkubo, a silk-weaving village near Fukushima, holdings averaged just over .5 *tan*. In a Shinshū village where the paper industry developed steadily during the Tokugawa period, the total number of families in the village increased between 1589 and 1872 from 82 to 253, and during the same period the average size of holdings declined from about 10 *tan* to 3.5 *tan*. (Hirasawa, *Kinsei Minami Shinano nōson*, p. 128.)

whatever with farming and no feeling for local traditions; it also tended to upset local property values and behavior patterns. An official document of 1835 gives the following picture of the dislocation caused by immigrant populations in the countryside around the silk town of Kiryū:

In recent years [the Kiryū silk-weaving industry] has prospered greatly, and people have accordingly quit raising silkworms. Raw silk is now bought from neighboring districts and even from other provinces, wholesale merchants having become numerous. Master weavers hire women to reel yarn and weave cloth in considerable numbers, and people have gradually been coming from distant places for this work. Many rent houses in the new district of the town and also in neighboring villages, with the result that land values have risen and the manner of living has naturally become luxurious. Since it is human nature to abhor work and to desire idleness, agriculture is of course neglected. Peasants hire servants and entrust cultivation to them, so that in recent years there has been a serious shortage of farm labor and wages have doubled. Farming has consequently become unprofitable, and more and more people have abandoned farming to live exclusively by trade and weaving.[15]

[The uppermost as well as the lowest stratum of peasants was growing away from farming to some extent, at least from farming's immediate day-to-day concerns.] Large holders gradually curtailed their farming operations as tenancy developed, and in some cases withdrew entirely from the management of land—though not from its ownership, the scale of which they steadily expanded. Freed in part from the routine supervision of cultivation, however, they increasingly turned their time and energy to trade and industry, both of which were rapidly expanding fields that offered opportunities for men with money.

Contemporaries were quick to notice the broadening of interest reflected in the tendency of the developing landlord class to invest in commodities as well as in land. Some late Tokugawa writers even suggested that the money of wealthy peasants, a few of whom were to be found in almost every district, came mainly from nonagricultural sources. Writing of the wealthy peasants whose fine homes dotted the landscape of his native country along the Inland Sea, Takemoto Ryūhei (1769–1820) asked himself how they became wealthy, and he unhesitatingly answered: "Not by farming alone; most also make *sake* or vegetable oil or operate pawnshops."[16] And Tanaka Kyūgu, who wrote of the area around Edo in the early eighteenth century, declared that dyeing textiles and making or dealing in *sake* and malt were the chief sources of wealth of the "rich families found everywhere in the country from the mountains to the seashore."[17]

Contemporary writers may have exaggerated, but there is no reason to doubt them on the main point that land was not the only important source of rural wealth in the late Tokugawa period. Someone had to market the local surplus and import what was needed from outside the village, organize local industry and supply it with raw materials and credit, provide transport services, and so on. And who if not the prosperous landholder was qualified for these tasks? All required capital or access to ample credit, and no one else in the village could meet this requirement; nor had anyone so much education, or so wide a circle of acquaintances outside the village to serve as commercial contacts. The prosperous landholder had an equally weighty advantage over anyone from the town who would do business in the village; personal relationships were still essential to confidence in most dealings in the village, and no outsider could know as much as the native about local markets, products, and workmen.[m]

Village trade and industry were consequently developed largely by local families. Their operations were generally on a very modest scale, but here and there were village businesses which had grown to serve an entire fief or province, or sometimes an even larger area. Thus one finds a family in Echigo in the eighteenth century which dealt mostly in cotton and wine, shipping to buyers as far away as Kyoto and Osaka, recording a single sale in 1718 amounting to 264 *ryō*.[18] The diary of a family in the Fukushima area in 1756 shows that it traded in raw silk, cocoons, raw cotton, indigo, rice, and soy beans, manufactured impressive quantities of *sake*, and loaned money to the local *daimyō*.[19] These were exceptional cases but by no means the only ones of the kind; every cluster of 10 or 20 villages was likely to have at least one family whose mercantile operations were on a fairly large scale.

[m] The importance of local knowledge may be judged from the following quotation from a tract written by a Buddhist monk in 1720. "In places where the silk industry flourishes, people in selecting a bride inquire about her skill in spinning and weaving before making a decision. Female children from the age of about six are trained in the art of spinning by their mothers, who care nothing for the material and time with the wheel that is wasted. . . . No material is wasted when cloth is woven with skill; it is light and even, so when it is dyed there are no blotches, and since it also wears well it brings a high price. But cloth woven clumsily wastes materials and is uneven and blotchy, and because it looks bad and wears worse it brings a poor price. . . . Buyers in the market, when they pick up a piece of cloth, can tell immediately that it was woven by so-and-so's wife or daughter in such and such a village." ("Kokka yōden," *KJKS*, VII, 72.)

Moneylending was another favorite line of business with wealthy village families, some of whom as village patriarchs had been the protectors of their less fortunate kinsmen and neighbors when the village was still a largely self-sufficient world of its own. In this traditional role moneylending—to help others rather than for private gain—had been a duty; but as times changed, the lending grew in scale and lost its altruistic quality. Extending operations far beyond the boundaries of a single village, some moneylenders came to perform the credit functions of country banks,[20] loaning large sums to all manner of borrowers scattered over a whole county or province—to *daimyō*, villages, irrigation districts, individual warriors, merchants, peasants. To cite one example of scale that was admittedly exceptional: the Watanabe family living in a village in Echigo Province received between 1749 and 1784 the gigantic sum of 63,135 *ryō* in payment of loans![21]

Nor were trade and moneylending the only fields to which such men turned their money and talents: industry was another. As we have seen, considerable division of labor had taken place in the main handicraft industries by 1750; most producers by that time depended on some other producer for raw materials and did not themselves produce for sale directly to consumers. Village merchants therefore performed an essential industrial function in buying and selling raw materials and semifinished goods, linking one producer and phase of production to others. Rarely did this role remain wholly passive. Wherever domestic industry developed vigorously, the merchant soon found himself supplying raw materials on credit and taking payment in finished goods that, as often as not, needed further processing to make them ready for sale. Sometimes he was obliged to see his materials through several stages of production in order to realize a return on them. From this stage of involvement in production it was no very great distance to taking charge of the entire process: putting out materials and tools regularly to peasant craftsmen, and paying them wages for working the materials into a finished product.[22] What proportion of domestic industry was organized after this fashion under the putting-out system by the late Tokugawa period is impossible to say, but there is evidence of the system on every hand, in nearly every important industry.[23]

Nor was this the highest stage of organization reached before the Restoration. Once merchants were accustomed to supplying workers with materials and tools and to taking responsibility for the entire productive process, it was inevitable that some of them would sooner or later see the advantages of tighter organization, and try to bring materials, tools, and workers all together in the same place.[24] In 1943, an old man who was describing the organization of the silk industry shortly after the Restoration in Fukushima Prefecture recalled that at the busy season of the year his family usually employed ten to 15 workers at silk reeling in the upper story of their house.[n] Enterprises of this size were not uncommon, and officials were forever lamenting the fact, fearful that agriculture was being deprived of essential labor.[o] There were also scattered manufactories that were on a much larger scale: a cotton mill in Izumi Province, for instance, had 80 looms in 1837;[25] a family in Ōshū employed up to 30 workers a day in producing silkworm eggs in 1873;[26] there were oil makers equipped with several water wheels for power, sugar makers with numerous expensive vats and presses for refining, innumerable brewers employing between 50 and 100 workers. Manifestly village merchants were already deeply implicated in the organization of industry, and the trend was toward larger units of production.

At the same time one must guard against the inference that a specialized business class divorced from an interest in land was emerging in the countryside. Rural merchants, manufacturers, and moneylenders, all frequently the same people, were typically rather large landowners by local standards; usually they even supervised the cultivation of part of their land. When one hears of a great merchant in Tōtōmi Province about 1860, he turns out to have held approximately 70 percent of the arable land in his village;[27] and a large holder in Yamato Province, with 40 percent of the arable of the village, is revealed also as a pawnbroker, fertilizer merchant, and oil maker.[28] These are typical cases: whether one begins by investigating conspicuous examples of village enterprise or of landholding, one ends by finding in all parts of the country that the two normally went together.[29]

While turning increasingly to trade and industry, then, wealthy

[n] The informant remembered clearly that one time in middle Meiji his family bought for nine *yen* a head four children in Yamagata Prefecture whom they used in both farming and silk reeling. This is an excellent illustration of how very diverse forms of labor were often intimately mingled, for these children worked side by side with workers hired at wages. (Fujita Gorō, *Nihon kindai sangyō no seisei*, Tokyo, 1948, p. 310.)

[o] The following edict issued in the Kishiwada fief in Izumi Province in 1790 is typical: "In recent years a great deal of cotton cloth for *haori* has been woven in this barony and the number of looms at work has greatly increased; and for this reason merchants employ a number of women operators in their homes, so that female farm labor and day labor has become exceedingly scarce." (Sumi, "Bakuhan kōki," p. 8.)

An Edo street scene. There is a group of warriors in the right foreground; one apparently of high rank is in ceremonial dress. (*Edo meisho zue.*)

A cotton goods shop in Edo. Two customers are being greeted inside the door, while just beyond them another customer is being shown bolts of cloth. The proprietor's family occupies the rear of the shop and the second floor. (*Edo meisho zue.*)

peasants did not liquidate their landed holdings; rather, they generally added to them. This is a fact of considerable significance. Land might be given over to tenants, but it still had to be farmed within the framework of the communal allocation of taxes and management of common land and water rights. [Along with other factors, such as the duty to care for family graves and shrines, this served to keep local families from deserting the country for the town. Only by staying in the village could they protect and promote their landed interests, which the action of the community touched at a thousand points.] So they remained, deeply involved in local politics. As a result the class antagonisms being generated by changes in agrarian society were, at one and the same time, both more and less dangerous for the peace of the countryside than would otherwise have been the case. Tensions were more quickly and intimately felt, but overt expression of them was more resolutely suppressed in favor of an appearance of community harmony —and they were the more explosive for that reason. [Deep beneath the everyday appearance of propriety and friendliness there were in many Japanese villages suppressed hatreds that merely needed some shock, some momentary lapse of customary restraint, to send them boiling to the surface.]

Perhaps it had always been this way; perhaps when the village had been more tightly knit and harmonious the secret antagonisms had gone even deeper and been more powerful.[*p*] But if so they had also been more effectively suppressed, and it was only as village organization loosened that they were given vent. [At all events, whether the loosening of village organization generated new tensions or merely gave existing ones new scope, the process is important to any understanding of the village in transition.]

We have touched on many reasons for this loosening; one we have almost completely neglected, however, is best observed in changes in landownership; that is the lack of perfect continuity in the composition

---

[*p*] Professor Lewis A. Coser's comments on hostility within primary groups are relevant here. "The closer the relationship, the greater the affective investment, the greater also the tendency to suppress rather than express hostile feelings. Whereas in secondary relationships, such as with business partners, feelings of hostility can be expressed with relative freedom, this is not always the case in primary relationships where total involvement of the participants may make the acting out of such feelings a danger to the relationship. In such cases feelings of hostility tend to accumulate and hence to intensify." (*The Functions of Social Conflict*, Glencoe, Illinois, 1956, p. 67.)

of both the upper and the lower strata of peasant society. Families were continuously moving in and out of both; although the movement was often so slow as to escape the notice of contemporary writers, it tended to disturb the web of traditional social relations through which the village worked to maintain peace and to enforce conformity. For the very essence of these relations was that they were personal and specific, and that neither families nor individuals were interchangeable within the system they formed.

Contemporary writers often give the impression of almost perfect continuity in the relative economic position of individual families; they state repeatedly that it was the large holders who acquired land and the small holders who lost it. The reasons they give for this are convincing; large holders, they say, farmed better than the small because they were in a better position to invest in fertilizer, animals, implements, and bribes to tax officials.[30] But contemporary observers who wrote in this fashion were referring to short-term change that was easily noticed. The small holder had first to become a middling holder before he could become a large one since families could not leap the entire gamut of economic gradations at a jump, and contemporaries saw part of the process only.

The actual pattern of the change in landownership was far more complex than the short view of contemporary writers suggests. Some peasant families who were great and powerful at the beginning of the Tokugawa period failed to make the transition from a natural to a money economy, lost their land bit by bit, and in time were reduced to poverty and even died out of the village. Still others made the transition in agriculture successfully, but fell victim to bad judgment or bad luck in some business venture; not everyone was prepared for so violent a change in economic behavior as success in trade, and even more in industry, required. On the other hand there were poor families who in time became wealthy and powerful—usually it seems by first accumulating a little capital from farming, then going into trade or moneylending.[q]

Mobility—both up and down—was highest in the areas where com-

[q] The most remarkable example I have come across is a family in Kai Province whose holding, as measured in estimated yield, expanded as follows: 10.7 *koku* (1680), 11.1 (1690), 33.1 (1697), 56.0 (1704), 66.0 (1711), 93.4 (1716), 202.1 (1728), 431.2 (1753), 449.5 (1755). (Ōishi Shinzaburō, "Edo jidai ni okeru nōmin no ie to sono sōzoku keitai ni tsuite," in *Kazoku seido no kenkyū*, I, edited by Nihon hōshakai gakkai, Tokyo, 1956, pp. 117–18.)

mercial farming and rural industry were best developed. Tanaka Kyūgu gives us a glimpse of one such place, the area around Hachiōji, which by the time he wrote was already a flourishing silk market:[31]

> It is rare [he says] that the original families who cleared the land survive to this day. Those who were originally rich have declined, and those who were first poor are now rich. Many persons who came to the village as servants from the outside have risen from these humble beginnings, gradually improving their position by trade and by buying paddy and forest land.

Kyūgu almost seems to have regarded violent reversals of family fortune as the usual thing. Although he exaggerated, one finds many cases that tend to bear him out. In Mino Province a family that was landless as late as the Meiwa era (1764–71) somehow managed to begin trading in cotton, and used the profits from this trade to extend its activity to rice and fertilizer, and to begin lending money; by 1819 it owned land yielding 190 *koku* annually and scattered through 15 villages.[32] A family in Shinshū with only a small holding in 1670 had accumulated 9.5 *chō* of paddy by the late Tokugawa period; it went on to acquire a surname and one of its members became a fiscal agent for the local lord.[33] Cases of dramatic decline were probably more frequent than cases of dramatic ascent, but they were less often recorded because downward progress frequently led to the extinction of a family.[r] For instance, the headman family of a village in Izumi Province held arable of over 100 *koku* yield at the end of the seventeenth century but, for reasons not entirely clear, it lost everything in the late Tokugawa period and eventually disappeared from the village.[34]

One must be careful not to repeat Kyūgu's mistake—to take as typical a class of cases that was merely numerous. Such cases were not typical and although it is impossible to say what *was*, cases of a very different kind, namely, families that were prodigies of longevity, who were great holders at the end of the sixteenth century or early seventeenth and still large (or larger) in the middle of the nineteenth, were

---

[r] There were also some cases of decline that did not end in extinction, and then the family papers were preserved. One outstanding case of this kind was a family of warrior origin that lived in a village in Aizu. In addition to holding extensive landed property in and around the village, during the eighteenth century this family lent money to both warriors and peasants and traded on a large scale in cotton, *sake*, and soy beans. Nevertheless, by the end of the century the family was in trouble, and in 1800 its head petitioned the local lord for a loan, saying that the family had recently come upon hard times and now hoped to revive its waning fortunes by investing in cotton looms and hiring operators to work them. (Fujita, *Nihon kindai sangyō*, pp. 240–48.)

at least very numerous. There were probably few villages outside the Kinai and the other scattered areas of intense urban influence that could not count at least one such family; and many such villages were also to be found in the Kinai.[8] These continuities to some extent offset the disruptive effect of large movements up and down the economic and social scale.

Not only was there sufficient social mobility to disturb traditional patterns of social relations, but the distance between social strata was becoming greater and communication accordingly more difficult. The traditional structure of the village was, of course, based on sharp economic distinctions, although the distinctions occurred within relatively narrow limits. Productivity traditionally had been too low and land too encumbered by obligations to permit economic differences of the kind made possible by increased productivity and growth of the market. Contemporary writers began to notice the new scale of rural wealth from about the beginning of the eighteenth century.

We have already encountered some notable examples of wealthy peasants; for instance, the Watanabe family of Echigo. How numerous the class was is impossible to say, but the land registers, though recording but one form of wealth, give the impression that there were perhaps one or two such families for every cluster of ten or so villages; and this corresponds with at least one contemporary estimate.[35] As always, however, one must make allowance for considerable regional diversities. In the Kinai, for instance, there were many villages with several wealthy families; but Furukawa Koshōken, who qualified if anyone did as an experienced traveler, has given us a picture of unrelieved poverty in Buzen Province (Kyūshū) at the end of the eighteenth century.[36]

Upon entering the country [he writes] one finds not a single peasant family that might be called wealthy; as far as the eye can reach neither white walls nor storehouses are to be seen. In both speech and character these people are much inferior to those of Chūgoku. In the mountainous parts, people do not even wear sandals, and they come into the house and sit down without washing. They do not eat rice except on festival days; millet is considered

---

[8] A family in the Kinai with 110 *koku* yield held 91 *koku* yield in 1871 (Sumi Tōyō, "Kinsei zenki Kinai sonraku no dōkō," *Hisutoria*, 13 (1955), p. 22); a family in present-day Okayama Prefecture with 110 *koku* yield in 1628 had 164 *koku* yield in 1822 (Taniguchi Sumio and Ishida Hiroshi, "Kinsei sonraku kōzō ni kansuru ichikōsatsu," *Shigaku kenkyū kinen ronsō*, Tokyo, 1950, p. 16); a family in Shinshū with 60 *koku* yield in 1665 held 150 *koku* yield in 1814 (Hirasawa Kiyoto, *Kinsei Minami Shinano mura no kenkyū*, Tokyo, 1951, p. 55); a family in Echigo held approximately 2 *chō* of paddy in 1683 and 21 *chō* in 1842 (Kitajima, "Echigo sankan chitai," pp. 27–28); and so on.

a fine food and is eaten regularly even in the temples. From these circumstances one may judge the manners of the area generally. It so happened that some merchants from Chōshū who were on their way to Bungo, Hyūga, and Ōsumi met inadvertently at an inn. They joked about the hardships of traveling in this area, and one said: "Let us go back to Japan."

Fear for the future was no doubt one reason that Tokugawa writers, most of them warriors, evinced the keen interest they did in the *"gōnō,"* as wealthy peasants were called. Fascinated by this new social phenomenon, they rightly regarded it as a threat to their way of life. If the mere sight of great wealth in the hands of peasants did not fill them with misgivings, bitter experience with the power of such wealth drove the lesson home. Large numbers of the military class of every rank depended on loans or contributions (*goyōkin*) from wealthy peasants to remain personally solvent. What better proof to them of institutional disintegration could there possibly be, unless it was the fawning respect for wealth that they perceived in every class and that they thought was destroying all sense of rank, and belittling the traditional virtues of frugality, industry, and modesty? "High and low compete in ostentation and luxury while government becomes more and more lax!" Fujita Yūkoku exclaimed, and then he subsided with a sigh: "This is an age when money buys anything."[37]

This was a favorite theme of political and economic writers. Love of money was corrupting all classes, none more dangerously than the peasants, who after all were the prime producers of the economy and the base of the social order. But the *gōnō* were the worst offenders of all; they lived (it was said) in the style of the city rich, foreclosed the land of their neighbors, welcomed crop failures for the opportunity of buying up land at distress prices, kept concubines, corrupted officials with gifts and bribes, were pretentious of culture, and much more. Buyō Inshi's indictment of them[38] is more or less typical:

Now the most lamentable abuse of the present day among the peasants is that those who have become wealthy forget their status and live luxuriously like city aristocrats. Their homes are as different from those of the common folk as day from night or clouds from mud. They build them with the most handsome and wonderful gates, porches, beams, alcoves, ornamental shelves, and libraries. Some give money to the Shōgun and receive the right to swords and surnames in return. . . . Others lend money to *daimyō* and local officials and . . . exercise influence in their localities and abuse the common peasants. Still others despise the minor officials and win favor with imperial princes, with members of the royal family who have taken Buddhist orders, and with people versed in court affairs. . . . Moreover, village officials and others of wealth entrust cultivation to servants; they themselves wear fine clothes and imitate the ceremonial style of warriors on all such occasions as weddings, celebrations, and masses for the dead.

There was more than a grain of truth in such descriptions; in numerous ways wealthy peasants were taking on the social characteristics of the warrior class. The most important distinction between the warrior and the peasant was that only the warrior had the right to bear a surname and to wear a sword; swords particularly were forbidden to peasants on the pain of severest punishment. Exceptions to the general ban on weapons were occasionally made, but until the latter half of the Tokugawa period they were confined to a relatively few village officials whose descent from warriors was both relatively recent and generally acknowledged. By the early nineteenth century, however, both the Shogunate and baronial governments as a financial measure were resorting to the sale of the right to both arms and names—the sale above all to wealthy peasants. Not even a pretense was made that the purchasers had aristocratic origins; a man had only to make a sufficient contribution to his lord's perennially straitened finances to qualify; who he was made little difference.

Nor was this all: warrior offices which carried the reality as well as the appearance of power were coming into the hands of peasants. This seems to have occurred most frequently in the Kinai, where petty lords, especially Tokugawa vassals called *hatamoto*, commonly lived in Edo and entrusted the collection of revenues to local agents called *daikan*. Partly for reasons of economy, but chiefly to facilitate the collection of revenue and the raising of local loans and contributions, absentee lords often appointed wealthy peasants to this enormously powerful and traditionally warrior office.[39]

In still other ways wealthy peasants were taking on warrior characteristics. From at least the early Tokugawa period the upper stratum of peasants had been literate, but by the last century of the period the literacy of wealthy peasants in many cases went far beyond its former utilitarian limits. Peasants began to cultivate the fine arts and invade the field of scholarship and speculative thought, all previously the special province of warriors and the city rich. One recalls the keen interest with which the villagers in Shimazaki's novel *Yoakemae* followed political developments in the capital, and how the son of the headman of the village went off to Edo with his father's blessing and financial support to study under a man who continued the scholarly tradition of the great Hirata Atsutane. This episode is by no means fanciful; many peasants who later were given court rank for their part in the Restoration studied in the late Tokugawa period under famous teachers in Kyoto and Edo, where they no doubt became intimate with the young warriors who were there on similar business.[40]

No higher testament to learning in any class exists than the agricultural treatises, which perhaps represent the finest achievement of Tokugawa scholarship. Miyazaki Antei, the author of the greatest of these treatises, may perhaps not be regarded as a peasant although he lived in a village; but numerous genuine peasant authors followed him. If they were less original in treating their subject—and who was not?—they had nevertheless read the authorities carefully, and were capable of clear, ordered exposition, proving that they had both discipline and talent, an uncommon combination in any age or class. And farming was not the only subject of peasant writing. Some wrote histories of their families or villages, others diaries into which they wove philosophical and social comment, still others treatises on village government; and many who did not write themselves read widely, and took a lively and intelligent interest in affairs far removed from events in the village. Such men occupied an intellectual world very different from that of the ordinary peasant. We get an idea of how different in reading the diary of the headman of a village in Settsu Province, who commented on the death of the Shōgun Ieharu and the fall from power of his favorite, Tanuma Okitsugu; recorded the news of a great fire in Kyoto in 1787, pedantically noting that it was ". . . a far greater conflagration than those of the Ōnin (1467–69) and Hōei (1704–11) eras"; noted whenever a certain Kyōgen company he was interested in came to Osaka, and so on.[41] The diary of a headman from a village on the Japan Sea who was going off to Edo on business near the end of the Tokugawa period contains a list of articles ordered from the capital by friends; the list included several books, one of them the *Nihon shoki!*[42]

Of the various arts that wealthy peasants cultivated in the late Tokugawa period—such as poetry, painting, calligraphy—the military arts were the least proper of all to their class. Buyō Inshi wrote that wealthy peasants ". . . keep masterless warriors around them and study military arts unsuitable to their status; they take teachers . . . and study the Japanese and Chinese styles of writing and painting."[43] It was quite true. A Bakufu order of 1805 stated: "We hear that in recent times peasants have retained masterless *samurai* and study military arts from them, and that peasants of like mind band together for practice."[44] At least one peasant's diary also mentions such groups practicing—with guns, too![45] Kimura Masazō wrote late in the Tokugawa period that ". . . in recent years many peasants have studied under *samurai* and masterless warriors who go about the country . . . teaching swordsmanship."[46]

Of course, neither swords and surnames nor learning and military training obliterated the distinctions between wealthy peasants and warriors. But they lessened the psychological distance between the two classes, and this may have prepared the way for a political alliance of elements of each during the crisis the country faced in the last decades of Tokugawa rule. But more important to us is the distance they certainly created between the rural rich and the mass of peasants: in embracing the culture of the warrior and the city, wealthy peasants were opening a gulf in understanding and sympathy that had not been seen in the countryside since the days before warriors were removed as a class from the land to the towns.

12

POLITICAL CONFLICT IN THE VILLAGE

As we saw in Chapter 5, the political system in the traditional village was based on cooperative agricultural groupings with enormous power over their members. This power was vested in head families which stood at the apex of kinship structure and at the center of farming organization. In very small villages, group and village might be coterminous; but in villages where more than one group existed, the power of each was checked to some extent by the others.

But it was also fortified by them; for head families in the village were linked by marriage ties and class interest, and collaboration rather than conflict was the normal state among them. Being the chief authors of tradition, they combined to restrict the right to hold office to their own number and perhaps a few of their leading branch families. Such restrictions, made sacrosanct by time and the approval of the local gods, strengthened the position of the head families as a class and of each such family in its own group.

This political system created no serious strain so long as the economy on which it was based remained essentially unchanged. Each family head then spoke for the united interests of its group in village councils; and each group rejoiced that it had so powerful a spokesman. But this stable identification of political, social, and economic power did not survive the development of the market.

Cooperative agriculture declined, leaving a group of competing families where there had once been unity. Economic life depended less and less on the group and more and more on the income, resources, and shifting business relations of individual families. With increasing competition among families there were great changes in relative economic position such as had not been possible before; in some cases the shifts were from one economic extreme to the other, but many less dramatic changes of importance were to be seen.

Such shifts in economic position were often not fully reflected by changes in political power. The monopoly of village office by a narrow clique of families was frequently perpetuated, though the original group might be somewhat enlarged and the relations among its members changed. The stubborn defense of old forms of power was bound, in the changed circumstances, to bring about a political crisis since village offices were prizes worth fighting for. Not only did they confer great prestige on their holders but, more important, they conferred authority to make community decisions, and community decisions were critical for nearly everyone in several ways.

The allocation of taxes was one. Not only did the village impose taxes of its own in order to maintain local roads, irrigation works, shrines, and other public buildings, and to pay the local headman (if he were given a salary); but it allocated the land tax and supplementary taxes (*komononari*) which the lord imposed on the village as a whole rather than on individual proprietors. It was of vital concern to everyone how these various taxes were allocated; together they frequently took 30 percent and perhaps more of what the village produced. Only a slight change of incidence would drastically affect the competitive position of individual families one way or another— insofar, that is, as competition had replaced cooperation. Little is known about the specific issues the allocation of taxes raised in the village, but it is not difficult to imagine what they were.

First was the question of whether taxes were to be based primarily on property assessments or on income. It was technically simpler to use property, but in that event income from nonagricultural sources, which was very large in some villages, would completely escape taxation. On the other hand, it was exceedingly difficult to know nonagricultural income accurately, and any attempt to investigate it was almost certain to result in misrepresentations and recriminations. But even the use of property as the base for taxation raised troublesome problems. Were animals, buildings, tools, ponds, and wasteland to be taken into account along with arable in assessing the value of holdings? People were bound to disagree no matter what the answer since these items of property bulked larger on some holdings than others. Nor were people more likely to agree on the method of assessing arable itself. Some would argue that the assessments of the land registers be used; others would point out that these assessments were badly out of date, in some villages having gone unrevised for a century or more: if they were to be used, therefore, the improving farmer whose yields had increased since the last assessment would be taxed at a lower rate, often far lower, than the man whose yields had remained the same.[1]

But, if the lord's assessments were unreliable, could the village be trusted to make its own? It was by no means easy to solve the technical problems of making assessments while achieving a reasonable degree of equity. Crop yields were a convenient index of the productivity of land, but which years' crops were to be taken as a base? Since statistical data on yields went back no further than men could remember them, which is to say four or five years at the most, and each man remembered only his own yields, there was bound to be disagreement. Then there was the vexing question of whether gross or net yield should be the relevant datum. Some fields yielded well but cost considerably more than others to work, because, for instance, it took an hour on foot to reach them, or terrace walls had to be maintained, and so on. If costs were to be taken into account, however, it was unfair to count only monetary costs; but how was the cost of unpriced items to be computed?

The administration of common land and water rights was another way village government unequally touched individual interests. If, for instance, people on the upper part of an irrigation system were to take as much water as they wanted, there might not be enough for people on the lower part. Rationing was necessary in such circumstances, but that necessitated measuring the volume of water—not an easy matter. Was water to be measured merely by the length of time the sluice gate of a ditch was open, without taking into account the speed of the current? That was potentially unfair since the flow was faster in some places than others, but on the other hand speed was difficult to measure exactly. Assuming the volume of water could somehow be satisfactorily measured, how should water be rationed? Should every family receive the same amount, or should the quantity be adjusted according to the amount of irrigated land?[a] The latter might seem the fairer method; but then many families would want to turn unirrigated fields into paddy, which would harm the interests of others, especially in years when water was short. In such years should new fields have the same claim to water as old, and if not by what amount should their claim be reduced?

The administration of common land raised similar problems. Did every family in the village have the right to an equal share in common land, or just the older families? After all, why should existing families

---

[a] Or, another way of discriminating was to tax "new fields" (*shinden*) more than "old fields" (*honden*) for the upkeep of the irrigation system; this is still done in some villages today. (Baba Akira, "Nōson ni okeru mizu no yakuwari," *Rekishi hyōron*, 43 (1953), 24–40.)

have their shares reduced merely because one of their number—for its own selfish reasons—founded a new branch family? Shares of different value might be established to meet this problem in part, but how were the different classes of shares to be assigned? How old did a family have to be to qualify for a full share? Equally difficult was the problem of measuring shares: if this were done by dividing the common into lots of uniform size, obviously some lots would be far more valuable than others because far more productive. But if productivity were to be considered—assuming it could be satisfactorily estimated—should not location and accessibility also be taken into account? There was no end to such questions; all of them were important; and there was only one way to be reasonably sure the answers would take one's interests into account: to share in the power of making them. For those outside the circle of privileged families that meant winning the right to hold office.

Political conflict broke out in a great many villages during the last century of the Tokugawa period.[2] How many villages were afflicted by this strife is impossible to say since the records lie buried in local documents that have only begun to be catalogued, but it seems clear that conflicts were most numerous in areas, such as the Kinai, where economic change was most marked. Since the traditional political system was restrictive everywhere, and was everywhere being undermined by economic change, we may suppose that even where conflicts had not yet broken out the ground for them was being secretly prepared. Wherever conflicts did break out the issues were similar: either a disenfranchised party demanded equal political rights in the village, including the right to hold office, or they demanded the dismissal of incumbent village officeholders, which was in effect an attempt to exercise the right of selecting officials. Rich and poor tended to be on opposite sides of the struggle, but there were many exceptions to this principle of alignment—too many to describe these conflicts as based mainly on economic classes.

One of the best-documented controversies was that in Kurashiki village located in Bitchū Province on the Inland Sea.[3] During the Tokugawa period Kurashiki developed as a center of cotton growing and as a local market; by 1695, the market was held six days monthly, suggesting an exceedingly lively local trade, although a local document of the time states rather plaintively, "Not too many people come."[4] Still, this was evidently no ordinary village, and later docu-

ments significantly refer to it sometimes as a "town." It probably began
to assume the aspect of a town about 1746, when it became the official
seat of a magistrate (*daikan*); perhaps more than any other factor this
encouraged the rapid population growth that followed. Whatever the
reason, the population of the village grew from 3,837 in 1695 to 7,199
in 1818.

Much of the population came from immigration, presumably of
poor peasants from the surrounding area attracted by the prospect of
employment, since the village population showed a heavy preponder-
ance of males throughout the eighteenth century.[b] Edicts originating
in the general area of the village, moreover, speak of a sizable nonfarming population, stating repeatedly that peasants were abandoning
farming because they could make a better living running shops.[c] The
official census of occupations for Kurashiki in 1770 confirms the charge:
it shows 888 families engaged in agriculture, 135 in handicrafts, 491
in commerce, and 319 in miscellaneous occupations. Even making
allowance for the smallness of business units and the fact that many
families classified as commercial or industrial also farmed, the figures
suggest a surprisingly urban environment. Of the families classified
as commercial, 19 were pawnbrokers, 18 wholesalers, 5 buyers of
secondhand goods, 22 *sake* manufacturers; 16 families dealt in fertilizer, 16 in tobacco, 15 in bean curd, 25 in tea, 4 in sundries, 32 in
oil, and 47 in rice and other cereals.[e] Kurashiki was indeed as much
town as village.

In the midst of such strenuous growth and change as the population figures suggest, it is not surprising that there was a marked concentration of land. By the early nineteenth century, a few enormously
large holders had emerged and the number of small, marginal holdings had greatly increased.[d] A change had also been taking place in
the organization of farming, for *genin* were present in considerable
numbers on large holdings in the early seventeenth century, but gen-

[b] In 1790, for instance, the excess of males reached nearly 1,000; at that date
there were 3,838 males and 2,997 females. (Naitō Seichū, "Kinsei sonraku no
kōzō henka to murakata sōdō," *Keizai ronsō*, LXXIV, 2 (1954), 43.)

[c] An edict of 1795, for example, stated: "In recent years a great number of
peasants have opened shops. When such persons succeed in making money, they
abandon their fields entirely. This is most serious and henceforth is ordered suppressed." (*Ibid.*, pp. 44–45.)

[d] In 1619, the largest holding in the village was 57 *koku* yield; but by 1829
there were four holdings over 100 *koku* and the largest was 374 *koku*! At the other
pole, holdings of 3 *koku* yield or less increased from a total of 103 in 1619 to 176
in 1829. (*Ibid.*, p. 46.)

erally disappeared during the eighteenth. Some probably became tenant farmers or tenant-owners, which would help account for the increase in the number of small holders.[e] In any event, the disappearance of *genin* bespeaks a shift on large holdings to tenant cultivation, and therefore a change in the character of large holders, who were becoming much larger and changing from working farmers to landlords.

Despite all these changes since 1600, however, the political system remained unaltered. No village office—headman, elder, or *hyakushō-dai* (peasant representative)—could be held by any person not a member of one of 13 families known as *koroku,* or "old registered." The title suggests that these families were enrolled in a register antedating those first registering other families, who were known as *shinroku,* or "newly registered." Although this is surmise, there can be no doubt that the 13 families were very old and powerful, since they appear in the early-seventeenth-century registers as large holders with four or five *genin* each; and from these facts it is not difficult to guess that each had once stood at the center of a cooperative farming group.

By the late eighteenth century, the position of these families had been much changed. Weakened by the decline in the importance of cooperation in farming, and by the large immigrant population that had moved into the village and stood wholly outside traditional social and economic organization, none of the 13 was as powerful as before, and several were decidedly weaker. For instance, one of the 13—a family that in 1643 had owned the largest holding in the village (56.887 *koku* yield) and occupied the office of the village elder—had by 1819 lost all its land but 6.527 *koku* yield; it continued going downhill thereafter until, in 1835, only 1.7289 *koku* yield remained. On the other hand some immigrant families had prospered. A certain Takezaemon, whose family had first moved into the village in the early eighteenth century, was reckoned the second wealthiest man in the village and early in the next century the third largest landholder; at that time he held land amounting to 224 *koku* yield and had 109 tenants! The headman and Takezaemon provide the most striking contrasts, but they were not the only cases of the kind.[f]

---

[e] In any case the increase was significant: the total number of holdings increased from 149 in 1619 to 242 in 1829. (*Ibid.*)

[f] For example: a wealthy peasant who had 65 *koku* yield joined the anti-Tokugawa forces at the time of the Restoration and afterward was a leader of the Liberal Party in Okayama Prefecture; in 1887, his family owned approximately 200 *chō* of land. (*Ibid.,* p. 53.)

No wonder the political monopoly of the 13 families—in a village of nearly 2,000 families!—became objectionable. By 1790 there were signs of trouble. Takezaemon, the wealthy immigrant, made a public demand that the people of the village be consulted in the allocation of the land tax,⁰ instead of the allocation's being made in private by the 13. When the headman of Kurashiki summarily rejected the petition, Takezaemon, joined by several others, appealed to the district magistrate, who resided in the village. The magistrate tried to persuade the petitioners to accept arrangements as they were. Instead, having thus discovered that they could expect no help from the magistrate, they began a public agitation and called a meeting of the villagers to discuss the matter. This bold step sufficiently alarmed the magistrate that he quickly issued an order conceding the point in dispute: henceforth, he said, all the villagers would meet with the village officials in the local temple and together they would allocate the taxes.⁶

Although this quieted the agitation for a time, it did not dispel hostility toward the privileged 13, and conflict flared up again in 1821 —this time over a matter of protocol. The headman, who had once been the largest holder in the village but in 1819 held only 6.527 *koku* yield, assumed the seat of honor at the celebration of the rebuilding of the village shrine that year, despite the fact that he had been able to contribute nothing to the expense of the occasion. The fiery Takezaemon, who had contributed generously, loudly protested and resigned from his five-family group, which was as near as he could come to resigning membership in the village. As was probably Takezaemon's intention, this act set off a series of recriminations that enflamed opinion against the 13; and at last 38 villagers, led by Takezaemon, joined in a petition to the magistrate asking that suitable persons be appointed to the office of "peasant representatives," hinting plainly that the incumbents of that office did nothing to protect the public interest against the headman and elders: thus they succeeded in attacking the headman and elders, too. The magistrate, as though to dismiss the charge as effrontery, raised the four incumbents in question to the currently vacant positions of elder. This was a most impolitic step, and it further aroused feeling against the village officials.

Between this event in 1823 and the end of the following year,

⁰ This was one of the commonest demands made upon village officials in the late Tokugawa period. It suggests that suspicion of dishonesty in the allocation of taxes was widespread. (Tsuda Hideo, "Hōken shakai hōkaiki ni okeru nōmin tōsō no ichiruikei ni tsuite," *RGKK*, 168 (1954), 7.)

there were 18 petitions and counterpetitions relating to the dispute. In the course of the controversy, Takezaemon and his party became increasingly bold: having first demanded the appointment of suitable persons as "peasant representatives," they went on to demand that the villagers as a whole be given a voice in the selection of all village officials and that the persons then serving as elders be dismissed from office; finally they demanded that the headman be required to submit all his accounts to public inspection, claiming that his refusal to do so had raised suspicion of peculation.

For the latter charge the petitioners received a severe reprimand from the magistrate. Since he quite evidently intended to back the 13, the petitioners dispatched representatives—no doubt at considerable expense—to Edo to appeal the case to the Shogunal government. After hearing the appeal, the official in charge ordered the headman to submit his accounts for ten years back for official inspection. Incriminating evidence was apparently found; for upon completion of the investigation four years later (government moved slowly even in those times of bureaucratic innocence), the Edo government issued an order depriving the headman, three elders, and all of the "peasant representatives" of their respective offices; and it directed that successors be selected by ballot by the holders (*takamochi*) of the village. An election was accordingly held, and lo! Takezaemon led all the rest.

Thus the struggle in Kurashiki ended in a clear-cut victory for the opposition; significant of the changing times, this was the usual outcome of such conflicts. Not in all villages was the outcome reached so peaceably, however. In Shijo village in Kawachi Province, for instance, the headman was charged with peculation and his dismissal demanded; a number of men invaded his home and beat his father, the former headman, so badly that five days later he died.[7] But despite the violence the dissidents prevailed, and their nominee was appointed as headman by the officials in charge of the case.

The struggle to revise the medieval structure of the village was not confined to the issue of political rights, but aimed to modify an ancient system of discrimination that reached every cranny of village life. Strangely, however, the contestants showed remarkably little interest in formulating guiding principles for a different kind of community. Insofar as they appealed to abstract principle at all, it was as an afterthought incidental to the specific issues at hand. One almost has the feeling that there was no hostility to discrimination and privilege as such, only to some versions of it—but that is perhaps stating the matter too strongly.

One sees the inclusive social character of these struggles most clearly in villages where the *miyaza* existed, since the structure of political privilege was then embodied in a very elaborate and extensive system of ritual. It will be recalled that the *miyaza* was a group of families who exercised exclusive ceremonial rights with respect to the village deity and enjoyed a privileged position in the village generally.[8] Although most commonly found in the Kinai, the *miyaza* was by no means confined to that region; there were others where it was perhaps as common and probably no large region to which it was wholly unknown. Nor were the types of privileges claimed by the *miyaza* peculiar to communities where the institution existed. Such privileges were virtually universal in rural communities and, indeed, were most firmly rooted in communities to which the *miyaza* was unknown; especially those where there could be no privileged *group* because a single family dominated the entire community, even claiming to be founder of all major lineages in it.[9] Far from representing an exceptional degree of inequality in village life, then, it seems probable that the *miyaza* appeared only where the structure of privilege was relatively insecure and required exceptionally elaborate institutional support.

Conflict over the *miyaza* divided villages cleanly between those who were excluded and those who were not, and sooner or later resulted in attacks on privilege in every department of village life. Typically, these struggles were fought through appeals and counter-appeals to higher administrative officials to annul or sustain the *miyaza's* prescriptive rights. Since these controversies were both common and prolonged in the Tokugawa period, one finds frequent reference to them in contemporary documents; in some villages people dimly remember them today.

Documentation, however, is fragmentary and badly scattered, and accordingly little is known about individual disputes. Considerable documentation on a few disputes has been gathered by Professor Andō Seiichi, who has generously made his materials available to this author. They concern disputes on three Kishū villages, and the remarks which follow are based mainly on them.[10] So few instances are represented in all, the evidence could be misleading as to the general character of *miyaza* disputes; on the other hand these cases fit the general pattern so far as it is known with the kind of evidence now available.

First a word about the region to which the documents refer. It is a long narrow valley formed by the Ki River, which provides water communications almost its entire length; the high mountains that rise up sharply on either side of the river form a flat alluvial plain about eight miles wide. As is attested by the exceedingly dense farming population crowded into it today, the valley is one of the richest farming areas in the country, favored by a mild climate, rich soil, and an excellent location. Opening to the east into the Nara plain, and at the opposite end into the sea, it not only was one of the first parts of the country to be settled but had the inestimable advantage for economic development of secure access to the rest of the country through the Inland Sea. In view of these natural advantages, it is hardly surprising that commercial farming developed there relatively early. How early is uncertain, but there is clear evidence of it by the end of the seventeenth century in the *Saizōki*,[h] an important agricultural treatise written about the Genroku period near the town of Hashimoto[i] in the upper valley.

Among other indications of an advanced stage of economic development to be found in the *Saizōki*—cash crops, commercial fertilizers, an intense concern with yields—is the frequent mention of wage labor. "In addition to the profits of farming [the author tells us in a typical passage] cultivators use their spare time to work for wages by the day or to engage in trade; some make in this way during a year between thirty and fifty *momme* [worth about one *koku* of rice in the early eighteenth century]."[11] Nor is the *Saizōki* the only evidence that wage labor was common in this area. An agreement was signed in 1713 by two villages near Hashimoto setting daily wages for the most important types of agricultural work: evidently labor was short and an attempt was being made locally to hold its price down. Eighty years later the shortage was still acute and seems to have become general. A document of 1790 from the government of the Kōya fief, which included much of the upper valley, speaks of the shortage explicitly and goes on to describe a consequence of it familiar in many places by this

[h] The *Saizōki*, written by a certain Saizō of Kamuro village near Hashimoto, purports to be a compilation of instructions given the author by his father. Part of the book deals with problems of village officials, but the greater part is devoted to showing how the family may be enriched through farming for the benefit of future generations. Among the unusual features of the book are figures on yields per *tan* of land and production costs per *koku* of rice.

[i] Boats for the lower valley loaded at Hashimoto, which was also a stopping place on the way from Osaka to Ise and other famous places including Mount Kōya. (Andō, "Kinsei zaikata shōgyō," p. 1.)

time: namely that large holders were having great difficulty working their land.[12] And still the labor shortage continued. In 1864 we find an order from Kōya requiring that holders and tenants within the borders of the fief rest their cotton looms for 50 and 20 days respectively from the eleventh day of the fifth month, that weaving might not interfere with the spring planting—showing, in addition to the shortage of agricultural labor, that the textile industry was in a flourishing condition.[13]

We have already traced the ways of the market in weakening the integrative force of cooperation and obligation in village life. Of these none was more destructive than an expanding labor market; for that meant the economic and social liberation of the small holder and *nago* from dependence on the group, and the decline of the group opened the way for competition and strife.

There is reason for thinking the struggle over the *miyaza* was most intense in communities located on the slopes rather than on the floor of the valley. These upland villages lacked the enormous integrative force that the irrigation system provided in most lowland villages; and since arable land in many such villages was exceedingly scarce and holdings almost uniformly small,[*] political and social inequalities had a less secure economic base than in villages where there was more arable land, less evenly distributed. Last, mountain villages were often more readily drawn into the market than other villages if transport and communication were not unduly difficult—admittedly a condition rarely met—for in charcoal making and lumbering these villages had potentially important industries ready to hand, and in addition upland was generally better suited than paddy to cash crops. In any case, all three Kishū communities for which we have documentation were either mountain or partly mountain villages.

The population of all three—Arakawa, Kudoyama, and Yamazaki by name—was divided cleanly into two groups of families: those who were members of the *miyaza* and those who were not—called *zakata* and *hirakata* respectively. As to the relative size of the groups, in one village there were 70 *zakata* and 320 *hirakata* families;[14] and although exact figures on the other two villages are lacking, in one the number of *zakata* increased toward the end of the Tokugawa period from

---

[*] There is a land register for just one of the three villages, a register of 1778 for Yamazaki village: it shows that the largest holding in the village at that date was worth only 6.536 *koku* yield. ("Denbata nayosechō," among Documents of Sugano family, Wakayama University.)

13 to 48, so the proportion of *zakata* before that time was certainly small. In other areas for which we have scattered data the proportion of *zakata* was likewise small.[k]

Family status as either *zakata* or *hirakata* was fixed more or less permanently, although occasionally a shift from the lower to the higher status was allowed, especially if a family belonging to the higher group died out. Otherwise membership in the *miyaza* passed down, like the family headship, from father to son, and passed down moreover to a single son in each generation. Branch families therefore did not inherit the *miyaza* status of their main families but became *hirakata*. So closely guarded was membership in the *miyaza*, in fact, that in some villages an adopted son who became head of a *zakata* family could not inherit membership unless his natural family were also *zakata*.[15] Thus, once established, the distinctions between the two groups in the village were perpetuated through the inheritance system.

It is impossible to know with certainty how communities first came to be divided into *zakata* and *hirakata*; the one certain thing is that the distinction goes back to a remote and misty past. There are reasons for thinking the chief basis for the distinction was family age. In the first place, *zakata* everywhere claimed to be the oldest families in their communities, in some cases alleging descent from ancestors who were contemporaries of the village deity: that is from the men who first cleared the land. On the other hand, *hirakata* were said to be relatively recent families, many of them immigrants,[l] which damned them doubly—as upstarts and as outlanders. Even the *zakata* admitted, though, that some *hirakata* families had been in the village several hundred years—such was the measure of age! Second, in some places *zakata* and *hirakata* were also called "old peasants" and "new peasants" respectively (*furubyakushō* and *shimbyakushō*). Third, all new families established in the village, even branches of *zakata* families, as we have seen, were automatically *hirakata*; hence the *zakata* as a group *must* have been older than the *hirakata*. Fourth, disabilities similar to those placed on *hirakata* were imposed on new families in nearly all communities whether there was a *miyaza* or not; and every-

[k] For instance: in 1825, 24 families belonged to the *miyaza* and 157 families stood outside it in a village in Sesshū. (Tsuda, "Hōken shakai hōkaiki," p. 9.)

[l] The size of Kudoyama village, which had a population of 400 families in 1756, certainly suggests a considerable immigrant population, attracted perhaps by employment opportunities in lumbering. (Documents 1:1; 1:8.)

where "*kyūka*" or "old family" was an honorific appellation and "*shin'ya*" or "new family" one of disesteem."

Naturally the *hirakata* denied everything, insisting that they were neither immigrants nor new families. They were as old (and hence as good) as the *zakata*, which came close to admitting that in principle family age and native-immigrant status were valid criteria for discrimination. But they were not convincing when it came to explaining why then they were nevertheless *hirakata*. The explanation was that membership in the *miyaza* required the payment of certain fees and that their ancestors had been too poor to belong"—which does not at all prove that they were not poor for the same reasons they were excluded.

Still other evidence on the point tends to support the *zakata* claim to an especial age as families. There were differences of status not only between *zakata* and *hirakata* but also among the *zakata* themselves; and since the latter distinctions pertained to ceremonial functions within the *miyaza*, we may suppose they were related in origin to those between *zakata* and other families. It is significant, therefore, that the titles distinguishing the various ranks among the *zakata* of one of the villages—Arakawa—were without exception titles belonging to officers of a medieval agrarian institution called *shō*[16] that was in some respects similar to the European manor and was at one time found over the greater part of the country. Nor was Arakawa an exceptional case. The title of the chief officer of the *miyaza* in many villages scattered over the Kinai was *kumon*, which was one of the commonest official titles to be found on the *shō*. It seems probable, then, that the preeminence of the highest-ranking *miyaza* families was longstanding, in some cases going back to perhaps the tenth century.° But what preeminence at that earlier time had been based on—whether administra-

---

^m See Chapter 5.

ⁿ There undoubtedly was an initiation fee, at least in some cases. A document listing the "precedents" concerning the *miyaza* in Arakawa village states: "A member of a *zakata* family may not make a payment of silver and assume a seat in the *za* before the age of eight." (Document 5:2.) There were in addition expenses incident to membership in the *miyaza*, such as contributing to the upkeep of the shrine and contributing to the expense of certain occasions more heavily than *hirakata*. For example, in Kudoyama village, a ceremony was held annually at which the birth of each female child during the year was announced. The parents of the newly born females bore the expense of the ceremony, *zakata* contributing three *shō* of rice per child and *hirakata* two *shō*. (Documents 2:1; 1:1.)

^o The *zakata* of Arakawa actually claimed that their privileges originated "about 800 years ago." (Document 4:8.)

tive office or family age—is quite uncertain. Whatever the answer, however, some *zakata* families were clearly among the oldest in the village.

Assuming family age to have been the essential distinction between *zakata* and *hirakata*, the struggle between the two groups would necessarily have cut across lineages, in general putting main and branch families on opposite sides of the conflict. A struggle of this kind could occur of course only where cooperative groups had largely ceased to perform the essential economic functions they had in the past. Although it is usually exceedingly difficult to identify main-branch relationships among families in a village at any very remote time in the past, it is possible to do so in one Shinshū village where there was a conflict over the ceremonial and political privileges of the *miyaza*. Members of the privileged group in this case were called *ōmae* while other families were called *komae*, roughly "great families" and "lesser families."[p] The lineage organization of this village, reconstructed from surviving genealogies, brings out two interesting facts. First, *komae* were without exception the branch families of *ōmae*;[17] and, second, *ōmae* with few exceptions were on the conservative side of the dispute, and *komae* were generally, though less solidly, on the other. In short, this dispute did rather consistently pit main and branch families against one another, showing how superficial cooperative groupings had become, and how powerful other interests now were.

The privileges of *zakata* families were essentially the same in all three of our Kishū villages. By far the most important privilege was the exclusive right to hold village office.[18] What power in village life this bespoke is described by the *zakata* of Arawaka who at the end of the nineteenth century recalled that they had once been the "brains and soul" of the village, and that they had dominated every aspect of village life. It is therefore not surprising to learn about another village from a gazetteer written in the late Tokugawa period that "Whenever a dispute arises, regardless of the right or wrong of the matter, the *hirakata* received the blame."[19] Such far-reaching power was not wholly conferred by political office but was strongly bolstered by

---

[p] These terms were widely used in Tokugawa times in a more general sense, to distinguish ordinary peasants (*komae*) from village officials, large holders, and others with a special position in the village (*ōmae*). It is significant that the term *ōmae* was also used in some places to designate the head family of a lineage. (*Kyōdoshi jiten*, compiled by Ōtsuka shigakkai, Tokyo, 1955, p. 71.)

office, once social and economic power began to fail. The question of the right to hold office therefore became the central issue in disputes between *hirakata* and *zakata*.

Other privileges claimed by the *zakata* were challenged at the same time, however. One was the exclusive right to exploit the common land of the village. In adjudicating the dispute in Kudoyama village, a magistrate stated that the *zakata* there claimed to be "in charge" (*shihai*) of the two mountains held as common land by the village, on the ground that they—the *zakata*—had lived in the village since the time of the village deity (*ujigami*). Apparently they claimed to own now as a group everything that the village had owned at that time, for the documents make it very clear that "in charge" meant the exclusive right of use, not merely management of the mountain for the benefit of the whole village.[20] Another *zakata* privilege claimed and challenged was the power to make for the community all decisions relating to irrigation. A *zakata* document of 1756 from Kudoyama reveals that the *zakata* leaders there rejected a petition from a *hirakata*, backed by others of the same status, to convert a certain field from upland to paddy. The power to make such decisions determined the allocation of a critical productive resource among the families of the village; and this particular decision precipitated a prolonged struggle between the two groups, whose interests were evidently affected oppositely by the change.[21]

Everywhere, of course, the *zakata* claimed exclusive ceremonial rights with respect to the community deity. This was inevitable: being the most somber and impressive expression of the community's corporate unity, the conduct of ceremonies directed toward the village deity reflected the hierarchical structure of the village, at least as it had existed at one time. Accordingly, only *zakata* could serve as shrine priests or in any of the other offices connected with the shrine; they made all decisions relating to the shrine, for example, its repair, its rebuilding, the timing of its various ceremonies; and they paid the greater part, if not all, of its expenses. Nor was the precedence of the *zakata* confined merely to administration of the shrine. "When the time comes to approach the deity (*ujigami*)," a petition of 1712 stated, "the members of the *miyaza* shall worship (*ogamu*) first and the *hirakata* may do so afterward."[22] The *hirakata* were not even allowed to attend some ceremonies associated with the village deity; as when the birth of a male child in a *zakata* family was announced to the *ujigami*, or when on an appointed day each month the *miyaza* assembled to offer wine to the *ujigami*.[23] On such occasions there was of course a strict order of ranking among the *zakata* themselves.[24]

Not all occasions were so exclusive; many the entire village attended. Such for instance were the meetings of the village assembly (*yoriai*) and the performances at the shrine or temple of Nō and Kyōgen. On such occasions, *zakata* and *hirakata* were strictly segregated. "On no account [says a document of 1713 from Yamazaki village] shall a *hirakata* be seated above a *zakata*."[25] An official, summing up the opposing claims in regard to seating in Kudoyama village at an annual ceremony on the eleventh day of the first month, said:[26]

First the Old Ones, Older Ones, and Oldest Ones [officers of the *miyaza?*] assemble at the shrine, make offerings, and drink ceremonial wine; then the other *zakata* and the *hirakata* assemble to receive wine. The seating order on this occasion is in dispute. The *zakata* claim that they are seated above and the *hirakata* below; the *hirakata* . . . say that only the headman and elders are seated above, and everyone else is seated according to age, whether *zakata* or *hirakata*.

No clearer evidence of failure to understand these disputes could be given than to imagine that the wrangling over seating order was petty and stupid. Questions of seating order went to the very heart of village organization, which was based on gradations of rank; let any of these break down and all would soon be in confusion. As the *zakata* of Yamazaki village put it: "Division of the village into *zakata* and *hirakata* is not limited to the *za* of the shrine; it includes all matters of seating and is so in all villages. To ignore it would be absurd and make government and other affairs in the village exceedingly difficult."[27]

"All matters of seating" meant on all occasions. For distinctions among *zakata* themselves, and between *zakata* and *hirakata*, although originating in the organization of Shinto ceremonies, carried over without perceptible softening into the ceremonies and management of Buddhist temples, despite the egalitarian character of Buddhist teaching. To illustrate: in Kudoyama, the *hirakata* petitioned the authorities for permission to build a Buddhist temple of their own, to be called Kwannon Temple,[q] because, on the occasion of masses at the existing

---

[q] It is significant that the shrine of the *ujigami* was located within the precincts of the temple. The *zakata* replied to the *hirakata* petition that they could not agree to the construction of the Kwannonji, since: "From early times there has been in the village a temple called Henjōji where all the people of the village

temple, the *zakata* entered the temple in order of rank, but no *hira-kata* was allowed to enter except the two leading families among them.[28] Discrimination between the two groups was allegedly carried over even into the play of children.[r]

None of these distinctions was unbearable or perhaps even especially distasteful, so long as cooperative agriculture prevailed, for then the distinctions seemed justified by differential functions. When distinctions ceased to have this meaning—apparently about the middle of the eighteenth century in the Ki River Valley—*hirakata* rebelled against them. Significantly, however, they did not demand outright abolition of the *miyaza* and the end of all distinctions; so deeply implanted was the notion of hierarchy, even the *hirakata* assumed that formal ranking in some form would continue. All they asked was that the existing system be revised. It was characteristic, for instance, that the *hirakata* in Kudoyama village asked for a Buddhist temple of their own rather than an end to segregation at the existing one. The most radical political demand heard was not, as one might expect, that group status be held irrelevant to the holding of village office, but that *hirakata* as well as *zakata* be permitted to hold such office. In one Kinai village, the *hirakata* went so far in recognizing the existing distinctions as to petition merely for political representation *as a group*: they asked that two village elders henceforth be selected from among *hirakata*.[29]

Although the central issue of disputes over the *miyaza* was the question of political enfranchisement, *hirakata* did not confine their demands to this issue in any of the three Kishū villages. As part of a general system of discrimination, differential political rights were difficult to attack alone, and demands for political reform soon included

worship and *where the ujigami is located and prayers are said to him*." (Document 1:1; my italics.) Nor was this mingling of Buddhism and Shinto rare. Among the "Ancient Precedents Concerning the *miyaza*" in Arakawa village was this one: "At the performance of Nō drama on the occasion of the moving-the-shrine-ceremony at Omifune shrine, the members of the *miyaza* without exception assemble at the temple called Kōsanji and receive ceremonial wine." (Document 4:8.)

[r] For example, see Nōson shiryō chōsakai (ed.), *Nōson no kōzō*, p. 149. Nor is this fact surprising since children's society in rural Japan mirrors in many ways the hierarchy of adult society. In some parts of Tōhoku, for instance, the son of a branch family until recently addressed the son of the main family as "elder brother" even when the latter was the younger of the two; and elsewhere the head of the youth group (*wakashū*) was typically chosen from a group of families providing headmen for the village. (Furushima, *Sanson no kōzō*, p. 165.)

demands for other kinds of reform too. The *hirakata* of Kudoyama demanded, for instance, in addition to the right to hold office, that they be allowed to enter the Henjōji temple on certain occasions; that anyone in the village be permitted to gather grass from the common; that on all kinds of occasions the officials of the village be seated in positions of honor but everyone else be seated according to age; that a certain ceremonial dinner that was held at public expense for the *zakata* once a year be abolished; that at certain Shinto ceremonies for the whole village *hirakata* be qualified equally with *zakata* to carry the sacred utensils.[30]

In some communities *hirakata* claims may have led to violence, but none of our three villages offers such an example. So far as the documents reveal, both sides confined themselves to appealing to the higher authorities to support their claims. In each case the conflict started with the *hirakata* submitting a petition asking for a magistrate's intervention on their behalf, the *zakata* following quickly with a counterpetition. In the resulting argument, one characteristic runs through the views of all three parties—*zakata*, *hirakata*, and the adjudicating officials alike. All accepted tradition as the ultimate standard of what should be and the only possible sanction for what was. Nowhere in the documents of any of the three villages did anyone appeal to an abstract principle of justice. The discrete events of the past were an authoritative guide to the present, and each party sought to show that its position conformed to them exactly. Other positions were described as representing "innovations" (*shimpō*), tantamount to charging those who held them with subversion. The direst consequences were predicted if tradition were sacrificed to innovation: the least that would happen was that the village would be thrown into confusion, local government would break down, the ruling class would be sorely vexed.

Of course, the argument that whatever was, was right, is not surprising coming from the *zakata* or the adjudicating officials, who were trying to defend existing arrangements against the demand for change. But the historical argument coming from the *hirakata*, who were trying to change existing institutions and should therefore (one supposes) be denying the validity of past practice and arguing for a clean sweep, is curious. All the same, we find *hirakata* appealing to history for vindication no less earnestly than the others. The *hirakata* of Kudoyama claimed they should be allowed to serve as headmen because one *hirakata* named Dembei had once served in that office; and that they should be permitted to serve as elders because certain *hirakata* had actually done so years before.[31] The *hirakata* in Yamazaki claimed the right, on the occasion of a certain ceremony, to enter a particular temple building in the village because once, 12 years previously, they had actually done so;[8] and so on.

Looking thus steadily to the past for justification, it is not surprising that *hirakata* had no vision of a future different in principle from what they had known. Indeed they had no quarrel with the past, only with the *zakata* version of it. Although this suggests a strong underlying conservatism, the particular version of the past they espoused was radically different from the dominant one, and the attempt to shape the present in accordance with it was in effect an attack on the whole structure of privilege inherited from the past. Nothing reveals this more clearly than the tenacity with which the *zakata*, heirs of the past, fought the *hirakata* program.

Although no violence marked the contention over the *miyaza* in any of our three villages, there was no lack of rancor. Even the pious language of the petitions fails to obscure the outraged feelings of the *zakata* of Kudoyama, for instance, commenting on an official decision in favor of the *hirakata*:[32]

The decision of the magistrate distressed us greatly, so we petitioned for a change of the order, knowing that the original decision was because the *hirakata* had tricked the magistrate. Their impropriety in doing so was unspeakable.

Consider the sequence of events leading up to this petition. Trouble began when the *hirakata* allegedly tricked the magistrate into making a favorable decision on a point concerning the use of arable land in the village. Outraged, the *zakata* petitioned the magistrate to change his order; he agreed to revise but not to annul it. Dissatisfied with this, the *zakata* sought to enlist the support of the *hirakata*, arguing that the revised order of the magistrate was the worst possible outcome for all concerned. The *hirakata* refused to cooperate and the *zakata* dropped the idea of another petition; meanwhile new issues between the two sides arose and were appealed to the magistrate, who decided against the *zakata*. Finally, despairing of success from more petitioning, they dispatched the village headman (a *zakata*, of course) to try to win the magistrate over privately. Unfortunately, as the *zakata* said subsequently in recounting the event: "The headman went

---

[8] The *zakata* did not deny this but said that the ceremony 12 years before was not the one the *hirakata* claimed; hence it constituted no precedent! (Documents 3:1; 1–2; 4:6.)

too far in his speech and was reprimanded and deprived of his office by the magistrate."[33]

The *zakata* now proposed to submit an apology from the entire village to the magistrate asking that the headman be pardoned; but the *hirakata* would not agree. The *zakata* therefore submitted the apology alone, only to have it rejected by the magistrate, who took the occasion to order that the headman's office, now vacant, be filled by election.[*] This made matters worse, and the *zakata* repeatedly asked the magistrate to reconsider. His answer was always the same: he would do so when he received a petition from the *whole* village to that effect. Since it was impossible to get *hirakata* agreement to any such petition, the issue remained unsettled and the village remained without a headman. Finally the *zakata*, going over the heads of the magistrate and even the lord, appealed to the magistrate in charge of shrines and temples in Edo (*jisha bugyō*). This was a desperate move since it entailed great expense and was a most dangerous breach of discipline, for which luckily they were merely reprimanded.[34]

Or take an amusing case showing the cunning with which communal warfare was waged. There had been a longstanding dispute between the two sides in Yamazaki village as to whether *hirakata* could participate on equal terms with the *zakata* in the ceremony held in conjunction with the periodic rebuilding of the village shrine, one of the most important of all village ceremonies. What once happened on the occasion of this ceremony had best be told in the terse language of the *hirakata* petition ten years after the event, when the dispute was still unsettled:[35]

It had been decided by the entire village meeting together that the time for beginning the ceremony should be the hour of the Ox. A drum was to be struck to announce the event to all. But before the appointed time, the members of the *miyaza* met and conducted the ceremony secretly—in order to carry it out properly, they said. We were shocked at this affront and protested repeatedly to the headman.

The documents available to us from Kishū record disputes that had already been in progress for many years by the late eighteenth century. How long is impossible to say in the case of Yamazaki village. We have one document of 1713 telling about a dispute that was still in progress in 1862![36] No wonder, then, that we see no definitive settlement of any of these disputes in the relatively short time covered

---

[*] It is not exactly clear what was meant by the word "election," but what seems indicated was an arrangement whereby the *zakata* would select a number of candidates from among themselves, and then the village at large elect one of them.

by the documentation. Indeed, a definitive settlement was out of the question so long as all parties, including the magistrate, took for granted the continuing existence of the two groups. So long as that was the case no settlement could result in more than a temporary equilibrium. This or that concession might satisfy the *hirakata* momentarily, but as long as they were denied complete equality they were certain sooner or later to renew the struggle.

Although for lack of documentation we cannot follow the history of this warfare further, we do know in general how it turned out. The victory of the *hirakata* was complete, for in these and other Kinai villages, almost without exception, the *miyaza* today either has ceased to exist or has been enlarged to include the entire village. It is possible, of course, that the political struggle between the same old groups has merely assumed new forms, but this seems doubtful. It certainly has not in villages where almost no one any longer even remembers which families belonged to the *miyaza* and which did not, and where public issues have changed too drastically for us to believe that parties have remained the same. But the struggle did continue long after the end of the Tokugawa period when we lose sight of it. Just once after that we catch a glimpse of the denouement, in an agreement made November 1899 by the *zakata* of Arakawa village, who were seeking vainly to save a cause already lost. In the agreement are expressed all the nostalgia of the conservative, and the bitterness of a proud and once powerful privileged class whose leadership has been thrust aside. The document is worth quoting at some length:[37]

We *toshiyori*[38] of Arakawa village are losing our quality. In ancient times . . . we were the officials who managed the affairs of the shrine and the legal and political matters of the village. We were the brains and spirit of the community. We occupied a privileged position in order to augment and safeguard the happiness of the people. The origin of that position is very ancient, and since its origin, though there have been many ups and downs, about eight hundred years have passed in all, and we continue the tradition unbroken. However, as a result of the Restoration [in 1868] many changes have occurred and our position with regard to legal and political matters is about to be destroyed. Now it consists of little more than the upkeep of the main part of the Shrine. Consequently, we who for many hundreds of years rendered good service are about to be swept aside. This is most lamentable. Therefore we have assembled as a group in the Mifune shrine and have resolved to strengthen our position in every way possible and thus to restore the former influence of this group.

[38] It is difficult to say in what sense the word *toshiyori* is used here, whether to mean a select group among the *zakata* or possibly as a synonym for *zakata*.

13

AGRARIAN CHANGE AND MODERN JAPAN

If a backward country, such as Japan was in 1850, is to modernize as rapidly as Japan did, it seems necessary that it satisfy a minimum of four conditions. First, it must have a leadership with a vision of a future radically different from the past. Second, the leadership must have control over a government with a high degree of authority and stability for decades; otherwise it will be unable to channel income into investment on the necessary scale, to overhaul or abolish traditional institutions that impede change, and to bring the people to the pitch of effort required to become something they are not. Third, the economy must afford the means of investing on a significant scale. Last, industry must have a satisfactory supply of labor. That these conditions could be satisfied in Japan in the second half of the nineteenth century was in no small part due to the agrarian changes of the preceding century and a half. Let us consider each condition in turn.

Japanese modernization as a rapid and deliberate movement began in 1868 with the Meiji Restoration. This event brought to power new men who used the authority of the state to drive the nation swiftly toward goals of industrial strength and military competence; the transformation of the country in the next few decades was largely their deliberate work. No one would deny that there were certain long-term trends in Japanese society and economy favorable to this work, but without a political revolution they might have come to nothing. How, then, did the revolution itself come about?

We know that many of the revolutionary leaders were warriors of relatively low rank who used their lords' fiefs (in which they had already won considerable power) as political and military bases to destroy the Shogunate and create a new government around the Emperor. But why did they choose to use power as they did, for sweeping reform rather than to restore the feudal system along lines more to their advantage? And how did lowly and often impecunious warriors[1] gain such power in the first place? We shall probably never know in satisfactory detail, since many of the critical episodes of the drama were backstage maneuvers in an atmosphere of conspiracy and suspicion. Although the agrarian background of politics of that period throws no direct light on these confused events, it helps us understand their outcome. But first something must be said of the place of the village in the political system.

The 250-odd fiefs in existence at the end of the Tokugawa period were similarly organized. Each was a more or less extensive territory held by a lord (*daimyō*) who lived in a castle town surrounded by armed retainers through whom he administered his lands. The administration consisted essentially of two echelons of officials: those who manned the central bureaus located in the castle or nearby in the town, and the district magistrates who were scattered about the fief. Each of the latter had an area in which he collected taxes, administered justice, maintained public order, carried out the orders of higher organs of government; in short, where he represented the lord in all of his manifold functions.

There were fewer of these district officials than seems possible today when we recall their heavy responsibilities. Although each had a staff of runners, secretaries, copyists, and servants, he was the only official between the village and the castle town, which in some cases was scores or, in the case of detached territories, even hundreds of miles away. Most surprising, perhaps, he usually had no military force at his command except a handful of armed men for guard duty. Nor were there warriors scattered through the villages who could rally quickly to his support with retainers, horses, and arms. Three hundred years earlier, in all but a few localities, the warriors had been removed from the countryside to the castle town in order to eliminate the danger to the lord of armed retainers directly in control of land and subjects. Thus the district magistrate, stationed in some tiny town or village surrounded by thickly settled hamlets stretching as far as the eye could see and well beyond, was charged with governing thousands of peasant families, with no immediate source of support more substantial than his insignia of office.

What made possible this extraordinary economy of force and officialdom was the competence and reliability of local government. Nowhere, for instance, did the lord undertake to levy taxes on individual peasants; rather, he laid taxes on villages as units, leaving each to allocate and collect its own, and to make up any deficit that might occur in the payments of individual families. This was but one of many administrative functions performed by villages in all parts of the country. Villages maintained their own roads and irrigation works, policed their territories, administered common land and irrigation rights; validated legal transactions among members, mediated disputes, and passed sentence and imposed punishment in petty criminal cases; enforced the lord's law and their own, stood responsible as a whole for a crime by any of their members, borrowed money, made contracts, sued and were sued. Aside from transmitting the lord's instructions to the villages, the magistrate normally did little more than help assess villages for taxes and receive their payments and hear the more serious civil and criminal cases they referred to him. Indeed, when local government was working well, he might even absent himself from his district for considerable periods, merely leaving an assistant in charge.

This administrative system was by no means merely a contrivance of the warrior class for its convenience; it had been evolving since prehistoric times. From the beginning of agriculture the village had a strong corporate life. The pattern of compact settlements testifies to the fact, as do the character of the tutelary deities and the ritual surrounding them. Even without these indications, however, one might guess at the character of the village from the authority the village exercised over its members and the need for continuous cooperation in farming.

As villages grew through immigration and the proliferation of families, a hierarchy of lineage, wealth, and political rights formed naturally in each, through the operation of the inheritance system and discrimination against immigrants. Cooperation in farming and the distributive system both were organized around these hierarchies; the villages were governed by them insofar as villages governed themselves. The evolving structure within the village was not radically modified until it was finally disrupted by the market, but the relations of the village to outside authority underwent many changes. The problem of government for successive military rulers was to make full administrative use of, without being menaced by, these stable local systems of power, typically headed by warrior families. By far the most successful attempt to solve this problem was the last, under the Tokugawa. It gave the village an extraordinary degree of autonomy *after* removing the warriors from it: an arrangement that brought the country two and a half centuries of peace, together with an unprecedented measure of popular welfare and justice.

But no balance between local government and higher authority could be final, and the sources of strength in the Tokugawa system were potentially sources of weakness. Power had been delegated downward so far, and on such a scale, that it could no longer be easily recovered. The system worked amazingly well; but everything depended on the continuing loyalty and discipline of the peasants. No breakdown of these supports of government was likely to occur—and none did, in fact—so long as the economic and social systems of the traditional village remained undisturbed. But what if these structures were violently upset: if the hierarchy of lineage, wealth, and political rights were disrupted from the outside?

No one in 1600 could have foreseen any such development. Yet the very success of the Tokugawa system created conditions favorable to change; cities grew, communications improved, productivity in agriculture increased, industry spread from town to countryside. Government did its best to isolate the village from the effects of these and other changes. But, as we have seen, the best efforts were unavailing and what was most feared happened: the stable structure of power in the village was upset.

Instability in the villages must have affected warrior politics within fiefs and nationally; for by 1860 the warrior class was deeply divided over foreign policy and the position of the Emperor. The contending parties would not have overlooked the opportunity to use village factions to their advantage since to control the villages of a fief was already to control half of its government. Besides, agrarian issues—posed by the spread of tenancy, the movement of population to towns and cities, and official trade monopolies—themselves contributed to the growing political crisis, forcing warrior parties to take positions on reform legislation certain to arouse intense interest—whether hostile or approving—in the villages.

It is not surprising, therefore, to find evidence of peasants taking part in the Restoration movement. Not only were loyalist sympathies common among the educated class of the village; a surprising number of peasants were given court honors for their part in the Restoration, and there must have been many more whose help was never so dramatically acknowledged. It is impossible to say with certainty how important peasant support was to the success of the Restoration; but it seems to have been of some consequence, and it was perhaps also important in turning the new government away from the temptation, undoubtedly present, to use victory merely to redistribute power within the warrior class.

That a backward nation's leaders are enlightened is not enough to guarantee success in modernizing; the leaders must have continuing support from the nation. Japan's new leaders commanded such support—despite what they demanded of the nation: nothing less than that it become an industrial society within a generation. One need only think what that overriding goal implied—in social dislocations, psychological strain, the disturbance of vested interests—to understand how difficult was the problem of organizing support.

To mobilize and hold support it was clearly necessary to formulate goals the nation could understand. But how state goals compellingly when they far transcend the experience of the community? How talk about national power, industrialization, or the march of science to a still agrarian people just emerging from feudalism? Japan's new leaders found the answer to this problem in translating these goals into a traditional language of loyalty and obligation. This was the language of feudal and family ethics expressing ideals central to the experience of nearly all Japanese. With suitable interpretation to make all little loyalties lead up to one great loyalty to the Emperor, these ideals called up prodigies of effort and self-sacrifice. No government could ask for more.

But, in thus using tradition on behalf of change, the new government soon found itself in a painful dilemma. Old values might sanction the building of a new society, but the new society could never be as hospitable to them as the old had been. In fact as an industrial society came into being, traditional values became increasingly irrelevant or obstructive, and steadily lost the power to command belief. Let me cite a few examples.

Rationalist thought, which an educational system dedicated to the advancement of science and technology was bound to promote, gradually called into question central elements of the political myth—imperial divinity and the family state. Modern industry gave rise to new and harsher class antagonisms that made the ideals of solidarity and duty to superiors harder to cherish. The authority of the family and the power of its symbols declined as the family lost economic functions to the market, and as the difference in outlook between generations widened. Nevertheless, the primary old values of loyalty and obedience did not collapse: they were continuously reinforced by stronger, more efficient measures of indoctrination and thought control by the state.

The groups in control of the state had no choice but to sustain orthodoxy as best they could. Without it there was no sanction for their monopoly of power, or for the wrenching changes of the forced march to industry and empire. If that effort should collapse, so must Japan's precarious international position, bringing loss of foreign markets, unemployment, perhaps social revolution. These were unthinkable alternatives. There was no way to go but ahead; but that way lay a further weakening of tradition which, the weaker it became, was the more needed to give stability and command effort. So leaders pushed ahead at any cost with supreme nerve or blind faith—it mattered little which. The ultimate price the nation paid was to be led without enthusiasm into a war that could not be won.

Long before this, however, the nation was paying in malaise for industrial success. Japanese life was wracked by the mounting tension of trying to live by the values of another age. Tensions did not take the form of ideological or political struggle between the parties who stood by tradition and those who would overthrow it. Such overt struggle might have been easier, or in any case would have put the stress between groups and parties rather than inside individuals. Except for Marxist intellectuals, however, no notable segment of the Japanese population openly disfavored the official ideology; no one could, without becoming an enemy of the state and in some real sense ceasing to be Japanese. But as time passed fewer and fewer people bore the weight of tradition comfortably; despite nearly universal protestations of loyalty and belief there was secret or unconscious alienation.

It is easier to guess than prove the existence of inner conflict deep beneath the surface of conduct. Still, testifying to it there were unwitting—and even some witting—flashes of candor. Take this passage from the novel *Sore kara*, by Natsume Soseki, in which a young man reflects on his father:[a]

His father had received the moral upbringing usual for samurai before the Restoration. This upbringing taught a code of conduct utterly removed from the realities of day-to-day living, yet his father believed in it implicitly— and this despite the fact that he was forever being driven by the fierce demands of business life. Over the long years he had changed with these demands, and now he bore little resemblance to what he once was, though he was quite unaware of this. Indeed, he was always boasting that it was his

[a] *Sōseki zenshū*, compiled by Iwanami Shigeo, Tokyo, 1936, V, 532.

strict warrior education that accounted for his success! But Daisuke thought differently. How could one fulfill the hourly demands of modern life and live by a feudal ethic! Even to try, one must wage war against oneself.

Or consider the case of Ishikawa Takuboku, one of Japan's most famous poets. Takuboku wrote a novel (*Kumo wa tensai dearu*) in which the hero, who is surely Takuboku himself, thinks existing society utterly corrupt and worthy only of destruction. While writing this novel, Takuboku wrote to a friend that he badly needed the money from its publication to discharge a long-neglected duty to his elder brother. What this duty was he did not say, but the term he used for it was *giri*—one of the central concepts of the ethics taught in the schools; and Takuboku was at this time a village school teacher, and his story's hero was the principal of a village elementary school. Conflicts like that of Takuboku, who seems a rebel against society's conventions while a slave to them, were not uncommon, and few aspects of modern Japanese culture would not reveal some evidence of them to careful analysis. Let me cite a few other examples.

Except on the far left, which did not count in the parliamentary struggle, no political party openly challenged the theory that all political authority derived from the Emperor. For parliamentary parties this theory had serious disadvantages since it placed governments beyond their control—cabinet ministers being responsible only to the Emperor. To overcome this inconvenience, almost continuously from 1880 to about 1935 one party or another advanced the view—strongly resisted by the military and the bureaucracy—that cabinet ministers should be responsible to parliament: the Emperor would still appoint ministers, but from the majority party in the lower house only. Those who held this view disclaimed any intention of encroaching on the power of the Emperor; they proved it (to their own satisfaction) by giving the doctrine of the Emperor as father of the people an ingenious if unconvincing twist. Since the Emperor was a wise and benevolent father who desired nothing but the welfare of his loving and filial subjects, there could be no conflict between throne and people; and to make the government responsible to parliament would merely bring the two closer together, thus making more effective the single will of both—now sometimes frustrated by selfish (and presumably unfilial) ministers! This argument was advanced by parties representing modern businessmen who, though aware of the stabilizing uses of the throne, were from time to time embarrassed and bullied by the governments that manipulated the throne's occult powers. The argument was, in essence, a radical attack on authoritarian government, hidden in a statement of the purest orthodoxy. There was no dishonesty in this— just divided minds and hearts.

Other examples come to mind: the drive to rationalize operations in business firms organized on the family principle; indoctrination in the values of the hierarchical family in an egalitarian educational system; the emperor cult and class struggle in the labor movement. But let us consider an important problem our argument raises. How was it that the old values continued to be strong enough to serve the purposes of the state and to create tension in men's minds? Why did the values rather not quickly lose their emotional power? The answer cannot merely be that the government sustained them through the educational system, military training, and public information media: for then what sustained the resolution of the government as its social base was transformed?

This brings us back to the character of agrarian change, which was determined as much by what did *not* change about farming as by what did. As was noted in the Introduction, change occurred within relatively narrow technical limits; and of the relatively unchanging elements of farming, the most important were the small size of the units, family organization of production, and the unsparing use of hand labor.[b] Whatever the reasons for these extraordinary continuities— and they are hotly debated—they had the effect of perpetuating the peasant family as an economic unit, thus allowing little change in its social character. The family's welfare continued to be of transcendent value, its authority immense. Solidarity and obedience were taught to the young as conditions of survival, and these traditional values carried over to behavior outside the family.

Another repository of tradition was the village. In many countries

[b] The continuing importance of the family in farming is revealed by the following figures, which show, on holdings of different size, the average percentage of labor that came from each of various sources in 1954: Ōuchi Tsutomu, *Nōka keizai*, Tokyo, 1957, p. 163.

Size of Holding (in *tan*)	Family	Hired by Year	Hired for Short Periods	Labor Received Through Various Forms of Social Obligation
Under 5	94.9	0.0	2.5	2.6
5–10	95.7	0.2	1.9	2.2
10–15	94.8	0.6	2.5	2.1
15–20	92.3	1.8	3.9	2.0
Over 20	88.2	4.2	5.4	2.2

industry broke up the peasant village and dispersed its population, or greatly weakened its solidarity by creating deep class divisions. Neither development occurred in Japan, at least not on a comparable scale. Family farming remained the almost invariable rule, preserving the pattern of compact settlements and blocking the growth of large capitalist farms. Landownership did tend to concentrate, but large owners turned their land over to families of tenants or part-tenants rather than work it themselves. Despite increasing differences of income and the growth of by-employments, therefore, the village remained predominantly a community of small peasants faced with similar problems of small-scale cultivation and marketing. Sentimental and organizational ties from an earlier period persisted with special force, and the authority of the village over its members remained exceedingly strong.

Rice culture also contributed to this result. Rice was cultivated wherever soil, climate, and terrain permitted, which is to say on at least part of most holdings. Because rice must be made to stand in water much of the growing season to get maximum yields, there was need in nearly every village for an extensive system of ditches, dams, dikes, ponds, tunnels, and water gates. Since these could be constructed and maintained only by community effort, their use was subject to community control. A rice farmer never owned or controlled all of the essential means of production himself, and he could not individually make all of the critical decisions of farming. He might wish, for instance, to turn an unirrigated field into paddy, but he would not be allowed to do so if this would impair the water supply of others. And, if this was the case, he would refrain from insisting on his wish since he had been taught he must and village opinion would be ranged solidly against him if he did not. The habit of obedience to community opinion where water was concerned likewise carried over to other community affairs (including the preservation of tradition), since any serious breach of solidarity directly threatened the communal foundations of farming.

Family farming and the emphasis on rice as a crop tended to preserve tradition among the peasantry in another way. These two factors kept farming less commercial than one might think in a country with as large an urban market as Japan. Most peasant families supplied all or nearly all of their own food, and food took a relatively large share of individual output. Hence, about one-third of the total agricultural income of the average peasant family in 1935 was received in kind, which is to say was consumed without marketing. Thus the Japanese peasant's involvement in the market was far from complete; commercial values did not penetrate a very large area of economic relations, which remained embedded in custom-bound social groups.[c]

Despite some weakening, the peasant family and village remained enormously powerful, conservative institutions. And it must be remembered that agriculture was not changing—or these institutions weakening—at the same rate in all parts of the country. There were great variations in this respect. In some places, for example, individual agriculture was a reality by the end of the Tokugawa period; in others it had just begun to appear. So the world of traditional values was not dead even in the early part of this century, but was full of life over large parts of Tōhoku, Hokuriku, and Kyūshū, and in some other areas.

Thus, although modernization generated in towns and cities new attitudes destructive of tradition, and greatly affected some important aspects of agriculture, the countryside remained a vast and populous hinterland of conservatism. Nor did the demographic ratio between town and country alter with the growth of industry as rapidly as in some countries. Owing to the intensive nature of farming, the agricultural population was almost perfectly stable from 1868 to 1940. As a result, persons employed in agriculture in Japan in 1930 accounted for 50.3 percent of the total labor force—as compared with 18.8 percent in the United States in 1940, 16.3 percent in Germany in 1933, and 6.2 percent in England in 1938! Here, then, was one of the most important reasons the state was able to sustain tradition even in the face of breathless change.

This brings us to a third condition for late but rapid modernization. Even though a government is strong and has the will to mod-

---

[c] Nor has the situation changed radically since the war. In 1954, the percentage of total agricultural income received in money by various classes of holders was as follows:

Size of Holding (in *tan*)	Percentage of Total Agricultural Income in Cash
Less than 5	42.8
5–10	58.0
10–15	64.8
15–20	68.5
Over 20	72.6

These figures bring out very clearly that the degree of commercialization is especially low on small holdings. (*Ibid.*, pp. 85,170.)

ernize, it must still find the means to invest on a grand scale in schools, factories, roads, harbors, railways, and so on, or its ambitions will come to nothing. If funds cannot be had from foreign sources, they must be taken from the domestic economy—which in most cases means from agriculture: thus the ability to modernize comes to depend largely on the productivity of agriculture and the willingness of the peasantry to part with current income for distant and half-understood goals.

This was Japan's predicament during the second half of the nineteenth century. Being fearful of the political consequences of foreign borrowing, the government financed investment almost entirely from domestic sources—mainly agriculture. The land tax accounted for 78 percent of ordinary revenues (the bulk of total revenues) from 1868 to 1881, and although the figure tended to fall after that it still stood at 50 percent in 1890. High as the rate of tax on land was, however, it did not represent an increase over the Tokugawa period. Already at the end of that period the take from agriculture by the warrior class was immense, and the Meiji government merely redirected it into new channels. Modernization was achieved, therefore, without reducing rural living standards or even taking the increase in productivity that occurred.

This bespeaks a very high level of productivity in agriculture by the end of the Tokugawa period, and it could not have been achieved except for the changes that had taken place in farming since 1600. These had freed the peasant of the goals of subsistence farming, concentrating his attention on raising crop yields, and they had given him new fertilizers, crops, and plant strains. At the same time they had loosened the control of the social group over his methods and routine, leaving him, within certain broad limits, free to farm as he would whatever others might do. This is but half of the story, however. Changes in farming had created a "surplus": but the traditional features of agrarian society made it possible for the government to continue to take the surplus over many generations. Had the rural population been moving away from tradition as rapidly as some other elements of the population, it is at least doubtful that so large a rate of investment or so fast a rate of modernization could have been sustained.

Finally, let us briefly consider the need for fit human materials for modernization. Industry clearly can develop no faster than the quantity and the quality of the labor force allow, which in practice usually means no faster than the character of agriculture permits, since workers must be recruited mainly from the farm population.[d] The offer of high wages (assuming such wages are feasible) does not alone assure a sufficient flow of labor, sufficiently trained. Market incentives may be too weak because they meet with a nearly universal aversion to factory employment or dislike of separating from family. Or there may be no difficulty in attracting labor but no quick or economical way of overcoming its ineptitude and psychological unfitness. (Throughout this argument I am assuming that force may not be used wholesale in place of incentives.)

It is easy to overlook the significance of labor in Japanese industrialization because it posed no major problem. For upward of two hundred years the agricultural labor force had been unwittingly preparing for the transition to factory employment. Commercial farming and the experience of working for wages had taught peasants to respond with alacrity to monetary incentives, and had given them a certain tolerance of impersonal relationships in pursuing monetary goals; but at the same time agriculture had not changed so much as to destroy the habit of loyalty and obedience. Another factor of importance was that wage labor had already begun to make the individual worker to some extent an economic unit. Wages after all were paid to him; and even if he turned them over to the family head, they were often saved in part to finance his marriage later on. In any case, working for wages had taught him that it was possible, and might also be advantageous, to cut family ties and make his way alone. This essential psychological preparation made it relatively easy to draw the peasant away from the village to the city. He came to the city already half-trained, too. Rural industry had given him a certain quickness of hand and eye, a respect for tools and materials, an adaptability to the cadences and confusion of moving parts; and city industry (or backward sectors of it where he could begin) was not technically so far advanced as to make his skills irrelevant. Few countries have embarked on industry with a superior labor force at hand.

But it was not only labor that rural Japan contributed to the city. Through the public schools and universities, many men (and some

[d] Alexander Gerschenkron points out that ". . . industrial labor in the sense of a stable, reliable, and disciplined group that has cut the umbilical cord connecting it with the land and has become suitable for utilization in factories is not abundant but extremely scarce in a backward country. Creation of an industrial labor force that really deserves its name is a most difficult and protracted process." ("Economic Backwardness in Historical Perspective," Bert F. Hoselitz (ed.), *The Progress of Underdeveloped Areas*, Chicago, 1952, p. 7.)

women) who were country-born rose to important positions in banking, industry, politics, education, letters, government, and so on. Indeed, an astonishing proportion of Japan's leaders in the past century have been men who reached adolescence in village environments. This bespeaks a high level of cultural achievement and aspiration in the countryside but also a narrowness of opportunity. Migration in Japan was a selective social movement. Men left their homes because they were restless and ambitious: because they saw elsewhere an avenue of advancement but barriers blocking it where they were.

For the past century therefore the villages have been exporting much of their best human material, or rather those best fitted for the relentless competitive struggle of urban life. Part of the dynamism of Japanese modernization must be found in this continuous flow of talented, aggressive, ambitious people. What was there in village life to produce such people in great number from the end of the Tokugawa period on? What social alchemy made of peasant boys men who could found international banks and trading companies? I do not know, but beyond question part of the answer is to be found somewhere in the history of change in rural Japan before 1868.

NOTES

ABBREVIATIONS

RGKK	*Rekishigaku kenkyū*	*NHRS*	*Nihon rekishi*
SGZS	*Shigaku zasshi*	*NGKK*	*Nōgyō keizai kenkyū*
SKSG	*Shakai keizai shigaku*	*NKSS*	*Nihon keizai sōsho*
NSKK	*Nihonshi kenkyū*	*KJKS*	*Kinsei jikata keizai shiryō*
	KSKS	*Kinsei shakai keizai sōsho*	

CHAPTER 1

1. Miyagawa Mitsuru, "Gōson seido to kenchi," *NSKK*, 19 (1953), 12.

2. *Ibid.*

3. Ōishi Kyūkei, "Jikata hanreiroku" (1781–94), *NKSS*, XXXI, 132–37.

4. Toyoda Takeshi, *Nihon no hōken toshi*, Tokyo, 1952, pp. 37, 148–49; and Sekiyama Naotarō, *Kinsei Nihon jinkō no kenkyū*, Tokyo, 1948, p. 232.

5. Furushima Toshio, "Edo jidai ni okeru Kinai nōgyō to kisei jinushi," *RGKK*, 144 (1950), 1.

6. *NKSS*, I, 70–71.

7. Scattered statistics on landholding in individual villages exist in impressive number, but no effort has been made to bring them together. Examples of village statistics may be found in Akiyama Hideo, "Kinsei shotō ni okeru Kinai sonraku no kenchi ni tsuite," *Hisutoria*, 5 (1952), 1; Sumi Tōyō, "Kinsei zenki Kinai sonraku no dōkō," *Hisutoria*, 13 (1955), 3; Hattori Kentarō, "Musashi no kuni Saitama-gun Mugikura-mura," *Mita gakkai zasshi*, XLVI, 2 (1953), 6; Ōtsuki Hiroshi, "Awahan ni okeru kinsei sonraku no keisei katei," *Keizai ronsō*, LXXIV, 2 (1954), 9.

8. See for example Oka Mitsuo, "Kinsei sonraku no tenkai to inasaku kankō," *RGKK*, 193 (1956), 25–26; and Takao Kazuhiko, "Edo zenki ni okeru Kinai sonraku no kōsei," *Kenkyū* (Kōbe daigaku bungakkai), 3 (1957), 60.

9. Hirasawa Kiyoto, *Kinsei Minami Shinano nōson no kenkyū*, Tokyo, 1955, p. 226.

10. See, for example, Shōji Kichinosuke, "Tokugawa jidai no Tōhoku nōgyō keiei kibo narabi ni jōyatoi," *SKSG*, XIV, 2 (1944), 19.

11. Fujita Gorō, *Kinsei ni okeru nōminsō no kaikyū bunka*, Tokyo, 1949, pp. 190–91.

12. An extensive literature has grown up dealing with various aspects of the *nago* class; perhaps the most useful studies are Ariga Kizaemon, *Nihon kazoku seido to kosaku seido*, Tokyo, 1943, and *Daikazoku seido to nago seido*, Tokyo, 1939; and Furushima Toshio, *Kinsei Nihon nōgyō no kōzō*, 2 vols., Tokyo, 1948.

13. Examples may be found in Oka, "Kinsei sonraku no tenkai to inasaku kankō," pp. 23–26; Miyagawa Mitsuru, Mizokawa Kiichi, and Tanaka Yutaka, "Tajima ni okeru daitochi shoyū no keisei to hensen" (I) *Kyōto Jimbun kagaku kenkyūjo chōsa hōkoku*, 1 (1952), 2–24; Harada Toshimaru, "Kinsei shukueki sonraku no shakai kōsei ni kansuru ichikōsatsu," *Hikone ronsō*, 5 (1954), 43; Nagahara Keiji and Nagakura Tamotsu, "Kōshin-jikyūteki nōgyō chitai ni okeru murakata jinushi no tenkai," *SGZS*, LXIV, 1 (1955), 7–15; Ōtsuki, "Awahan," pp. 3–8; Andō Seiichi, "Kinsei shoki nōson kōzō no tenkai" (II), *Rekishi kyōiku*, III, 11 (1955), 14–25.

14. Furushima, *Kinsei Nihon nōgyō no kōzō*, p. 49.

CHAPTER 2

1. Furushima, *Kinsei Nihon nōgyō no kōzō*, p. 586.

2. Also see Mihashi Tokio, "Edo jidai ni okeru nōgyō keiei no hensen," in Miyamoto Mataji (ed.), *Nōson kōzō no shiteki bunseki*, Tokyo, 1955, p. 6.

3. Andō Seiichi, "Kinsei Kyūshū ni okeru nōminsō no bunka," *Kyūshū keizai shi kenkyū*, Tokyo, 1953, p. 104.

4. Shimada Takashi, "Suwahan nōgyō keiei no ichirei," *Keizaigaku*, 25 (1952), 45.

5. *Ibid.*

6. Andō, "Kinsei Kyūshū ni okeru nōminsō no bunka," p. 104.

7. Fujita, *Nōminsō no kaikyū bunka*, p. 77.

8. Furushima Toshio, *Nihon hōken nōgyōshi*, Tokyo, 1941, p. 141.

9. *Nihon keizai sōsho*, edited by Takimoto Seiichi, Tokyo, 1914, III, 1104.

10. *Nihon kinsei sompō no kenkyū*, edited by Maeda Masaharu, Tokyo, 1950, document 67.

11. Ichikawa Yūichirō, *Saku-chihō Edo jidai no nōson seikatsu*, Nozawa, 1955, p. 77.

12. Kodama Kōta, *Kinsei nōson shakai no kenkyū*, Tokyo, 1953, p. 275; Nagahara and Nagakura, "Kōshin-jikyūteki nōgyō," pp. 13–15.

13. Kitajima Masamoto, "Edo jidai no nōmin no ie," in Nihon hōshakai gakkai (ed.), *Kazoku seido no kenkyū*, Tokyo, 1956, I, 57.

14. Takeuchi Toshimi, "Sanson ni okeru hōkōnin," *SKSG*, IV, 5 (1934), 79–96.

15. Kitajima Masamoto, "Watanabeke no jinushiteki seikaku ni tsuite," *Essa kenkyū*, 2 (1952), 72–73.

16. Kanai Madoka, "Suwahan ni okeru bakuhan taisei no kakuritsu," *Shinano*, IV, 10 (1952).

17. "Zenkoku minji kanrei ruishū," in Yoshino Sakuzō (ed.), *Meiji bunka zenshū*, Tokyo, 1929, VIII, 303.

CHAPTER 3

1. Ariga, *Kazoku seido*, p. 640.
2. This discussion on the character of labor services is based mainly on Ariga, *Kazoku seido*, pp. 611–39.
3. Mori Kahei, *Nago seido to nōchi kaikaku*, Tokyo, 1951, p. 30.
4. Adapted from Ariga, *Kazoku seido*, pp. 636–38.
5. Adapted from Ariga, *Kazoku seido*, pp. 636–37.
6. Ōtō Tokihiko, "Bunke to saishi," *Minkan denshō*, VIII, 2 (1942), 18; and Hori Ichirō, *Minkan shinkō*, Tokyo, 1951, pp. 128–29.
7. Yanagida Kunio, *Sanson seikatsu no kenkyū*, Tokyo, 1937, pp. 379, 385; Kitano Seiichi, "Dōzoku soshiki to oyakata kokata kankō shiryō," *Minzokugaku nempō*, III (1940–41), 161–91; Hori, *Minkan shinkō*, pp. 134–35, 139.
8. Maeda, *Nihon kinsei sompō*, document 65, pp. 62–63.
9. Harada Toshimaru, "Higohan nōson ni okeru kazoku no kōzō," *Ōita daigaku keizai ronshū*, II, 2 (1952), 118; and Ōtsuki, "Awahan ni okeru kinsei sonraku no keisei katei," p. 18.
10. Mori, *Nōchi kaikaku*, pp. 90–91; Miyagawa Mitsuru, "Gōson seido to kenchi," pp. 12–21, and "Taikō kenchi to kazoku kōsei" (4), *Hisutoria*, 11 (1955), 31.

CHAPTER 4

1. A somewhat more extended discussion in English of the relation of property and the family headship may be found in Ariga Kizaemon, "The Family in Japan," *Marriage and Family Living*, XVI, 4 (1954), 362–68; see also *Minzokugaku jiten*, edited by Yanagida Kunio, Tokyo, 1952, pp. 325–27.
2. This compilation was translated into English under the supervision of John H. Wigmore and entitled *Materials for the Study of Private Law in Old Japan, Transactions of the Asiatic Society of Japan*, XX, Supplement, Parts I, II, III, IV, V, Yokohama, 1892.
3. Wigmore, *Private Law*, V, 95–109.
4. *Ibid.*, pp. 98–99.
5. *Ibid.*, p. 102.
6. *Ibid.*, pp. 98, 105.
7. *Ibid.*, pp. 96, 102, 109.
8. A study made in 1951 by Professor Fukutake of four widely scattered villages revealed that the main elements of the inheritance system were still intact. Fukutake Tadashi, *Family System and Population of Farming Communities in Japan*, Tokyo, 1952, pp. 1–29.
9. Nakamura Jihei, "Sengo nōson no bunke," *Nōgyō sōgō kenkyū*, VI, 3 (1952), 173.

10. *Ibid.*, pp. 160–61.

11. *Ibid.*, p. 159.

12. For other notable instances too complex to describe here, see Imai Rintarō and Yagi Akihiro, *Hōken shakai no nōson kōzō*, Tokyo, 1955, pp. 1–46.

13. Shiozawa Kimio, "Iwate-ken Kemuyama-mura no ichinōka keiei," *Keizaigaku*, 28 (1953), 100, 108, 116.

14. Wigmore, *Private Law*, V, 103.

CHAPTER 5

1. A detailed schematic representation of the irrigation system of a Shinshū village made in 1771 is to be found in Ōishi Shinzaburō, "Kinseiteki sonraku kyōdōtai to ie," *Tōyō bunka*, 18/19 (1955), 7–8. It shows that there were a total of 105 fields, each numbered in the order it received water. Since it took a week to make the entire rounds at the planting, it is evident that some fields must have received water for only a few hours. This underlines the importance of stable cooperative groupings for the cultivation of rice, especially when one considers that in some places during the Tokugawa period the transplanting had to be accomplished in no more than ten days.

2. There are literally scores of short reports from all over the country on these groups in learned journals representing various social science interests; the largest number is to be found in *Minkan denshō*. By far the most detailed and suggestive studies are Ariga, *Kazoku seido* and *Daikazoku seido to nago seido*; also excellent are Kitano Seiichi, "Dōzokudan shiryō," *Minzokugaku kenkyū*, III, 2, and "Kōshu sanson no dōzokuteki soshiki to oyakata kokata kankō," *Minzokugaku nempō*, II.

3. Yanagida Kunio, *Zokusei goi*, Tokyo, 1943, pp. 1–32.

4. Komura Hajime, "Kinsei shotō kenchichō naukenín ni tsuite no oboegaki," *SKSG*, XIX, 6 (1954), 93.

5. Ōishi Shinzaburō, "Tochi shoyū to sonraku kōzō," *SKSG*, XIX, 1 (1953), 87–97.

6. Kodama Kōta, *Kinsei nōmin seikatsu shi*, Tokyo, 1951, p. 163; and Furushima Toshio (ed.), *Sanson no kōzō*, Tokyo, 1949, pp. 166–67.

7. Ōtō Tokihiko, "Bunke to saishi," *Minkan denshō*, VIII, 2 (1942), 385.

8. Kitano Seiichi, "Dōzoku soshiki to oyakata kokata kankō shiryō," *Minzokugaku nempō*, III (1940–41), 234.

9. Umeki Tadaaki, "Shōya tekagami," *KJKS*, VII, 172.

10. Wigmore, *Private Law*, pp. 104, 108.

11. Ōishi Shinzaburō, "Tochi shoyū to sonraku kōzō, *SKSG*, XIX, 1 (1953), 96–99.

12. Nomura Kanetarō (ed.), *Goningumi no kenkyū*, Tokyo, 1943, pp. 87–88; Asada Mitsuteru and Nakamura Shūichirō, *Nihon shihonshugi shakai keisei shi*, Tokyo, 1949, p. 105; Irimajiri Yoshinaga, "Tokugawa

bakuhan seika no nōgyō kikō," in *Hōken shakai no kōzō bunseki*, edited by Tsuchiya Takao, Tokyo, 1950, p. 198.

13. Fujita Gorō, *Hōken shakai no tenkai katei*, Tokyo, 1952, pp. 4–39; Haraguchi Kiyoshi, "Bakumatsu seisō no ichikōsatsu—Tosahan o chūshin to shite," *RGKK*, 142 (1949), 33. Leaders of these uprisings sometimes became semilegendary heroes to whom monuments were erected and rites celebrated.

14. Maeda, *Nihon kinsei sompō*, p. 150.

15. Oda Kichijō, *Kagahan nōsei shikō*, Tokyo, 1929, p. 173.

16. Kitano Seiichi, "Dōzokudan shiryō," *Minzokugaku kenkyū*, III, 2 (1946), 240–41; and Ariga Kizaemon, *Nihon kon'in shi ron*, Tokyo, 1948, pp. 22–24.

17. Maeda, *Nihon kinsei sompō*, Document 64.

18. *Ibid.*, Document 67.

19. *Ibid.*, pp. 90–150.

20. Paul S. Dull, "The Political Structure of a Japanese Village," *The Far Eastern Quarterly*, XIII, 2 (1954), 187.

21. Umeki, "Shōya tekagami," pp. 169–71.

CHAPTER 6

1. An excellent short account of the castle town, which accounted for most of this urban growth, is John W. Hall, "The Castle Town and Japan's Modern Urbanization," *Far Eastern Quarterly*, XV, 1 (1955), 37–56. This article also provides a useful guide to the Japanese literature on the subject.

2. Furushima Toshio, *Nihon hōken nōgyōshi*, p. 304, and *Kinsei ni okeru shōgyōteki nōgyō no tenkai*, Tokyo, 1950, pp. 18–19; and Harada Tomohiko, *Chūsei ni okeru toshi no kenkyū*, Tokyo, 1942, pp. 235–61.

3. Furushima, *Kinsei ni okeru shōgyōteki nōgyō*, p. 147.

4. For excerpts from the ambassador's diary, Akiyama Kenzō, *Nisshi kōshō shiwa*, Tokyo, 1935, pp. 122–41.

5. Kobayashi Yoshimasa, *Nihon shihonshugi no seisei to sono kiban*, Tokyo, 1949, p. 23.

6. Fujita, *Hōken shakai no tenkai katei*, p. 235.

7. Quoted in *Nihon sanshigyō hattatsu shi*, edited by Takahashi keizai kenkyūjo, Tokyo, 1941, I, 134.

8. *Ibid.*

9. *Hōken shakai no kōzō bunseki*, edited by Tsuchiya Takao, Tokyo, 1950, p. 219.

10. *Ibid.*, p. 221.

11. *NKSS*, VIII, 530; also Kobayashi, *Nihon shihonshugi no seisei to sono kiban*, p. 24.

12. The best general study of the organization of the silk industry in the Tokugawa period and especially good on the role of the Kyoto guilds is Takahashi, *Nihon sanshigyō*, I. Invaluable for a close-up view of the silk

industry in a locality is Shōji Kichinosuke, *Meiji ishin no keizai kōzō*, Tokyo, 1954, pp. 150–96.

13. Nakamura Shūichirō and Asada Mitsuteru, *Nihon shihonshugi shakai keisei shi*, Tokyo, 1949, p. 128.

14. *Ibid.*, p. 130.

15. Takahashi, *Nihon sanshigyō*, I, 126.

16. Adachi Ikutsune, "Bakumatsu ni okeru shōgyōteki nōgyō no hattatsu kōzō," *Jimbungaku hō*, I (1950), 70; and Furushima Toshio and Nagahara Keiji, *Shōhin seisan to kisei jinushisei*, Tokyo, 1954, p. 32.

17. Shinobu Seizaburō, *Kindai Nihon sangyō shi josetsu*, Tokyo, 1942, p. 51.

18. Kitajima Masamoto, "Kōshinchi ni okeru nōminteki shukōgyō no seikaku," *NSKK*, 12 (1950), 13–21.

19. *Ibid.*, pp. 13–21.

20. Nomura Kanetarō, *Mura meisaichō no kenkyū*, Tokyo, 1949, p. 794.

21. Takao Kazuhiko, "Settsu Hirano-gō ni okeru watasaku no hatten," *Shirin*, XXXIV, 1/2 (1951), 2.

22. Furushima and Nagahara, *Shōhin seisan*, p. 36.

23. Ono Emio, "Yamato ni okeru kinsei kōyugyō no hattatsu," *Hisutoria*, 12 (1955), 45, 47, 50.

24. In the same year, Ōkubo produced 6,000 rolls of silk cloth; silk bought approximately 2 *ryō* per roll in this area somewhat earlier. (Shōji Kichinosuke, *Kawamata chihō habutae kigyō hattatsu shi*, Fukushima, 1953, pp. 4, 13.) Professor Shōji has cited in a personal letter the price of rice in the Fukushima area in 1875 as 1.68 yen per *koku*; generally one *ryō* had the same value as one yen.

25. Kitajima, "Kōshinchi," pp. 16–17.

26. Shinobu, *Kindai Nihon sangyō*, p. 51.

27. Most of these budgets are to be found in Toya Toshiyuki, *Kinsei nōgyō keiei shiron*, Tokyo, 1946, pp. 42–73.

28. *Ibid.*, pp. 53, 87–88.

29. Furushima, *Kinsei ni okeru shōgyōteki nōgyō no tenkai*, p. 143.

30. A document of 1792 from the barony of Akita stated: "Labor by the month and day (!) has become very short in the villages with the result that the farmers are distressed." (Furushima and Nagahara, *Shōhin seisan*, p. 88.)

31. Shōji, *Meiji ishin*, p. 160.

32. The text of the diary is in Toya, *Kinsei nōgyō keiei shiron*, pp. 169–338.

33. *Ibid.*, pp. 341–43.

CHAPTER 7

1. By far the best general treatment of this subject is Furushima Toshio, *Nihon nōgyō gijutsu shi*, Tokyo, 1949, 2 vols. Also valuable, though less comprehensive in the one case and less detailed in the other, are Toya, *Nōgyō*

keiei, and Tohata Seiichi (ed.), *Nihon nōgyō hattatsu shi*, Tokyo, 1953, I.

2. Contemporaries saw this very clearly. See Suyama Don'ō (1657–1732), "Gōson nōjiroku," *NKSS*, IV, 425–26.

3. There is no good comprehensive study of the science of agronomy during the latter half of the Tokugawa period, but Furushima Toshio (*Nihon nōgaku shi*, Tokyo, 1946, Vol. I) takes the story up to the end of the seventeenth century; the manuscript of Volume II covering the remainder of the Tokugawa period was burned during World War II.

4. The *Nōgyō zensho* has been printed in many collections; I have used the text edited by Tsuchiya Takao in the *Iwanami bunko*, Tokyo, 1949. All citations are from this edition.

5. *Nōgyō zensho*, pp. 23–28.

6. The *Nōgu benri ron* first appeared in 1826; it is reprinted in *Tsūzoku keizai bunko*, edited by Takimoto Seiichi, Tokyo, 1931, XII.

7. Hayakawa Kōtarō (ed.), *Muramatsuke sakumotsu oboechō*, Tokyo, 1936, pp. 81–90.

8. The *Nōgyō zensho* was also frequently quoted in works from the hands of peasants; an example is to be found in a manuscript written by an Etchū peasant in 1788 and entitled "Shika nōgyō dan" (*KJKS*, VII, 310).

9. This untitled treatise is printed in *Kawachi Ishikawa-mura gakujitsu chōsa hōkoku*, edited by Nomura Yutaka, Sakai, 1953, pp. 365–80.

10. *Ibid.*, pp. 370–75.

11. See the "Hyakushō denki," which was written anonymously about the year 1700, in *NKSS*, XXXI, and the "Hōnen zeisho" (1685), *NKSS*, I.

12. Furushima and Nagahara, *Shōhin seisan*, p. 159.

13. Tohata Seiichi (ed.), *Nihon nōgyō hattatsu shi*, I, 17.

14. For examples see Gotō Yōichi, "Jūkuseiki San'yōsuji nōson ni okeru funō keiei no seikaku," *SGZS*, LXIII, 7 (1954), 49–51, and "Kinsei kōki minami Kantō chihō no nōgyō gijutsu," *NHRS*, 96 (1956), 55–59.

15. Shōji, *Meiji ishin*, p. 40.

16. Furushima, *Nōgyō no kōzō*, p. 240.

17. Kobayashi, *Nihon shihonshugi no seisei to sono kiban*, pp. 43–44.

18. Furushima and Nagahara, *Shōhin seisan*, pp. 42–43, 160–61.

19. Furushima, *Nōgyō gijutsu*, II, 646–56.

20. Gotō, "Jūkuseiki San'yōsuji nōson ni okeru funō keiei no seikaku," p. 12.

21. Imai and Yagi, *Hōken shakai no nōson kōzō*, p. 47.

22. Toya, *Nōgyō keiei*, pp. 441–42.

23. Furushima, *Nōgyō no kōzō*, pp. 373–80.

CHAPTER 8

1. Imai and Yagi, *Hōken shakai no nōson kōzō*, pp. 1, 144.

2. For example, see Miyagawa, "Taikō kenchi" (4), *Hisutoria*, 11 (1955), 43–44, and *ibid.* (3), *Hisutoria*, 10 (1954), 44.

3. Nomura, *Meisaichō no kenkyū*, p. 260.

4. Andō, "Kinsei Kyūshū ni okeru nōminsō no bunka," p. 108; also Furushima and Nagahara, *Shōhin seisan*, p. 88.

5. A good general treatment of population policy is Sekiyama, *Nihon jinkō*, pp. 184–225; also see *Fukuoka-ken nōchi kaikaku shi*, edited by Fukuoka-ken nōchi kaikaku shi hensan iinkai, Fukuoka, 1950, I, 424.

6. This is quite clear from surviving loan agreements. See the splendid article by Mori Kahei, "Igeshijichi hōkōnin no kenkyū," *NSKK*, 12 (1950), 48–63; also the more broadly interpretive treatment by Fujita, *Hōken shakai no tenkai katei*, pp. 181–257.

7. This was in 1795. Quoted by Fujita, *Kinsei ni okeru nōminsō*, pp. 61–62.

8. Mori, "Hōkōnin no kenkyū," pp. 60–61.

9. *Ibid.*, pp. 58–61.

10. Imai and Yagi, *Hōken shakai no nōson kōzō*, pp. 144–47.

11. Shimada, "Suwahan nōgyō keiei no ichirei," pp. 47–48.

12. *Ibid.*, pp. 48–49.

13. Furushima and Nagahara, *Shōhin seisan*, p. 88.

14. Fujimoto Takashi, "Bakumatsu Buzen ni okeru kisei jinushi no seikaku," *Keizaigaku kenkyū*, XIX, 2 (1953), 153.

15. Text of the diary for 1846 in Toya, *Nōgyō keiei*, pp. 134–55.

16. Ōtsuki Hiroshi, "Awahan ni okeru yōran sembai seido no seiritsu katei," *Keizai ronsō*, LXXIV, 5 (1954), 64.

17. Tsuchiya, *Hōken shakai no kōzō bunseki*, p. 275.

18. Imai and Yagi, *Hōken shakai no nōson kōzō*, p. 158.

CHAPTER 9

1. Mihashi, "Edo jidai ni okeru nōgyō keiei no hensen," in Miyamoto, *Nōson kōzō no shiteki bunseki*, p. 16.

2. Fujita Yūkoku, "Kannō wakumon" (1779), *Nihon keizai taiten*, XXXII, 228.

3. Shiono Tokio, "Bakumatsuki ni okeru chūnōsō no dōkō," *Hisutoria*, 10 (1954), 72; Ōtsuki, "Awahan ni okeru yōran sembai seido no seiritsu katei," p. 64; and Nomura, *Meisaichō no kenkyū*, pp. 260, 736.

4. Fukuoka-ken, *Fukuoka-ken nōchi*, pp. 423–24; Tsuchiya, *Hōken shakai no kōzō bunseki*, p. 275; Nomura, *Meisaichō no kenkyū*, p. 736.

5. Tsuchiya, *Hōken shakai no kōzō bunseki*, p. 276.

6. Hirasawa, *Kinsei Minami Shinano*, p. 103.

7. "Minkan shōyō," *NKSS*, I, 260–61.

8. Quoted by Furushima, *Nihon nōgyō gijutsu shi*, II, 720.

9. "Jikata hanreiroku," pp. 368–74.

10. Kajinishi Mitsuhaya, "Kindai Echizen seishigyō to ryūtsū," *SKSG*, XIX, 1 (1953), 16.

11. Toya, *Nōgyō keiei*, pp. 130–31.

12. Wakita Osamu, "Jinushisei no hatten o megutte," *RGKK*, 181 (1955), 14.

13. Hirasawa, *Kinsei Minami Shinano*, pp. 81–86.

14. Ōishi Shinzaburō, "Tochi shoyū to sonraku kōzō," p. 99.

15. Furushima Toshio and Sekijima Hisao, *Yōeki rōdō sei no hōkai katei*, Tokyo, 1938, pp. 266–67.

16. Furushima, *Nōgyō no kōzō*, pp. 499–502.

17. Furushima and Sekijima, *Yōeki rōdō sei*, p. 327.

18. Nakazawa Benjirō, *Nihon beika hendō sho*, Tokyo, 1933, pp. 241–42.

19. Document in Furushima and Sekijima, *Yōeki rōdō sei*, p. 432.

20. Ariga Kizaemon, *Nihon kazoku seido to kosaku seido*, Tokyo, 1943, pp. 513–42.

CHAPTER 10

1. In 1934, 68.4 percent of all farm families worked less than one *chō* of land, whereas only 3.7 percent worked more than 2 *chō*. (Ōuchi Tsutomu, *Nōka keizai*, Tokyo, 1957, p. 15.)

2. Differences of scale are commonly significant for cooperation in peasant societies. In Wales, for instance: "Large farms are better equipped than others and their smaller neighbors depend on them a great deal. On the other hand, the large farm requires additional labour on many occasions, and in borrowing its machines the little farmer incurs the obligation to give a day's work now and then in exchange." (Alwyn D. Rees, *Life in a Welsh Countryside. A Social Study of Llanfihangel yng Ngwynfa*, Cardiff, 1951, p. 93.)

3. For a typical case, see *Kisei jinushisei no kenkyū*, edited by Fukushima daigaku keizai gakkai, Tokyo, 1955, pp. 108–9.

4. Furushima and Nagahara, *Shōhin seisan*, p. 187.

5. Quoted by Gotō, "Jūkuseiki San'yōsuji nōson ni okeru funō keiei no seikaku," p. 58.

6. Tōdai . . . chōsakai, "Shinshū Ochiai chōsa hōkoku," pp. 64–65.

7. Matsuki Tsuyoshi, "Hirosakihan ni okeru shuzōgyō, shuzō shihon oyobi sono keiei keitai ni tsuite," *SKSG*, XLIX, 4 (1938), 110.

8. This account is based on Shimada Takashi, "Bakumatsu, Meiji shoki Kemuyama-mura no rōdō soshiki," *Keizaigaku*, 28 (1953), 65–91; and Shiozawa, "Iwate-ken Kemuyama-mura no ichinōka keiei," pp. 129–33.

9. *Taishō jūnen fukenbetsu kosaku kankō chōsa shūsei*, edited by Tsuchiya Takao, Tokyo, 1942–43, 2 vols.

10. The discussion of types of rent is based primarily on Ariga, *Kazoku seido*, and *Hompō ni okeru kariwake kosaku* (Nōrinshō), Tokyo, 1934.

11. For an example of reversion to *kariwake* from a more advanced type of rent, see Shōji, *Meiji ishin*, p. 142.

CHAPTER 11

1. Nearly all of 78 mortgages dating from the first three-quarters of the nineteenth century from villages in the vicinity of Fukushima show loans between one and five *ryō*. There were, however, a few large loans— for 150, 100, 75, and 60 *ryō*—and, unlike the small loans, the mortgages in these cases stipulate without exception that the loan was to be used for investment in sericulture, *sake* making, or simply "business."

2. Thomas C. Smith, "The Land Tax in the Tokugawa Period," *Journal of Asian Studies*, XVIII, 1 (1958), 3–19.

3. Sumi Tōyō, "Bakuhan kōki Sennan kigyō chitai nōmin no tōsō," *Hisutoria*, 14 (1956), 13.

4. On the origin, organization, and functioning of guilds, see Miyamoto Mataji, *Nihon kinsei ton'yasei no kenkyū*, Tokyo, 1951, especially pp. 287–330. The power of the guilds provoked the hostility of both peasant producers and village merchants. On the producers, see Shiono, "Bakumatsuki ni okeru chūnōsō," p. 68. On the merchants, see Andō Seiichi, "Kinsei zaikata shōgyō no tenkai," *Kishū keizai shi kenkyū sōsho*, V (1956), 1–25; and "Tsuyamahan ni okeru zaikata shōgyō no hattatsu," *Keizai riron*, 34 (1956), 1–31.

5. Imai and Yagi, *Hōken shakai no nōson*, p. 63.

6. Both advantages were thoroughly understood; see the Tokugawa edicts explaining the rationale of fixed taxes. (Nishimura Shō, "Jōmensei ni kansuru ichikōsatsu," *Rekishi kagaku*, V, 6 (1936), 79–80.)

7. The cooperative spirit languishes noticeably today. In one of his satirical sketches of village life, Kida Noboru says: "I cannot agree with the view that the Japanese peasant is lazy. Oh, the peasants no doubt seem that way when they loll about doing cooperative work, but let something once touch their private interests and it is a different story." (*Buraku kōfuku ron*, Tokyo, 1958, p. 120.)

8. For examples of villages where all holdings can be traced over a considerable period of time, see Imai and Yagi, *Hōken shakai no nōson*, pp. 50–53; and Harada Toshimaru, "Kinsei sonraku ni okeru kakaku ni tsuite," *Hikone ronsō*, 6 (1955), 9–10.

9. See such a graph for a Shinshū village in *Kinsei nōson no kōzō*, edited by Nōson shiryō chōsakai, Tokyo, 1952, p. 143.

10. For other instances, see Andō Seiichi, "Kinsei shoki Kyūshū no nōson kōzō," in *Nōson kōzō no shiteki bunseki*, edited by Miyamoto Mataji, Tokyo, 1955, p. 34; *Kinsei jinushisei no seisei to tenkai*, edited by Furushima Toshio, Tokyo, 1952, p. 10; Imai and Yagi, *Hōken shakai no nōson*, pp. 84–85; Tsuchiya, "Nōminsō no bunka," in *Hōken shakai no kōzō bunseki*, pp. 242–44; Naitō Seichū, "Bitchū Kurashiki ni okeru shinroku to koroku no kōsō," *Keizai ronsō*, LXXI, 2 (1953), 46; Ōtsuki, "Awahan ni okeru kinsei sonraku no keisei katei," pp. 10–16; and Miyagawa, Mizokawa, and Tanaka, "Tajima ni okeru daitochi shoyū," p. 2. Many other examples may be found by the most casual perusal of the literature on the land system.

11. Ōuchi Tsutomu, *Nōgyō mondai*, Tokyo, 1951, p. 175.

12. On this origin of *nago*, see Ariga, *Kazoku seido*, pp. 404–79.

13. Furushima, *Kinsei ni okeru shōgyōteki nōgyō no tenkai*, p. 83; Endō Masao, *Nihon kinsei shōgyō shihon hattatsu shi ron*, Tokyo, 1936, pp. 114–32; and Koseki Toyokichi, "Ansei 4-nen Kawakita-mura fūdo torishimari sashidashichō no kenkyū," *Tosa shidan*, 40 (1932), 118–19.

14. Nakamura Akira, "Bakumatsuki ni okeru nōson kōgyō no tenkai," *NSKK*, 28 (1956), 27.

15. Shinobu Seizaburō, *Kindai Nihon sangyō shi josetsu*, Tokyo, 1942, p. 11.

16. "Kannōsaku," *NKSS*, XX, 585–86.

17. Quoted in *Hōken shakai no kōzō bunseki*, edited by Tsuchiya Takao, Tokyo, 1950, p. 229.

18. Kitajima Masamoto, "Echigo sankan chitai ni okeru junsui hōken-sei no kōzō," *SGZS*, LIX, 6 (1950), 37.

19. Fujita Gorō, *Nihon kindai sangyō no seisei*, Tokyo, 1948, pp. 241–42.

20. Fujimoto, "Bakumatsu Buzen ni okeru kisei jinushi no seikaku," p. 148.

21. Kitajima, "Watanabeke," pp. 76–78.

22. For detailed illustration of the workings of the system, see Shinobu Seizaburō, *Kindai Nihon sangyō shi josetsu*, pp. 9–119; and Shōji, *Meiji ishin*, pp. 150–98.

23. For illustrations, see Thomas C. Smith, "Landlords and Rural Capitalists in the Modernization of Japan," *Journal of Economic History*, XVI, 2 (1956), 170.

24. The question of how far this development had gone and how widespread it was is the central issue of a now protracted debate known among Japanese historians as the "manufacturing controversy." Although inconclusive, this debate has been fertile of ideas and research; it is summarized in Kimura Motoi, *Nihon hōken shakai kenkyū shi*, Tokyo, 1956, pp. 273–84.

25. Toya, *Nōgyō keiei*, p. 33.

26. Shōji, *Meiji ishin*, pp. 169–70.

27. Ōishi Shinzaburō, "Tochi shoyū to sonraku kōzō," pp. 102–3.

28. Ono Emio, "Yamato ni okeru kinsei kōyugyō no hattatsu," pp. 54–55.

29. For other examples, see Kitajima, "Kōshinchi ni okeru nōminteki shukōgyō," pp. 18–19.

30. Tsuchiya, *Hōken shakai no kōzō bunseki*, pp. 234–35.

31. *Ibid.*, p. 229.

32. Nakamura Akira, "Bakumatsu ni okeru nōson kōgyō no tenkai," *NSKK*, 28 (1956), 33.

33. Furushima Toshio, "Bakumatsuki ni okeru tochi shūchū no seikaku," *SKSG*, XIX, 6 (1954), 77–79.

34. Sumi Tōyō, "Bakumatsu kōki Sennan kigyō chitai nōmin no tōsō," *Hisutoria*, 14 (1956), 10.

35. Takemoto Ryūhei (1769–1820), "Kannōsaku," *NKSS*, XX, 586.

36. Furukawa Koshō, "Seiyū zakki" (1794), *NKSS*, IX, 48–49.

37. Quoted by Tsuchiya, *Hōken shakai no kōzō bunseki*, p. 224.

38. Buyō Inshi, "Seji kemmonroku" (1816), *KSKS*, I, pp. 48–49.

39. For an account of how this office was sometimes used by the holder to his own economic advantage, see Furushima Toshio, "Bakumatsuki ni okeru tochi shūchū no seikaku," pp. 73–81.

40. Thomas C. Smith, *Political Change and Industrial Development in Japan: Government Enterprise, 1868–1880*, Stanford, 1955, p. 38.

41. Kobayashi Shigeru, "Hōkensei hōkaiki ni okeru Kinai nōmin no ideorogii no tenkai," *Hisutoria*, 14 (1956), 28.

42. Thomas C. Smith, "The Japanese Village in the Seventeenth Century," *Journal of Economic History*, XII, 1 (1952), 7.
43. "Seji kemmonroku," *KSKS*, I, p. 49.
44. *Nihon zaisei keizai shiryō*, compiled by the Ministry of Finance, Tokyo, 1924–25, II, 1058.
45. Toya, *Nōgyō keiei*, p. 218.
46. Ōyama Shikitarō, *Nōheiron*, Tokyo, 1942, p. 140.

CHAPTER 12

1. On the failure to revise assessments periodically, see Smith, "The Land Tax in the Tokugawa Period," pp. 1–19.
2. Tsuda Hideo, "Hōken shakai hōkaiki ni okeru nōmin tōsō no ichiruikei ni tsuite," *RGKK*, 168 (1954), 1–15; Asao Naohiro, "Bakumatsu ni okeru ryōshu to nōmin," *NSKK*, 29 (1956), 54–76; Furushima and Nagahara, *Shōhin seisan*, pp. 129–32; Hattori, "Musashi no kuni Saitama-gun Mugikura-mura," pp. 1–23; *Kinsei nōson no kōzō*, edited by Nōson shiryō chōsakai, pp. 145–96; Shōji, *Meiji ishin*, pp. 211–16.
3. This account of the struggle in Kurashiki village is based on Naitō Seichū's brilliant study. ("Kinsei sonraku no kōzō henka to murakata sōdō," *Keizai ronsō*, LXXIV, 2 (1954), 39–60.
4. *Ibid.*, p. 42.
5. *Ibid.*, p. 46.
6. *Ibid.*, p. 55.
7. Asao, "Bakumatsu ni okeru ryōshu to nōmin," p. 60.
8. The fullest treatment of the organization of the *miyaza* is Higo Kazuo, *Miyaza no kenkyū*, Tokyo, 1942; however, this work is weak on the historical development of the institution and should be supplemented by Imai and Yagi, *Hōken shakai no nōson*, Chapter III, and Wakamori Tarō "Miyaza no kaishō katei," *Nihon minzokugaku*, I, 2.
9. Ariga Kizaemon, *Sonraku seikatsu*, Tokyo, 1948, pp. 114–38.
10. The documents are hereafter referred to by the following numbers:

1:1. Henjōji document. "Osorenagara kakitsuke o motte negaiage tatematsuri-sōrō," 1756.
2:1. Henjōji document. "Saibanchō," undated.
3:1. Sugano family document. "Sashiage-mōshi issatsu no koto," 1713.
3:6. Sugano family document. "Otoriatsukai yakuteisho no koto," 1848.
3:10. Sugano family document. "Oboe," 1780.
3:11. Sugano family document. "Sadame," 1843.
4:1. "Jizamurai gomen negai kakihikae," 1812.
4:2. "Hōreki nenkan yakusho kiroku," 1752.
4:3. "Shōya-toshiyori-chū gijō rempanjo," 1752.
4:4. "Gosengūshiki zaretsu shitai nijūshichimei narabini ryō godaikan okugaki kahan," 1758.
4:5. "Nagusa-kōri Wasa-shō Wasake yuishojō," undated.

4:6. "Oboe," 1757.

4:8. "Meiji nijuichinen . . . toshiyori keiyakusho," 1888.

4:9. "Miyaza kōrei oboe," undated.

5:1. Arii family document. "Gijō oboe," Hōreki era (1751–63).

5:2. Arii family document. "Arakawa toshiyorichū korei ni yori miyaza gijōki," 1805.

5:3. Arii family document. "Otazune no ken ni tsuite osorenagara okotae-moshiage tatematsuru oboe," 1791.

5:4. Arii family document. "Mōshi-watashi," 1795.

11. Andō Seiichi, "Kinsei zaikata shōgyō no tenkai," p. 2.

12. *Ibid.*, p. 21.

13. *Ibid.*, p. 20.

14. Document 1:1.

15. Document 5:2.

16. Document 5:1.

17. *Kinsei nōson no kōzō*, edited by Noson shiryō chōsakai, Tokyo, 1952, pp. 147–88.

18. Documents 3:6; 3:10; and 2:1.

19. *Nankai Yuasa shi*, a hand-written manuscript; undated but evidently of the late Tokugawa period.

20. Document 2:1.

21. Document 1:1.

22. Document 3:1.

23. Documents 2:1 and 3:1.

24. Document 4:6.

25. Document 3:1.

26. Document 2:1.

27. Document 3:1.

28. Documents 1:1 and 2:1.

29. *Nankai Yuasa shi*.

30. Document 2:1.

31. Documents 5:3 and 2:1.

32. Document 1:1.

33. Document 1:1.

34. Document 1:1.

35. Document 3:5.

36. Documents 3:1 and 3:10.

37. Document 4:8.

CHAPTER 13

1. For a contrary view, see Albert Craig, "The Restoration Movement in Chōshū," *Journal of Asian Studies*, XVIII, 2 (1959), 187–99.

BIBLIOGRAPHY

I have not thought it necessary to compile a comprehensive bibliography on Tokugawa agrarian history; such a listing would be excessively long and is unnecessary since several good bibliographies already exist. I have therefore attempted to list only the more important items consulted; those cited no more than once in the text have usually been excluded. First citations of all books and articles in the notes, however, carry full bibliographic data, and may be found by using the Index. Those who wish a fuller bibliography than the one given here are referred to *Nihon keizai shi daisan bunken*, edited by Honjō Eijirō (Tokyo, 1953), to the excellent annual bibliographical issue of *Shigaku zasshi*, and to Volume 22 of *Sekai rekishi jiten* (Tokyo, 1955).

A few very general remarks on the kinds of materials available for a study of peasant life in the Tokugawa period may be useful, however. By far the richest materials are the village administrative documents (mostly registers of various kinds kept by the headman) and the private papers of individual families (mostly account books). The former give detailed knowledge of statistical changes in the composition of villages with respect to population, families, occupations, fields, buildings, and animals; the latter give intimate if fleeting glimpses of farm management and household economy. Together the two have imparted to studies of agrarian history since World War II a concreteness previously lacking. These materials, however, are not only generally unpublished but unfortunately likely to remain so; most of them are uncollected and even uncatalogued and repose in varying states of disorder in local temple, shrine, and family archives.

Some village documents have been published, although generally in small batches of limited value. There are a few notable exceptions such as the admirable *Mura meisaichō no kenkyū*, edited by Nomura Kanetarō, and the new series *Dai Nihon kinsei shiryō* begun in 1953 by the Historiographical Institute at Tokyo University. With the latter publication continuing, it is evident that the tendency to scattered publication is largely a thing of the past; but the series at the present writing (1958) does not yet cover a sufficient range of subjects, through a long enough time period, to be as useful as it promises soon to become.

Printed collections of laws, edicts, and administrative orders abound. Though of course useful, their contents on agrarian affairs are generally well known, and in any case they tell more about how rulers would have had things than how they actually were. An important exception is a compilation on customary law made by the government in the early Meiji period and translated by John H. Wigmore and his associates under the title *Mate-*

rials for the Study of Private Law in Old Japan, which gives a wealth of information on custom in various parts of the country, especially in rural areas, with respect to such matters as contracts, commercial transactions, inheritance, marriage, divorce, and adoption.

To supplement the worm's-eye view of peasant life given by village documents, there are the broader views to be found in the writings of contemporaries on a great variety of subjects including agriculture, farm tools, water works, local customs, administration, and general social and economic problems. These give a larger and livelier, though less circumstantial, picture of peasant life than do the various registers; they are also valuable as guides to shifting contemporary opinion on agrarian problems. Most of these treatises have now been published in one or another of the several great collections of Tokugawa political and economic writings cited below.

Few documents of any kind throw light on social and religious life in rural areas; at the best they give an occasional fact, inadvertently and incompletely recorded. This is not surprising since these subjects had little direct administrative significance and, further, were so well known locally that no one felt impelled to record them in detail. Nevertheless they are essential to understanding village life, even those aspects of it amply recorded. Here the near-present affords the best historical materials; for social and religious practices of the past have not changed so radically as to be now entirely beyond recall, and for thirty years or more Japanese ethnographers under the inspiration of Professor Yanagida Kunio, and recently more formal social scientists also, have been busy describing and analyzing these practices. It is consequently possible to make out with fair accuracy at least the general outlines of peasant social and religious life in the Tokugawa period.

MANUSCRIPT COLLECTIONS

Ariike monjo 有井家文書, Arii Motozaburō Shi 有井元三郎氏所藏, Arakawa-mura, Naka-gun, Wakayama-ken.

Fugeshi-gunson kokōmenki 鳳至郡村戸高免記, undated, no. 164, Kanazawa City Library.

Haibara-gun monjo 榛原郡文書, Keiji hakubutsukan 刑事博物館, Meiji University, Tokyo.

Harake monjo 原家文書, Hara Shi 原氏所藏, Haruki, Osaka Prefecture.

Henjōji monjo 遍照寺文書, Henjōji 遍照寺所藏, Hashimoto, Wakayama-ken.

Hondake monjo 本多家文書, Keiji hakubutsukan 刑事博物館, Meiji University, Tokyo.

Ichiba-mura monjo 市場村文書, Kishū keizai shi kenkyūjo 紀州經済史研究所, Wakayama University, Wakayama.

Nakagawake monjo 中川家文書, Kishū keizai shi kenkyūjo 紀州經済史研究所, Wakayama University, Wakayama.

Ōnishike monjo 大西家文書, Shiryōkan 史料館, Shinagawa-ku, Tokyo.

Samegai-mura monjo 醒井村文書, Shiryōkan 史料館, Shiga University, Hikone.

Suganoke monjo 菅野家文書, Kishū keizai shi kenkyūjo 紀州經濟史研究所, Wakayama University, Wakayama.

Sugaura monjo 菅浦文書, Shiryōkan 史料館, Shiga University, Hikone.

Ura-mura monjo 浦村文書, Shiryōkan 史料館, Shiga University, Hikone.

U-Roku ryōgun kōmenki 羽鹿兩郡高免記, undated, no. 168, Kanazawa City Library.

Yamadake monjo 山田家文書, Shiryōkan 史料館, Shinagawa-ku, Tokyo.

Yamaguchike monjo 山口家文書, Shiryōkan 史料館, Shinagawa-ku, Tokyo.

PRINTED DOCUMENTS

Goningumi no kenkyū 五人組の研究, edited by Nomura Kanetarō 野村兼太郎, Tokyo, 1943.

Hompō ni okeru kariwake kosaku 本邦ニ於ケル刈分小作, Nōrinshō nōmukyoku 農林省農務局, Tokyo, 1934.

Kagahan nōsei shi kō 加賀藩農政史考, edited by Oda Kichinojō 小田吉之丈, Tokyo, 1929.

Kawachi Ishikawa-mura gakujutsu chōsa hōkoku, kinsei sonraku shiryō 河內石川村學術調査報告, 近世村落資料, edited by Nomura Yutaka 野村豊, Osaka, 1952.

Materials for the Study of Private Law in Old Japan, translated under the supervision of John H. Wigmore, *Transactions of the Asiatic Society of Japan,* XX, Supplement, Parts I, II, III, IV, V, Yokohama, 1892.

Mura meisaichō no kenkyū 村明細帳の研究, edited by Nomura Kanetarō 野村兼太郎, Tokyo, 1949.

Nihon kinsei sompō no kenkyū 日本近世村法の研究, edited by Maeda Masaharu 前田正治, Tokyo, 1950.

Ofuregaki Hōreki shūsei 御觸書寶曆集成, edited by Ishii Ryōsuke 石井良助 and Takayanagi Shinzō 高柳眞三, Tokyo, 1934-41, 5 vols.

Taishō jūnen fukembetsu kosaku kankō chōsa shūsei 大正十年府縣別小作慣行調査集成, edited by Tsuchiya Takao 土屋喬雄, Tokyo, 1942-43, 2 vols.

Zenkoku minji kanrei ruishū 全國民事慣例類集 in *Meiji bunka zenshū* 明治文化全集, VIII, edited by Yoshino Sakuzō, Tokyo, 1929.

WRITINGS OF CONTEMPORARIES

Buyō Inshi 武陽隱士, *Seji kemmonroku* 世事見聞錄 (ca. 1817), in *Kinsei shakai keizai sōsho* 近世社會經濟叢書, edited by Honjō Eijirō 本庄榮次郎, Tokyo, completed in 1927, I.

Chihō ochibo shū 地方落穗集 (ca. 1788), anonymous, in *NKSS* 日本經

濟叢書, edited by Nihon keizai sōsho kankōkai 日本經濟叢書刊行會, Tokyo, completed in 1917, IX, 1-334.

Hōnen zeisho 豐年稅書 (1685), anonymous, in *NKSS* 日本經濟叢書, edited by Nihon keizai sōsho kankōkai 日本經濟叢書刊行會, Tokyo, completed in 1917, I, 49-109.

Koga Koshōken 古川古松軒, *Saiyū zakki* 西遊雜記 (1794), in *Nihon shakai keizai sōsho* 日本社會經濟叢書, edited by Honjō Eijirō 本庄榮次郎, Tokyo, completed in 1927, IX, 1-199.

Konishi Atsuyoshi 小西篤好, *Nōgyō yowa* 農業餘話 (ca. 1840), in *NKSS* 日本經濟叢書刊行會, edited by Nihon keizai sōsho kankōkai, Tokyo, completed in 1917, XIX, 523-600.

Miyazaki Antei 宮崎安貞, *Nōgyō zensho* 農業全書 (1697), edited by Tsuchiya Takao 土屋喬雄, 6th printing, Tokyo, 1949.

Ōhata Saizō 大畑才藏, *Chihō no kikigaki* 地方の聞書 (ca. 1700), in 近世地方經濟史料, edited by Ono Takeo 小野武夫, Tokyo, completed in 1932, II, 399-433.

Ōishi Kyūkei 大石久敬, *Jikata hanreiroku* 地方凡例錄 (1791-94), in *NKSS* 日本經濟叢書, edited by Nihon keizai sōsho kankōkai, Tokyo, completed in 1917, XXXI, 1-682.

Ōkura Eijō 大藏永常, *Nōgu benri ron* 農具便利論, in Tsūzoku keizai bunko 通俗經濟文庫, edited by Takimoto Seiichi 瀧本精一, Tokyo, 1931, XII.

Takemoto Ryūhei 武元立平, *Kannōsaku* 勸農策 (ca. 1810), in *NKSS* 日本經濟叢書, edited by Nihon keizai sōsho kankōkai, Tokyo, completed in 1917, XX, 575-604.

Tanaka Kyūgu 田中丘隅, *Minkan shōyō* 民間省要 (ca. 1721), in *NKSS* 日本經濟叢書, edited by Nihon keizai sōsho kankōkai, Tokyo, completed in 1917, I, 229-740.

Umeki Tadaaki 梅木忠章, *Shōya tekagami* 庄屋手鏡 (1813), in 近世地方經濟史料, edited by Ono Takeo 小野武夫, Tokyo, completed in 1932, VII, 169-75.

BOOKS

Ariga Kizaemon 有賀喜左衞門, *Nihon kazoku seido to kosaku seido* 日本家族制度と小作制度, Tokyo, 1943.

Ariga Kizaemon 有賀喜左衞門, *Nihon kon'in shi ron* 日本婚姻史論, Tokyo, 1948.

Ariga Kizaemon 有賀喜左衞門, *Sonraku seikatsu* 村落生活, Tokyo, 1948.

Fujita Gorō 藤田五郎, *Hōken shakai no tenkai katei* 封建社會の展開過程, Tokyo, 1952.

Furushima Toshio 古島敏雄, *Edo jidai no shōhin ryūtsū to kōtsū* 江戸時代の商品流通と交通, Tokyo, 1951.

Furushima Toshio 古島敏雄, *Kinsei Nihon nōgyō no kōzō* 近世日本農業の構造, Tokyo, 1948.

Furushima Toshio 古島敏雄, *Nihon nōgaku shi* 日本農學史, I, Tokyo, 1946.

Furushima Toshio 古島敏雄, *Nihon nōgyō gijutsu shi* 日本農業技術史, Tokyo, 1949–50, 2 vols.

Furushima Toshio 古島敏雄, *Kinsei ni okeru shōgyōteki nōgyō no tenkai* 近世における商業的農業の展開, Tokyo, 1950.

Furushima Toshio 古島敏雄 and Nagahara Keiji 永原慶二, *Shōhin seisan to kisei jinushisei* 商品生產と寄生地主制, Tokyo, 1954.

Harada Tomohiko 原田伴彦, *Chūsei ni okeru toshi no kenkyū* 中世における都市の研究, Tokyo, 1942.

Hirasawa Kiyoto 平澤清人, *Kinsei Minami Shinano nōson no kenkyū* 近世南信濃農村の研究, Tokyo, 1955.

Hōken shakai no kōzō bunseki 封建社會の構造分析, edited by Tsuchiya Takao 土屋喬雄, Tokyo, 1950.

Hori Ichiro 堀一郎, *Minkan shinkō* 民間信仰, Tokyo, 1951.

Imai Rintarō 今井林太郎 and Yagi Akihiro 八木哲浩, *Hōken shakai no nōson kōzō* 封建社會の農村構造, Tokyo, 1955.

Kawaura Kōji 川浦康次 and Shiozawa Kimio 鹽澤君夫, *Kisei jinushisei ron* 寄生地主制論, Tokyo, 1958.

Kazoku to sonraku, Vol. I 家族と村落, edited by Toda Teizō 戸田貞三, Tokyo, 1942, 2 vols.

Kinoshita Akira 木下彰, *Nihon nōgyō kōzō ron* 日本農業構造論, Tokyo, 1949.

Kisei jinushisei no seisei to tenkai, Kyōto-fu Otokuni-gun Kuga-mura no jisshōteki kenkyū 寄生地主制の生成と展開 京都府乙訓郡久我村の實證的研究, edited by Furushima Toshio 古島敏雄, Tokyo, 1952.

Kitamura Toshio 喜多村俊夫, *Nihon kangai suiri kankō no shiteki kenkyū* 日本灌漑水利慣行の史的研究, Tokyo, 1950.

Kodama Kōta 兒玉幸多, *Kinsei Nōson shakai no kenkyū* 近世農村社會の研究, Tokyo, 1953.

Kodama Kōta 兒玉幸多, *Kinsei nōmin seikatsu shi* 近世農民生活史, Tokyo, 1951.

Miyamoto Mataji 宮本又次, *Nihon kinsei ton'yasei no kenkyū* 日本近世問屋制の研究, Tokyo, 1951.

Nakamura Kichiji 中村吉治, *Kinsei shoki nōsei shi kenkyū* 近世初期農政史研究, Tokyo, 1938.

Nōson shiryō chōsakai 農村史料調査會, *Kinsei nōson no kōzō—Shinshū Suwa-gun Fujimi, Ochiai ryōson no rekishi* 近世農村の構造—信州諏訪郡富士見落合兩村の歴史, Tokyo, 1952.

Ōuchi Tsutomu 大內力, *Nōka keizai* 農家經済, *Nihon tōkei kenkyūjo keizai bunseki shiriizu 6*, Tokyo, 1957.

Sanson no kōzō 山村の構造, edited by Furushima Toshio 古島敏雄, Tokyo, 1949.

Sanson seikatsu no kenkyū 山村生活の研究, edited by Yanagida Kunio 柳田國男, Tokyo, 1937.

Sekiyama Naotarō 關山直太郎, *Kinsei Nihon jinkō no kenkyū* 近世日本人口の研究, Tokyo, 1948.

Shibata Minoru 柴田實, *Shōen sonraku no kōzō* 庄園村落の構造, Osaka, 1955.

Shimizu Mitsuo 清水三男, *Chūsei shōen no kiso kōzō* 中世庄園の基礎構造, Tokyo, 1949.

Shimizu Mitsuo 清水三男, *Nihon chūsei no sonraku* 日本中世の村落, Tokyo, 1942.

Shinobu Seizaburō 信夫清三郎, *Kindai Nihon sangyō shi josetsu* 近代日本産業史序説, Tokyo, 1942.

Shōji Kichinosuke 庄司吉之助, *Meiji ishin no keizai kōzō* 明治維新の經濟構造, Tokyo, 1954.

Sonraku kōzō no shiteki bunseki 村落構造の史的分析, edited by Nakamura Kichiji 中村吉治, Tokyo, 1956.

Takahashi keizai kenkyūjo 高橋經濟研究所, *Nihon sanshigyō hattatsu shi*, Vol. I 日本蠶絲業發達史, Tokyo, 1941.

Toya Toshiyuki 戸谷敏之, *Kinsei nōgyō keiei shi ron* 近世農業經營史論, Tokyo, 1949.

Warichi seido to nōchi kaikaku 割地制度と農地改革, edited by Furushima Toshio 古島敏雄, Tokyo, 1953.

ARTICLES

Andō Seiichi 安藤精一, "Kinsei shoki Higo no Kuni nōson no shakai kōsei" 近世初期肥後國農村の社會構成, *Keizai riron* 經濟理論, 9 (1952), 39–51.

Andō Seiichi 安藤精一, "Kinsei shoki nōson kōzō no tenkai" 近世初期農村構造の展開, *Rekishi kyōiku*, III, 10, 11 (1955), 39–42, 14–25.

Andō Seiichi 安藤精一, "Tsuyamahan ni okeru zaikata shōgyō no hattatsu" 津山藩における在方商業の發達, *Keizai riron* 經濟理論, 34 (1956), 1–31.

Andō Seiichi 安藤精一, "Kinsei Kyūshū ni okeru nōminsō no bunka" 近世九州における農民層の分化, in *Kyūshū keizai shi kenkyū* 九州經濟史研究, edited by Miyamoto Mataji 宮本又次, Tokyo, 1953, pp. 99–116.

Andō Seiichi 安藤精一, "Kinsei shoki Kyūshū no nōson kōzō" 近世初期九州の農村構造, in *Nōson kōzō no shiteki bunseki* 農村構造の史的分析, edited by Miyamoto Mataji 宮本又次, Tokyo, 1955, pp. 1–27.

Aoki Takahisa 青木孝壽, "Kita Shinano ni okeru Bunroku kenchi" 北信濃における文祿檢地, *SGZS*, LXIII, 1 (1954), 58–68.

Araki Moriaki 安良城盛昭, "Taikō kenchi no rekishiteki igi" 太閤檢地の歷史的意義, *RGKK*, 167 (1954), 12–24.

Endō Shinnosuke 遠藤進之助, "Kinsei shoki kenchi ni okeru 'mura' no seiritsu" 近世初期檢地における『村』の成立, *SKSG*, XX, 2 (1954), 54–75.

Fujita Gorō 藤田五郎, "Kinsei ni okeru nōminsō no kaikyū bunka" 近世における農民層の階級分化, in *Shakai kōsei shi taikei* 社會構成史大系, Vol. 13, edited by Watanabe Yoshimichi 渡部義通 and others, Tokyo, 1949.

Gotō Yōichi 後藤陽一, "Jūkuseiki San'yōsuji nōson ni okeru funō keiei no seikaku" 一九世紀山陽筋農村における富農經營の性格, *SGZS*, LXIII, 7 (1954), 48–68.

Harada Toshimaru 原田敏丸, "Higohan nōson ni okeru kazoku no kōzō" 肥後藩農村における家族の構造, *Ōita daigaku keizai ronshū* 大分大學經濟論集, II, 2 (1951), 111–35.

Harada Toshimaru 原田敏丸, "Kinsei sonraku ni okeru kakaku ni tsuite" 近世村落における家格について, *Hikone ronsō* 彦根論叢, 6 (1955), 1–12.

Iibuchi Keitarō 飯淵敬太郎, "Tōhoku-chihō ni okeru tochi shoyū no keitai" 東北地方における土地所有の形態, in *Tochi seido no kenkyū* 土地制度の研究, edited by Jimbun kagaku iinkai 人文科學委員會, Tokyo, 1948, pp. 47–62.

Ikeda Takamasa 池田敬正, "Kinsei zenki no Kinai sonraku to nōmin kazoku no hatten" 近世村落の畿内村落と農民家族の發展, *Hisutoria* ヒストリア, 12 (1955), 61–72.

Imai Rintarō 今井林太郎, "Kinsei shotō ni okeru kenchi no ichikōsatsu" 近世初頭における檢地の一考察, *SKSG*, IX, 11/12 (1940), 116–21.

Itō Tasaburō 伊東多三郎, "Iwayuru heinō bunri no jisshōteki kenkyū" 所謂兵農分離の實證的研究, *SKSG*, XIII, 8 (1943), 1–50.

Kawai Yūnosuke 河井勇之助, "Kinsei shotō Ōmi-chihō kenchichō no kenkyū" 近世初頭近江地方檢地帳の研究, in *Shigaku kenkyū kinen ronsō* 史學研究紀念論叢, edited by Hiroshima bunrika daigaku shigakka kyōshitsu 廣島文理科大學史學教室, Tokyo, 1950, pp. 95–123.

Kitajima Masamoto 北島正元, "Echigo sankan chitai ni okeru junsui hōkensei no kōzō" 越後山間地帶に於ける純粋封建制の構造, *SGZS*, LIX, 6 (1950), 1–39.

Kitajima Masamoto 北島正元, "Edo jidai no nōmin no 'ie'" 江戶時代の農民の『家』, in *Kazoku seido no kenkyū* 家族制度の研究, Vol. 1, edited by Nihon hōshakai gakkai 日本法社會學會, Tokyo, 1956, pp. 53–77.

Kitajima Masamoto 北島正元, "Kōshinchi ni okeru nōminteki shukōgyō no seikaku" 後進地における農民的手工業の性格, *NSKK*, 12 (1950), 13–21.

Kitano Seiichi 喜多野清一, "Dōzokudan shiryō" 同族團資料, *Minzokugaku kenkyū* 民族學研究, III, 2 (1946), 94–110.

Kitano Seiichi 喜多野清一, "Dōzoku soshiki to oyakata kokata kankō shiryō"

同族組織と親方子方慣行資料, *Minzokugaku nempō* 民族學年報, III (1940–41), 161–91.

Kitano Seiichi 喜多野清一, "Kōshū sanson no dōzokuteki soshiki to oyakata kokata kankō—Yamanashi-ken Kita-tsuru-gun Yuzuhara-mura Ōgaki o chūshin to shite—" 甲州山村の同族的組織と親方子方慣行—山梨縣北都留郡桐原村大垣を中心として—, *Minzokugaku nempō* 民族學年報, II (1939), 41–95.

Kodama Kōta 兒玉幸多, "Edo jidai nōson ni okeru kazoku seiin no mondai—tokuni jinan ika ni tsuite—" 江戸時代農村に於ける家族成員の問題—特に二男以下に就いて—, *Rekishi chiri* 歴史地理, LXV, 4 (1935), 43–60.

Komura Hajime 小村弌, "Kinsei shotō kenchichō naukenin ni tsuite no oboe-gaki" 近世初頭檢地帳名請人についての覺書, *SKSG*, XIX, 6 (1954), 89–101.

Miyagawa Hidekazu 宮川秀一, "Nayosechō kisai ni kansuru nisan no mondaiten ni tsuite" 名寄帳記載に關する二、三の問題点について, *NHRS*, 90 (1955).

Miyagawa Mitsuru 宮川滿, "Gōson seido to kenchi" 郷村制度と檢地, *Nihonshi kenkyū* 日本史研究, 19 (1953), 1–28.

Miyagawa Mitsuru 宮川滿, "Taikō kenchi to kazoku kōsei" (1) 太閤檢地と家族構成, *Hisutoria* ヒストリア, 8 (1953), 1–17.

Miyagawa Mitsuru 宮川滿, "Taikō kenchi to kazoku kōsei" (2) 太閤檢地と家族構成, *Hisutoria* ヒストリア, 9 (1954), 18–35.

Miyagawa Mitsuru 宮川滿, "Taikō kenchi to kazoku kōsei" (3) 太閤檢地と家族構成, *Hisutoria* ヒストリア, 10 (1954), 27–49.

Miyagawa Mitsuru 宮川滿, "Taikō kenchi to kazoku kōsei" (4) 太閤檢地と家族構成, *Hisutoria* ヒストリア, 11 (1955), 23–47.

Mori Kahei 森嘉兵衛, "Kinsei nōmin kaihō no shakai keizaishiteki igi" 近世農民解放の社會經濟史的意義, in *Nōmin kaihō no shiteki kōsatsu* 農民解放の史的考察, edited by Shakai keizai shigakkai 社會經濟史學會, Tokyo, 1948, pp. 51–97.

Nagahara Keiji 永原慶二, "Nihon ni okeru nōdosei no keisei katei" 日本における農奴制の形成過程, *RGKK*, 140 (1949), 1–12.

Nagahara Keiji 永原慶二 and Nagakura Tamotsu 長倉保, "Kōshin-jikyūteki nōgyō chitai ni okeru murakata jinushi no tenkai" (2) 後進＝自給的農業地帯における村方地主の展開, *SGZS*, LXIV, 2 (1955), 36–49.

Nagashima Fukutarō 永島福太郎, "Kujiya kō" 公家家考, *SGZS*, LXIII, 3 (1954), 27–51.

Naitō Seichū 内藤正中, "Kinsei sonraku no kōzō henka to murakata sōdō" 近世村落の構造變化と村方騒動, *Keizai ronsō* 經濟論叢, LXXIV, 2 (1954), 39–60.

Nakamura Jihei 中村治兵衛, "Sengo nōson no bunke" 戦後農村の分家, *Nōgyō sōgō kenkyū* 農業綜合研究, VI, 3 (1952), 147–87.

Nishioka Toranosuke 西岡虎之助, "Kinsei shōya no genryū" 近世庄屋の源流, *SGZS*, XLIX, 2, 3 (1938), 1–20, 71–112.

Nishitani Katsuya 西谷勝也, "Dōzoku to chi no kami" 同族と地の神, *Minkan denshō* 民間傳承, XV, 2 (1951), 25–28.

Ōishi Shinzaburō 大石愼三郎, "Edo jidai ni okeru nōmin no ie to sono sōzoku keitai ni tsuite" 江戸時代における農民の家とその相續形態について, in *Kazoku seido no kenkyū* 家族制度の研究, Vol. I, edited by Nihon hōshakai gakkai 日本法社會學會, Tokyo, 1956, pp. 79–121.

Ōtō Tokihiko 大藤時彦, "Bunke to saishi" 分家と祭祀, *Minkan denshō* 民間傳承, VIII, 2 (1942), 14–20.

Ōtsuki Hiroshi 大槻弘, "Awahan ni okeru kinsei sonraku no keisei katei" 阿波藩における近世村落の形成過程, *Keizai ronsō* 經濟論叢, LXXIV, 2 (1954), 3–21.

Shimada Takashi 島田隆, "Suwahan nōgyō keiei no ichirei" 諏訪藩農業經營の一例, *Keizaigaku* 經濟學, 25 (1952), 34–60.

Shōji Kichinosuke 庄司吉之助, "Bakumatsu Tōhoku nōgyō no seisan keitai to jinushi keiei" 幕末東北農業の生產形態と地主經營, *RGKK*, 136 (1948), 11–19.

Sumi Tōyō 鷲見等曜, "Bakuhan kōki Sennan kigyō chitai nōmin no tōsō" 近世前期畿内村落の動向, *Hisutoria* ヒストリア, 14 (1956), 1–20.

Sumi Tōyō 鷲見等曜, "Kinsei zenki Kinai sonraku no dōkō" 幕藩後期泉南機業地帶農民の闘爭, *Hisutoria* ヒストリア, 13 (1955).

Takao Kazuhiko 高尾一彦, "Settsu Hirano-gō ni okeru watasaku no hatten" 攝津平野鄉に於ける綿作の發展, *Shirin* 史林, XXXIV, 1/2 (1951), 1–21.

Takao Kazuhiko 高尾一彦 and Wakita Osamu 脇田修, "Genroku jidai ni okeru Kinai sonraku no hatten" 元祿時代における畿内村落の發展, *Nihonshi kenkyū* 日本史研究, 20 (1953), 1–28.

Takeuchi Harutoshi 竹内治利, "Higashi Shinshū chihō ni okeru kinsei sonraku no seiritsu to hatten" 東信州地方における近世村落の成立と發展, *NHRS*, 77 (1954), 17–22.

Takeuchi Toshimi 竹内利美, "Kenchi to bunke kanshū—Nagano-ken Kamiminochi-gun Sakae-mura no jirei—" 檢地と分家慣習―長野縣上水内郡榮村の事例, *SKSG*, VII, 7, 8 (1937), 97–114, 63–84.

Takeuchi Toshimi 竹内利美, "Mura no seisai" 村の制裁, *SKSG*, VIII, 6 (1938), 1–31.

Takeuchi Toshimi 竹内利美, "Sanson ni okeru hōkōnin" 山村に於ける奉公人, *SKSG*, IV, 5 (1934), 79–103.

Tsuchiya Takao 土屋喬雄, "Nōminsō no bunka" 農民層の分化, in *Hōken shakai no kōzō bunseki* 封建社會の構造分析, edited by Tsuchiya Takao 土屋喬雄, Tokyo, 1950, pp. 215–81.

Tsuda Hideo 津田秀夫, "Hōken shakai hōkaiki ni okeru nōmin tōsō no ichiruikei ni tsuite" 封建社會崩壊期における農民闘爭の一類型について, *RGKK*, 168 (1954), 1–15.

Wakita Osamu 脇田修, "Jinushisei no hatten o megutte" 地主制の發展を
めぐつて, *RGKK*, 181 (1955), 12–23.

Wakita Osamu 脇田修, "Sekka watasaku chitai ni okeru nōmin no dōkō"
攝河綿作地帶における農民の動向, *Keizai ronsō* 經濟論叢, LXXIV, 5
(1954), 35–58.

INDEX

Affines, 6–8, 18, 23, 145
Agricultural diaries: of Ishikawa family, 84–86; on rice production, 95, 99; on animal rental, 144; and village mercantile operations, 167
Agricultural treatises, 87, 98n, 178; *Nōgyō zensho*, 88–92, 126n, 132n; *Nōgyō isho*, 92n; *Chōbō fudoki* 94n; *Saizōki*, 189
Aichi Prefecture, 90
Aizu barony (*han*), 73, 113
Aizu Province, 37n, 98n, 174n; as hemp source, 77; size of holdings, 162n
Aki Province: branch families, 21n; rice production, 99; wage labor, 144
All Souls' (*bon*), 31
Ancestral rites, 31–32, 37, 53–54
Andō Seiichi, 188
Animals, farm, 33, 41, 142; loan and rental of, 25, 144
Arable land: partitioning of, 41–43; assessment of, 181; mentioned, 104, 190, 198
Arakawa, 190, 192f, 196n, 200
Ariga Kizaemon: on labor services, 28, 137; on headmen, 58n; on rents, 152
Ashi Tōzan, 75
Awa Province: *koya* in, 17n; *genin* in, 35n; and "new families," 55n; indigo production, 69

Bakufu, 15, 178
Banishment (from village), 61f
Baronial governments (*han*), 14, 177
Bekke, see Branch family
Bingo Province, partitioning in, 40
Bitchū Province, political conflicts in, 183–87
Bizen Province, homestead ownership, 42n

Bloch, Marc, 4n
Boshū, comparison with Choshū villages, 94n
Branch family (*bekke*), 19–23, 145–47; and ritual acts, 29–31; relation to main family, 31, 45–48, 53–57, 141, 193; and partitioning, 38–43, 45–46; labor services, 47–48; and *mutaka*, 163–64; as *hirakata*, 191; mentioned, 32n, 108, 196n
Brewing industry, 84, 149, 169. *See also Sake* making
Buckwheat, 26
Buddhism, 57, 195f
Budgets, of peasants, 81–82
Buntsuke (subordinate registration), 20n
Buyō Inshi, on *gōnō*, 176–78
Buzen Province: *nago* in, 10; branch families, 21n; landless families, 164n; poverty in, 175–76
By-employments, 129–30, 134, 146–47; mentioned, 118, 136, 158

Capital equipment, 25, 141–42
Cash crops, 69, 72, 82, 102, 159. *See also by name*
Castle towns 1, 4, 67f, 202
Ceremonial services, 29–32. *See also Miyaza*
Chikuzen Province: indigo, 69; *nago* in, 135n
China: silk from, 75; farm employment, 129n; arts of, 178
Chōbō fudoki, 94n
Choshū, comparison with Boshū villages, 94n
Cities, *see* Urban growth
Cognates, 6–8, 18, 23, 145
Commercial farming, 4f, 67, 85; geo-